BEHIND THE PRIVET HEDGE

BEHIND THE PRIVET HEDGE

Richard Sudell, the Suburban Garden
and the Beautification of Britain

MICHAEL GILSON

REAKTION BOOKS

For Susan

Published by
REAKTION BOOKS LTD
Unit 32, Waterside
44–48 Wharf Road
London N1 7UX, UK
www.reaktionbooks.co.uk

First published 2024
Copyright © Michael Gilson 2024

All rights reserved

No part of this publication may be reproduced, stored in a retrieval system, or transmitted, in any form or by any means, electronic, mechanical, photocopying, recording or otherwise, without the prior permission of the publishers

Printed and bound in Great Britain by Bell & Bain, Glasgow

A catalogue record for this book is available from the British Library

ISBN 978 1 78914 8602

CONTENTS

Introduction: On the Train to Roehampton with Edith Sitwell and D. H. Lawrence *7*

1 'A little garden city' *17*

2 'An industrial slave? Never' *36*

3 Trouble at the Whit Monday Garden Show *52*

4 The Birth of Beautification *73*

5 Sudell the Flower Evangelist *92*

6 'Taste is utterly debased' *112*

7 'There were little bridges, gnomes and things' *134*

8 An Unrivalled Influence on a New Nation of Gardeners *156*

9 'A new Britain must arise on better lines than the old' *187*

10 The Landscape Architect Struggles to Make a Mark *210*

11 'An important and influential figure' *230*

12 The Importance of Play *254*

13 Sudell Urges Us to Invite Betty Uprichard into our Garden *278*

14 'Sudell has been proved right' *299*

References *307*
Acknowledgements *323*
Photo Acknowledgements *324*
Index *325*

Privet hedge on Roehampton Estate, now called Dover House.

Introduction:
On the Train to Roehampton with Edith Sitwell and D. H. Lawrence

I'm on a train heading to London from the South Coast on a sunny September Saturday. With a degree of excitement, I'm going to visit the Roehampton Garden Society's Autumn Show in the community hall of St Margaret's Church, Putney. A few years ago this would have seemed an unlikely trip. Now it all makes perfect sense. As the train leaves Chichester, I see through the dirty window the evidence of random housing development beginning to choke the old Roman city. Workmen in fluorescent bibs and yellow helmets scurry around muddy pockets of land erecting an astonishing number of 'executive' houses in small spaces. From what I can see the garage and driveway for the SUV is taking precedence over any attempt to give would-be owners anything approximating to a decent-sized garden. Not good for the builder's density ratio nor their balance sheet.

Soon we are into the Arun floodplains. On the horizon is the town that takes its name from the river, its castle and cathedral, dominating symbols of combined spiritual and temporal might. But even this imperious landscape is under threat: the Arundel bypass planned through the valley will surely bring a petrol station, industrial park and four-bedroomed house hamlet with it. As the train grinds its way to London rows of gardens abutting the line after East Croydon appear, each presenting itself for the briefest of inspections by this travelling audience, a snatched glimpse into private lives and personalities. South Croydon, Selhurst, Thornton

Heath, Norbury, Streatham Common, Balham and so on. Decking here, barely controlled wisteria there, a trampoline every now and again. Next a huge white gleaming PVC conservatory eating up outdoor space for those with no time for tiresome weekend weeding. Surprisingly, over the fence appears a neglected area, long grass and an old swing, through which a cat prowls, followed by a pristine plot divided into immaculate lawn, bordered by hydrangea, anemone and rose, nearest the house, and raised vegetable beds and greenhouse next to the rail line. A determined resident is pushing a wheelbarrow towards the runner beans, passing through the honeysuckle-clad archway marking the boundary between pleasurable relaxation and purposeful labour.

As we pass the last garden I think of my grandfather, a municipal landscape gardener, whose own plot was a marvel of immaculate exactitude and expert seasonal planting for colour, dominated by a silver birch and weeping willow hybrid he had grafted himself. That tree strikes me as an odd thing now, but at the time served as a cool hiding place for my brother and me.

I think also of my father's love of flowers and quiet pride in our small garden. A Tilbury docker, he found peace and tranquillity, away from the metal-on-metal grind of giant cranes lifting containers from the bowels of Seven Seas-crossing leviathans, by sipping a beer on our tiny patio and watching the butterflies dance around his marigolds. We are now making our way towards Victoria, and thoughts of them in their gardens summon up D. H. Lawrence and his interwar essay on Nottingham miners, whose simple love of colour in their own backyards was an antidote to the pitch-black misery that awaited them below ground:

> I've seen many a collier stand in his back garden looking down at a flower with that odd, remote sort of contemplating which shows a real awareness of the presence of beauty. It would not even be admiration, or joy, or delight, or any

of those things which so often have a root in the possessive instinct. It would be a sort of contemplating: which shows the incipient artist.[1]

But because I'm on a quest this day and because those London plots have revealed what usually is hidden in such private places – namely that our gardens reveal everything about ourselves and, despite how hard we might resist the notion, their history is intricately and irretrievably interwoven with politics – I find myself thinking of critic and poet Edith Sitwell as the train comes to a halt outside Clapham Junction.

Raging snob Sitwell, who grew up in Renishaw Hall, Derbyshire, with its eighteenth-century Italianate gardens and army of labourers to tend them, was infamous for falling out with other artists and writers. In Tuscany in the early twentieth century (she affected to not remember when) she ran into Lawrence and took an instant dislike to him, his 'matted, dank look' and the fact that he was, in her view, over-keen to impress on her his 'son of toil' credentials. He was, she later said, like 'a plaster gnome on a stone toadstool in some suburban garden'.[2]

Feel the poison. Apart from the prepositions, every word in that sentence is dripping with uranium-grade disdain. Suburbia is the easy target in the crosshairs. No artist could ever come from such a place, she is saying. Grade II-listed country house and inherited wealth maybe, but from the land of overblown roses and crazy paving? How absurd. Ironic really given Lawrence's own hatred of the houses of suburbia, flexing his tempestuous machismo by describing them as 'horrid little red rattraps'. By the way, note the 'some'. Sitwell can't even be bothered to locate the garden. After all, they are everywhere, slowly destroying Albion with vulgar taste and uppity attempts at self-improvement.

Incidentally, the Sitwells were able to afford their country homes and 120-hectare (300 ac) landscape because they owned the sort of mines that Lawrence's colliers longed to escape from to gaze upon the simple beauty contained within the very much smaller pieces of land at the back of their tied cottages. See what I mean about gardens and politics? As the train starts to roll forward again, I think of Lawrence allegedly using Renishaw as inspiration for Wragby Hall, the home of the eponymous heroine of *Lady Chatterley's Lover*. That's the problem with garden and landscape history. You pull at a thread and you just can't stop.

By now, though, we are into Battersea and to the left, in a small gap between dull modern flats, I spy the park, transformed in 1951 into the Pleasure Gardens for the Festival of Britain. They attracted tens of thousands of visitors daily to enjoy installations like the Tree Walk and to gaze open-mouthed at the bonkers Lewitt and Him Guinness Clock. Here was a time of astonishing confidence in modern Britain where the environment in which we lived was at the heart of the national debate, the culmination of decades of theorizing about the future shape of our towns and cities and the open spaces we had a right to. Argument that such matters could be the subject of proper planning, central regulation even, did not bring forth instant howling condemnation from free marketeers back then.

Instantly, on my right, I am dragged back to the present and a twenty-first-century two-fingered salute to that ethos and design theory; a monstrosity of laissez-faire, a money-talks development that has been allowed to disfigure the face of Thameside London. Like a high-rise ghetto, miles of glass-fronted rabbit-hutch flats completely encase the Grade II* listed Battersea Power Station designed by Giles Gilbert Scott. Its iconic towers are now invisible behind (what appear to be) indiscriminately erected, dreary grey shrouds of concrete. In the summer, drying clothes, bikes and bric-a-brac clutter up minuscule porches behind the glass, giving the impression of a Brazilian favela minus the defiant joy. Here a one-bedroom box will set you back £830,000. It's as if no one cared about what was going on as this thing splurged into the sky in front of millions of commuters every day, as if planners (in the twenty-first century a dirty word if ever there was one) had just thrown in the towel in the face of devil-may-care politicians and global capital.

But we should not assume that calamitous mistakes are only made in the here and now. My journey is about to reveal more proof that we rarely learn our lesson when it comes to imposing theories of living on powerless populations. End of the line for my travels is Putney station and from there I will walk to Roehampton, now called the Dover House Estate, and the garden show. I'm early, so I take an extra five minutes to walk to the close-by Alton Estate. As I walk along Putney Heath Road I hear in my head Alton Estate designer Bill Howell, a Modern Movement zealot, all Received Pronunciation vowels, speak of his mission 'to turn the tide back from the suburban dream . . . this is what we must do; we don't want to rush out and live in horrid little suburbs and semi-detached houses.'[3]

And what of his vision now? I sit by the bus stop at Alton and take in the 1950s brutalist slab block towers rising all around me, home to around 12,000 residents. The most famous of these buildings are the five five-storey blocks of Highcliffe, which had modernists salivating, and perhaps you can see why. Built on concrete stilts or legs, an admittedly impressive construction feat, the slabs almost slide into the green sloping hills that announce the northern edge of the estate. All around are trees and grassland. And yet it has the unmistakable feel of desolation, the only signs of activity in the landscape the foraging of thousands of grey squirrels who have seemingly colonized the place. Highcliffe is thrown at this landscape by architects full of the creative machismo that comes with the new and without a thought to a concept of community. They've had to call the flat blocks and maisonettes that make up Alton 'Neighbourhoods' in an attempt to engender feelings among residents that this is home rather than a failed experiment visited upon them. A shabby block of shops is mostly shuttered. Incredibly, you could throw a stone from here and have it land in Richmond Park, one of eight Royal Parks in London and a Site of Special Scientific Interest.

It wouldn't have occurred to Howell and the design teams at Alton to acknowledge the 1,010 hectares (2,500 ac) of nature reserve on the border of their project. A golf course now forms a physical and, perhaps, mental barrier between the two. In the late 1950s these architects were mesmerized by Le Corbusier and his Unité d'habitation principle (more of this later) of high-rise communities, almost literally steamrollering any dissent that might question the social price of such ideas. Of course, Howell and his cohorts never actually lived in these places themselves nor, of course, the horrid little suburbs.

On the off chance, I Google Alton to see what I might discover. The first link I see has a headline screaming, 'The run-down London estate on the edge of posh Richmond Park where some days it's "hell".' It's a story from August 2021 on a newspaper website called *MyLondon*.[4] The subhead beneath reads 'Many children on the estate have never set foot in Richmond Park', followed by a first line of the story which has residents '"crying out" for help as they await regeneration plans'. They fear proposals to build more high-rise blocks will further damage the area. Wandsworth Borough Council is doing its best to revive this benighted place, but Howell and co. have dealt it a desperate hand.

The *MyLondon* story is shocking, revealing, as it does, that it is not the distance to the park that puts off the children of Alton Estate but the fear that they will be 'intimidated' by the lushness of Richmond Park and the wealth on show symbolized by the £2-million-plus houses that line it. Alton has become a prison of the mind. And yet, a five-minute walk the other way is the patchwork of allotments at the centre of Dover House, evidence for another vision of how we might live, this one from forty years before the Alton Estate's construction. Leaving Alton and retracing my steps along Putney Heath Road I turn into the semi-rural track that is Putney Park Lane.

Suddenly a different world is entered, as if the stile I navigate as I enter is the gateway to the Secret Garden itself.

Here the coolness provided by a canopy of lime trees on either side of the track immediately deadens the constant sound of rumbling London traffic. Further in are Arts and Crafts cottage houses with gardens, front and side or back. Little pockets of green space pop up to surprise, and the sound of a lawnmower is heard somewhere in the near distance, a much-derided soundtrack of the suburbs. The development, then simply called the Roehampton Estate, was built for almost exactly the same sort of people that decades later found themselves at Alton.

Down this lane is St Margaret's Church and my destination, the Roehampton Garden Society (RGS) Autumn Show. I enter the light airy chapel, built in 1892, and remember that in the interwar years worshippers from old, moneyed Putney would sit on a separate side of the aisle from their new working-class neighbours from inner-city London. Sometimes they even attended different services until the intervention of the vicar, insisting on Christian togetherness.

Under my feet is the crypt, the appropriate setting for a 'dark night of the soul' meeting in 1923 in which Richard Sudell (the hero of this book) began the work of recovering the purpose and stability of the newly formed society after a financial scandal. Why the crypt was chosen for that June evening meeting, the first and only time the Roehampton Estate Garden Society (REGS) – as it was then called – met there, is not clear. As summer rain fell outside, the subject of how money had gone missing from the Aunt Sally stand at the Whitsun Fete was just one of the fierce debates that echoed around the stone walls.

Back to the present, and the society that Sudell founded one hundred years ago is preparing for the show in the newly built community centre adjacent to the church. Inside, Jackie Savage, past president, barely has time to raise her eyebrows in greeting as the exhibits are displayed, the produce for sale set out and the tea and cake stand readied. The impressive bustle and sense of purpose is likely as it has been at this time every year for the last century. Before the doors open, I take the chance for an exclusive preview of the exhibits. They are remarkable. Robert Linton's winning 'Three Pears' (section D, No. 64) looks like a Cézanne. 'The trick is to celebrate the successes and not fuss about the failures – a good lesson for life,' Robert tells me. It's no wonder that Vivien Fowler's 'Winter Harvest Collection' (section B, No. 19) has taken first prize, basket teeming with corn on the cob, chilli peppers, King Edward spuds, garlic, carrots and tomatoes, centred by orange and yellow nasturtium. Vivien has done well to bring tomatoes to the show, for most of the growers on the estate have suffered blight this year.

Elsewhere there are categories for dahlias (hugely popular), mixed cut flowers, aubergines, leeks, cucumbers, French beans, marrows, mixed herbs and so on. And it is fiercely competitive, judged under Royal Horticultural Society rules and regulations. I can find no one from the Alton Estate exhibiting here. How could they? As I leave, the show still in full swing, to take my social, architectural and landscape history journey in reverse I reflect how proud Sudell would have been of Jackie, Robert and Vivien, one hundred years on, for their tireless, enthusiastic commitment to growing and beautifying in no matter how small a space. It was a cause for which he spent his lifetime evangelizing and for which he has yet to receive proper recognition.

As the train trundles out of the capital, I remember Vivien's words about the 'privilege and pleasure' it is to own her Roehampton allotment. 'Digging up my potato bed to source five perfect potatoes is not my favourite show activity but it is compulsive! And even if you don't win a prize, it's the "showing" that is important – otherwise there wouldn't be a show!' But I also reflect on her concern that the gains made a century ago by Sudell, and many, many others, are in danger of disappearing:

In London and in most big cities the pressure on available land for housing means that new allotment sites will not happen – and indeed some existing sites are threatened. People want to grow their own produce and Roehampton Garden Society has a four-year waiting list for a plot. Perhaps Planning Laws in the future could include community growing spaces in their Codes?

My journey only took a day, but now we must travel back to the beginning of the last century to help us understand how this country's reputation as a 'land of gardeners' was made, how now-forgotten battles made this so, how the suburban garden, loathed by the few, silently loved by the many and whose history is rarely told, was the heart of a very British revolution. We will see how one man was right at the centre of this, not on the front pages, but deep down in the soil of new practice, helping in the battle to beautify this island inch by hard-dug inch.

Vivien Fowler's winning Winter Harvest Collection exhibit at the Roehampton Garden Society's Autumn Show, 2021.

Part of the Roehampton Estate under construction, 1926.

1
'A little garden city'

On an early summer's evening in 1924, if you had happened to be strolling beneath the laburnum and almond trees on a new housing estate many of its tenants considered paradise on earth, you might have been struck by the sound of loud applause coming from the community centre. Inside at the annual general meeting of the Roehampton Estate Tenants' Association (RETA) – there had only been one previous such occasion – the audience, mostly men in smart suits, was there to hear about the minutiae of life in their new environment. Rent book issues, play area upgrades, repairs to boilers and home inspections were on the agenda. So what had caused these residents to spontaneously express their joyous appreciation at this stuffy meeting?

One man was responsible for the approbation, someone who had spent the last two years introducing and demonstrating to tenants, many fresh from cramped inner-city slums, a new skill they had never previously needed, imbuing a passion that would help transform the face of depressed, shell-shocked post-war Britain. He was Richard Sudell, chairman of the Roehampton Estate Garden Society (REGS) and RETA. Sudell was reporting back on progress. Two years before, when the garden society had first been established, this showpiece 'cottage estate' built by the London County Council (LCC) had been half-finished, with a little more than six hundred houses on site, each including something many new residents had never had before, namely a small patch of adjacent land. Those early years were a real leap into the unknown, for while the LCC builders provided residents with homes they could hitherto only have dreamt of, the gardens were a different matter. Witness this editorial in the *Roehampton Estate Gazette*, a parish pump magazine that was a remarkable symbol of an early community spirit among tenants and for which Sudell wrote a gardening advice column from its very first issue.

> Who among us cannot recall the grim struggle of the early days of our tenancy among the wilds of this, our garden suburb. The ring of spade on brick, concrete and tin can did reverberate across the road during the mellow evenings of early autumn of 1921. Barbed wire entanglements, concrete pillboxes, lumps of old iron, enough bricks to build a home and a few old boats made up the rich and varied assortment of litter with which the ground was impregnated. The net result was in front a jungle, in rear a howling wilderness, inside a very fed up and disillusioned householder.[1]

That was where Sudell came in. A gardener since the age of fourteen, he was a remarkable character, an imprisoned First World War conscientious objector who would, against the odds, go on to play a leading role in the foundation of professionalized landscape architecture. But for now he was a grassroots evangelical with a strong conviction that everyone, not just the privileged few, should have access to open space, fresh air and horticultural beauty. His time had come. For two years he had organized the tenants of Roehampton into a fearsome gardening force, offering instruction to his new neighbours, promoting competitions and flower shows, lecturing on allotment growing, organizing the purchase of communal gardening tools and writing letters to the LCC urging it to deliver on its promise to plant more trees. Members of the society who paid their two-shillings-a-year fees would gain access, 'at very low charge', to a shared lawnmower and roller.

And so Roehampton began to burst into colour. Petunias, pansies, dahlias, daffodils, geraniums, sunflowers, hollyhocks, poppy, nasturtium, lupine, lavatera, polyanthus, antirrhinums and asters brought dazzling hues to grey earth or even windowsills. Life began to spring forth, heartily and needfully encouraged by those who were shadowed by the death and destruction of the First World War.

At that meeting, just before he was to leave the estate, Sudell told them what they had achieved. He gave them details of the success of the annual garden show, gave examples of excellence and promised he would continue to push the LCC for more help and extra funding in the neighbourhood. It was then that our evening walkers would have heard first a ripple and then widespread applause as Sudell sat down on the podium. We know this because the *Gazette* reported it so.[2] Roehampton, with its tenants' association, garden society and community newsletter, had become in a few short years the archetypal example of what was to both cause the residents to rejoice and, later, provide critics with material for ridicule: the suburb.

By today's standards of haphazard 'market-led' house building the development of these new environs was an astonishing achievement, a centrally planned expansion of decent living conditions fuelled partly by the demands from the many working-class men returning from the horrors of the Great War that they should not return to the slum conditions they had left. The recognition of the sacrifice they had made drove a political groundswell for social change that was astutely recognized by Prime Minister David Lloyd George. But it is equally true to say that his 'A Country Fit for Heroes' homes building campaign, launched in 1919, was also a product of anxious glances over his shoulder at the Bolshevik revolution in Russia of 1917: 'Britain would hold out against the dangers of Bolshevism, but only if the people were given confidence, only if they were made to believe that things were being done for them.'[3] There is little doubt too that medics and army recruiters had been shocked by the unhealthy and unfit state of many of the men conscripted to fight in the war, most of whom came from urban slums. Even George V opined that 'an adequate solution of the housing question is the foundation of all progress.'[4] A much-read book at the time, *The Home I Want*, written by returning soldier Richard Reiss of the North Lancashire Regiment, carried the subtitle 'You cannot expect an A1 population out of C3 homes'.[5]

New homes, gardens and allotments would thus be the emollient to soothe potential unrest, and the antidote to a shortage of fighting-fit men in the future. As we shall see, allegations that gardens were 'opiates' of the masses protecting against real social change had been aired before. That criticism would soon be employed again as the suburbs grew. It was estimated that at the end of the First World War there were 600,000 families without houses. In total more than 5 million new houses were built in the interwar years, more than 3 million in the private sector and in excess of a million in the public, wiping out this shortage and indeed creating a surplus, a remarkable period of productivity. Many of the new estates were inspired by the Garden City movement, new homes and gardens moving into spaces left by the fragmentation of the old, landed estates, broken by changing economics that made them unaffordable to all but the most well-resourced of the aristocracy. Here then was the real beginning of a British reputation for love of gardens and gardening, paving the way for the ritualized visit to the garden centre and the explosion of written advice on home and garden for the aspirational. It was also contested – a time when the shape of Britain and how people lived and the environment in which they did so really mattered.

The mechanisms for this vast change in social policy were to be Acts of Parliament driven by those at the forefront of the Garden City movement. Echoing examples like George Cadbury's model village Bournville, in Birmingham, the 1918 government-commissioned

Tudor Walters Report recommended densities on the new estates of a maximum of twelve houses to the acre and back gardens of about 400 square yards. Estates were to be made attractive through 'planning the lines of the road and disposing the spaces and buildings as to develop the beauty of vista, arrangement and proportion'.[6] The Housing Act of 1919, also known as the Addison Act after its author, the then Minister of Health, Dr Christopher Addison, enshrined these principles and gave generous subsidies to local authorities of up to 75 per cent of cost to build affordable homes for rent. The Act called for local councils to provide 500,000 homes over the next three years, although when the economy dived into depression in the early 1920s this had to be revised as funding was cut. Eventually a little more than 200,000 homes were built under the legislation. Successor Acts in the interwar years gave less generous subsidies but still allowed councils to build more than 1 million homes for rent in the period. Nevertheless, Addison enshrined in Britain for the first time the principle of the provision of decent council housing for rent.

Garden City pioneers seized their chance to position themselves in the driving seat for this change. For instance, architect and town planner Raymond Unwin, who had been part of the team that designed the first garden city at Letchworth before the war, was a hugely influential member of the Tudor Walters Committee. Unwin was a remarkable figure who had been inspired by artist William Morris's Arts and Crafts movement. His architectural and design partnership with brother-in-law Barry Parker, another Arts and Crafts disciple, made its cause improving housing for the working class, both inside and out, resulting in many new houses in the early twentieth century reflecting their newly spacious design style. In 1919, as the Tudor Walters Committee was convened, Unwin was chief architect to the newly formed Ministry of Health, giving him huge influence over its deliberations and the report it produced.

Unwin had earlier designed Letchworth for the 'father' of the garden city, Ebenezer Howard, in 1903. Howard's 1898 book *Tomorrow:*

A Peaceful Path to Real Reform became the bible of the movement, providing practical detail on designing new communities of no more than 32,000 people in order to free them from inner city slums, arrest the decline of lives connected to the land and indeed to protect that land from the encroachment of modern cities.[7] His Garden City Limited company built both Letchworth, before, and Welwyn after the war. Fearing the government would never mobilize with enough urgency to make these radical changes in the living environment, he just got on with it, buying the land and bringing in designers, architects and builders himself. The theoretical bloodline stretched back to Thomas More's *Utopia*, a 1515 treatise on an idealized society, which contained one of the first proposals for the construction of a new town. In the early nineteenth century so-called utopian socialists, such as Robert Owen at New Lanark and Charles Fourier in France, revived the philosophy. In the same century 'religious utopians' who built model villages, such as Titus Salt with Saltaire, William Lever with Port Sunlight and Cadbury at Bournville, continued the cause. All believed that industrialized urbanization, for which they were of course partially responsible, had created communities that were 'irretrievably inappropriate for the well-being of the human condition, either physical or moral'.[8]

At the root of Howard's Garden City movement was an attempt to improve the poor sanitary conditions that urbanization and its squalor had visited upon the country. In many ways the cities and towns now stood for corruption and degeneracy while the countryside, and its idealized rural past, was pure and moral. Ironically, given the ancestry of the movement with its beneficent industrialists, the vision looked back to a pre-industrial England, a golden era, which appeared to have forgotten abject rural poverty and serfdom. A return to nature would revitalize the human spirit. The debt of the Tudor Walters Report to philanthropist and Quaker George Cadbury was clear. Cadbury brought his chocolate works out of the back streets of Birmingham and created his own 'Factory in the Garden', to be called Bournville after the local stream, in fresh fields on the outskirts of town. Next door on 48 hectares (120 ac) of land, he built the Bournville estate, begun in 1894 and totalling more than three hundred homes for rent, that would make it easy for 'working men to own houses with large gardens free from the danger of being spoilt ... by interference of the enjoyment of sun, light and air'. For Cadbury it was simple: 'the only effective way is to bring men out of the cities and into the country and to give every man his garden where he can come into touch with nature and thus know more of nature's God.'[9] As early as 1909 the *Journal of the Royal Institute of Public Health* was joining the chorus of approval describing a layout of the estate that was designed so there was no overcrowding of houses. The cottages themselves were either semi-detached or in blocks of four, each standing in a plot of land averaging 500 square yards. The enthusiasm for the estate drips from the page: 'There are front gardens gay with flowers, and back gardens rich with fruit and vegetables. There are parks, playgrounds and open spaces.'[10] Sudell, as we shall see, had intimate knowledge of Bournville and it is highly likely that it was here that his own passion for the Garden City movement began. While not quite a model village, Roehampton followed the Bournville blueprint almost to the letter, its picturesque cottages, gardens and greens reflecting the return to nature demanded by the Garden City movement.

By the time Sudell moved to Roehampton, in 1921, council estate building was in full swing. Across town the Becontree estate in Dagenham would soon be the largest public housing project in the world, home to 100,000 tenants in 26,000 homes. With Unwin's backing, and given the acute need for housing, the Garden City ethos had mutated into the construction of garden suburbs. These were, in some senses, now in danger of directly undermining one of Howard's principles of protecting rural areas. Nevertheless, Sudell's attendance at the opening of Putney Park House as a community centre for the estate shows how committed he was to the social

Richard Sudell with his second wife, Ida.

principles of the movement, even if the practical design philosophy of building separate communities was effectively already dead.

Returning for the ceremony in 1924, shortly after he had moved away from the estate, the *Wandsworth Borough News* quotes him thus: 'Mr R. Sudell, who was formerly on the committee but has now left the neighbourhood, said he wanted the co-operative spirit to continue among the tenants and to see if they could not make that into a little garden city.'[11] Sudell, from a Quaker background himself, believed that the right to have a decent living environment and access to gardens and fresh air was crucial if society was to progress. And of course, with this right came an individual responsibility for the collective good of the estate, the enthusiastic support for community improvement. For an increasing number of critics, the growth of this new suburbia and the explosion of interwar house building was a cause of planning concern and snobbish ridicule. For Sudell there was, more importantly, practical work to do in encouraging his neighbours to throw themselves into self-improving work on their gardens.

It might seem ironic that Sudell, an absolutist conscientious objector during the war, was a beneficiary of the 'Country Fit for Heroes' house-building policy. It might also be tempting to dismiss him and his garden society as a mundane minor footnote in this story of sweeping social change. That would be a mistake, for deep down in the reality of the freshly dug earth, the practicalities of gardening are the roots of a fascinating story of how this nation was transformed between the wars and beyond. While political debate about the post-war shape of the country raged, Sudell was leading his neighbours to plant their lawns and begin their horticultural odyssey. 'The first consideration in planning a garden is its aspects,' he wrote in the second-ever edition of the *Gazette* in December 1922. 'Wherever possible paths should be made to run North to South.'[12] This sort of practical advice was exactly what his neighbours needed, as would millions of others across Britain in the next decades as a virtually unquenchable thirst to improve immediate environment gripped the nation. Now came communal lawnmowers, garden fetes, biggest marrow competitions, crazy paving, the rise of the rose, immaculate lawns, horticultural one-upmanship. All of these things – perfect fertilizer for British comic sensibilities around twitching curtains and dull conformity – tell a story of a new community: the suburbanites.

Soon town-planning theorists and advocates of the Le Corbusier-powered Modern Movement would heave into view. In fierce debates both before and after the Second World War they demanded housing that was at the cutting edge of design and promoted communal living, giving residents new spaces and vistas, often rising into the sky, while also preserving rural idyll from sprawling expanding suburbs. They poured scorn on the huge new council estates. Also in their sights were private-sector ribbon developments stretching out from big cities. In London, speculative house building on land that spread out with the development of the Metropolitan rail line had them aghast at the rise of mock-Tudor houses and gardening one-upmanship among neighbours of what was to be forever known as Metro-land. But what of the residents themselves? The theorists would be ignoring a simple fact. Many of these new house dwellers, especially the tenants of the cottage estates that councils built, had come from deprived inner-city areas and cramped tenements where communal living was a necessity, not an option. Others would remember the desperate conditions and the daily battle to survive in the squalid trenches of mainland Europe during the war. They had little interest in semi-communal living as a concept. Their new homes and, perhaps more importantly, gardens gave them something they had rarely had before. Privacy.

While the meaning of the word is disputed, it is hard to think of any other proper etymological derivation for *privet*, as in hedge, other than *private*. For that indeed is what these robustly growing

Example of a small front garden on Dover House Estate, 2021.

shrubs came to symbolize in Roehampton and hundreds of other suburbs like it. The privet hedge gave new suburban dwellers protection and a seclusion they had rarely experienced in their former cramped inner-city environments. As we shall see, the new residents of these houses are often missing from the debate about one of the biggest social and economic changes in modern British history, although now and again they poke through like one of the weeds in the crazy paving they spent their weekends battling. Witness the testimony of John Edwin Smith, who as a young boy moved with his family into one of the other LCC estates, Downham. Smith recalled, just like the new tenants across town at Roehampton, how all that his family discovered upon moving in was a 'lump of clay' where the garden might be. Like many newly situated tenants, his father, a foreman bricklayer, went to work in the garden with a gusto that was typical of thousands of others:

> I remember [my father] making a circular flower bed and ringing it with lumps of old stone and concrete that had been found among the building materials. I think [he] took a few cuttings from the privet hedge and put them either side of the path leading to the front door, so that we had continuous privet hedge all round.[13]

This was not the definition of community that theorists, who did not live in these places themselves, had imagined. Sudell understood the motivations of people like the bricklayer perfectly. His support for this grassroots movement often led him to be viewed with sniffy suspicion by some contemporaries within landscape architecture, a profession he did much to establish. There is a recurring theme in much of the instructional writing he undertook for the *Gazette*, the gardening journals he would go on to edit and in the many articles and gardening books he wrote right up to the late 1950s. For Sudell a small garden was a chance for residents to gain relief from the 'turmoil of the day' or 'exclusion from the world', leitmotifs of a philosophy that would put him in the crosshairs of the modernists who detested the privatizing spaces suburban gardens symbolized.[14]

And this wasn't just an architectural debate. The gardens were also contested spaces for horticulturalists and garden designers. The interwar suburban garden, promoted by Sudell and others, had a simplicity that, for critics, could drift into kitsch. This was the era of crazy paving, statuary in the smallest of gardens, even garden gnomes, regimented planting regimes, bedding out, the ubiquity of the rose, especially in the front garden, and of course the privet hedge. But these gardens were clearly modern in that they spoke of a style suited to the new times, on a scale and in circumstances never seen before, and as such are rich in historical meaning, worthy of study rather than dismissal. Strict formalism characterized the suburban approach. Order and compartmentalization were important, a definite move away from turn-of-the-century gardener and writer William Robinson's wild cottage gardens, and the Arts and Crafts-inspired profusion of small country-house planting that became associated with garden designer Gertrude Jekyll.

Egalitarian and unique, using new materials, extensive paving, bright colours, geometrical forms and pared-back choice of planting, the new gardens were, it could be argued, harbingers of a design theory that the Festival of Britain in 1951 did much to promote. They were in effect an assault on a post-war dull grey world, with clean lines and bright, primary colours as weapons of transition. In some ways crazy paving, so often suggested in Sudell's garden instruction, for instance, serves as a useful introduction to elements of the debate that surrounded suburban garden development. Derided by many, the pathways added to the formality of the garden, necessitating those straight lines and delineated spaces. But this formality was rooted, for Sudell and others, in a realization that many of the people who were now gardeners did not have the time to create works of garden art; for them the stylizations of the country-house approach were a virtual impossibility given the need to work long hours to pay new rents or mortgages and feed families. What Sudell was concerned with was the labour-saving garden, a thing of beauty in the environment in which many people now lived, and achievable with an abundance of planting advice. In other words, it was practical. 'Many busy people owning small homes have no less garden love than their more leisured friends. But then circumstances demand that their gardens must be maintained side by side with other occupations and must not be too exacting,' wrote Sudell in one of his many instruction articles.[15]

It is perhaps worth remembering that Jekyll, the horticultural darling of the Arts and Crafts movement, whose painterly 'country house' planting schemes remain widely copied and admired, had eleven full-time gardeners to keep her 6-hectare (15 ac) garden at her home at Munstead Wood in Surrey looking wild and naturalistic. Sudell's need to nudge along Britain's new gardeners and gently persuade them, primarily through an explosion of painfully practical instruction manuals, was something he and other suburban garden pioneers understood in a way that many designers and architects who would lead bodies like the Royal Horticultural Society (RHS) and the soon-to-be established Institute of Landscape Architects (ILA) did not.

Despite the eventual parting of the ways between Arts and Crafts and early twentieth-century design ethos, the estate on which Sudell began his mission had a remarkable variety of houses in the style of the former. Influenced by Unwin and Parker, the houses were built in clusters with side gardens, three allotment sites and trees preserved from the old estates of Dover House and Putney Park House. The LCC had bought these estates, a combined 59 hectares (147 ac), for £120,000. Dover House, built around 1787, was the former home of legendary American banker J. P. Morgan. He inherited it from his father, who was also a banker in London and used Dover House as a country estate. Under J. P. the estate grew to 57 hectares (140 ac) on which prize Jersey cattle grazed, the famous Morgan strawberry was cultivated under yards of glass, and the twenty-bedroomed house was festooned with art estimated to be worth £50 million. After J. P. Morgan died, his son showed no interest in the estate and, after a spell as an amputee hospital during the First World War, it was sold to the LCC. Dover House was demolished in 1923.[16] The LCC had its own architects' department, and two young members of staff, Thomas Blashill and W. E. Riley, influenced by Unwin and Parker, helped it build some of the most progressive housing and public buildings in the country at the time, including Roehampton: 'They sought to bring the working-class cottage the dignity, individuality and quality of design and materials that a wealthy private person would expect in his country house.'[17] As well as Roehampton, Blashill and Riley designed Totterdown Fields in Tooting and White Hart Lane in Tottenham, 'all consisting of humane Arts and Crafts influenced two-storey cottages of the type built at Letchworth and Hampstead Garden Suburb.'[18]

> Cottages are arranged with varying degrees of formality around communal green spaces, the size and shape of which varies considerably. Clustering cottages around intimate green spaces was undoubtedly a deliberate attempt to create a sense of place and engender a feeling of community within the Estate as a whole.[19]

From the start, initially at least, the adherence to Unwin-inspired Garden City thinking was total: 'Houses were termed as cottages. The pavements were very wide and planted with almond and laburnum trees, as were the front gardens, which were edged with privet.'[20] Roehampton quickly became the LCC's showcase new estate, even though Becontree was far larger. The plan was to follow 'Hampstead Garden Suburb in its allegiance to the romantic concept of "growing out of the earth"'.[21] While many of the new residents were from inner-city London, getting a place in this new, emerging dreamland was anything but easy. There were undoubtedly hundreds of families who had never lived in such a spacious environment and certainly never had a garden, yet the new tenants were extensively interviewed in their existing homes to test for suitability for residence, with the LCC director of housing explaining the estate would appeal only to 'those of the working class whose standards and ideals are the highest'.[22] The estate earned the nickname 'Uniform Town' because it was home to so many relatively better-off workers such as policemen, postmen, middle-ranking civil servants and tram drivers. Before they were kicked off, one family even had a part-time maid. Research shows that in 1930 white-collar worker heads of households made up 36 per cent of the estate, significantly higher than some other LCC estates, although this figure had fallen to 30 per cent by the end of the decade, with 17 per cent unskilled. In 1927 some of the early, larger houses were being rented for 30 shillings a week, way beyond the reach of inner-city slum dwellers, although rents did vary considerably.[23]

We should be careful, however, not to overplay the new estate as a metaphorical waiting room for the emerging middle classes. Many families did arrive from crowded, deprived parts of the capital and soon found Roehampton to be their salvation, even though paying the rent was a constant source of worry. The Belton family was perhaps typical of the sort of new residents who came to live on the estate. Tina Belton remembered: 'There were eight of us living in three rooms in Paddington, and we were overcrowded. We had to find new accommodation because of my father's health, he had TB [tuberculosis].'[24]

Similarly, Ivy Woollett, who moved onto the estate in the early 1920s after her father, a skilled motor coach builder, finally secured a tenancy after a five-year wait, recalled many periods when he was out of work and money was tight. Nevertheless, it was worth it:

'So when she [her mother] got this house, with a bathroom and a back garden we could play in and our own front door, she thought she was in heaven.'[25] Certainly Lt Cmdr Alfred Cooper Rawson, a Conservative councillor on Wandsworth Borough Council and Putney resident, was distinctly unwelcoming to all new arrivals, white collar or otherwise. The old estates, Cooper Rawson wrote to the local newspaper, the *Wandsworth Borough News*, as the planning process began, 'were entirely unsuitable for working class dwellings'.[26] In the same edition a story on the planned estate was headlined 'A Putney Bombshell'. Cooper Rawson was spared the worst that the new arrivals could visit upon his semi-rural idyll when he was elected MP for Brighton in 1922; he was knighted in 1929. He wasn't alone in protest. There were calls for a public inquiry into the plans, and even suggestions that existing residents from the Upper Richmond Road and the old Roehampton village could club together to buy the land to stop the LCC building. Resident Peggy Sturman held perhaps typical views. She said she thought the new estate, 'would get a run-down appearance and that perhaps the tenants in it wouldn't look after it, you know properly. I suppose we looked upon them as all being very, very poor people from the bad areas of the East End and that sort of thing.'[27]

The views from Putney were widely shared by the upper and middle classes, who, while willing to see their countrymen fight and die in the Great War, were less keen on the possibility that those people could share a little of the spoils of victory by gaining increased access to space on the island they had fought to defend. What was remarkable was that the new community of Roehampton soon began to gel and to evince a sense of purpose that might have come as a shock to existing residents. The Roehampton Estate Tenants' Association was formed in early 1921 and shortly after that the REGS in January 1922, quickly superseding in membership a moribund, if more grandiose-sounding, Roehampton Horticultural and Cottage Garden Society, which would eventually be folded into the new upstart. The first edition of the *Roehampton Estate Gazette* was published at the end of that year, displaying a clear determination to uphold the standards of the estate that we might even call busybodying these days, but driven by a mixture of pride at new beginnings and relief at escape from a miserable past. The views of existing nearby residents did begin to change once they saw the early houses and felt the sense of community emanating from the estate. Witness the changing testimony of Peggy Sturman: 'We used to walk around there, and it was really, really, quite a sight. Everyone seemed to take tremendous pride in the estate.'[28]

Cover of the *Roehampton Estate Gazette* (December 1922). Sudell wrote for it for two years after leaving Roehampton.

The LCC finished the estate in 1927 under various Housing Acts, a range of subsidies allowing more than 1,200 homes, ranging from five-room houses to two-room flats and housing a population of more than 5,000, to be constructed. It was certainly not going to loosen its managerial grip after the tenant interviews. The rent book with its pages of rules and regulations quickly became the bible to live by and the clipboard-wielding housing inspectors' regular visits meant gardens had to be kept pristine, neighbours' disapproval working in tandem with check sheets to keep things in order. The threat of eviction from the Land of Milk and Honey was a powerful weapon.

Into this mix came Richard Sudell with his first wife, Emily, who was from Hackney and a tireless organizer, advocate and eventually author herself. The couple married in Staines, Middlesex, in 1920 and later moved into 65 Huntingfield Road, the end of a three-cottage terrace situated at the bend of the road but set far enough back to allow a tiny front and larger back garden. Sudell was itching to get started on his horticultural project, as can be seen from the fact that he was already secretary of the London Gardens Guild (LGG), a body set up to encourage the beautification of the capital, particularly its poverty-stricken areas. Gardens and open spaces would be the LGG's weapons in this campaign, as we shall see later in this story. At the first meeting of the potential garden society on 22 January 1922, held in a meeting room at Putney Park House itself, which had been retained by the LCC, Sudell gave a speech to fifty attendees in which he spelt out the benefits of an association. Undoubtedly the prime mover, he urged his neighbours to form a society under the umbrella of the LGG as other estates were doing. Such a group would be able to hold flower shows, lectures and competitions and benefit from the discount buying of seeds and bulbs through the guild. This initial meeting was chaired by Mr Berry, a senior manager of the LCC Housing Department, such was the importance placed by the authority on these matters. According to the minutes of the meeting, 'the chairman in opening proceedings described the object of calling the tenants together in respect of beautifying the estate by means of planting and tending their gardens.' 'Beautification' was a word that was growing in importance for many progressives in the capital looking to tackle the terrible effects of extreme poverty and the ill health that came with it. At the end of the meeting Sudell was elected the society's first chairman.[29]

In just two short years Sudell threw himself with incredible zeal and considerable charm into the project. Here he was getting his hands dirty for the cause, literally by helping neighbours in their gardens and metaphorically by writing letters to the LCC, organizing shows and authoring instruction articles. He was a small symbol of the social and, by association, landscape history of the time. He stands as a living embodiment of a movement that wanted no more wars, demanded social change and was prepared to take practical steps towards building a better world, no matter how small the corner of it they could affect. Late into the night during August 1923, for example, the hammering of typewriter keys could be heard from 65 Huntingfield Road. A financial crisis caused by the suspect bookkeeping of a departed treasurer had left no money to pay for printing invitations and accounts for the forthcoming AGM: 'Since there were no funds, the committee thankfully accepted the offer of Mr Sudell to type out 600 notices concerning the meeting.'[30]

2
'An industrial slave? Never'

In a small prison cell 10 feet by 4 feet, a man is sewing mailbags. Apart from prison officers, he has not seen another soul for seven days. He is forbidden to speak, has only bread and water for sustenance and does not have the luxury of a mattress to sleep on. How does a gentle 23-year-old, already a callous-handed gardening veteran of ten years, something of an expert in orchids, get here, in solitary confinement in Winson Green prison, Birmingham, amid murderers and robbers and where the hangman's noose still swings? The jail, with its imposing 6-metre (20 ft) Gothic front gate, is only 48 kilometres (30 mi.) from the model village of Bournville and Woodbrooke College, the Society of Friends' study centre founded in his former home by chocolate factory owner George Cadbury with the help of another Quaker and chocolatier, John Rowntree.

It was at Woodbrooke on a clear day in spring 1916, having effectively sought sanctuary, that Richard Sudell was arrested by police officers in front of fellow students and taken away to face a tribunal. A few months before, the Military Service Act enforcing conscription had been enacted. 'In the middle of a glorious afternoon our fellow student, Mr Sudell, left under escort to testify to the faith that is in him on the question of military service. He was tried on Monday morning and sent to Warwick.'[1] Sudell was a conscientious objector and would remain one throughout the war, one of just 1,300 estimated 'absolutists' who refused any service to the war effort or alternative occupations that were offered to keep objectors out of prison or other forms of incarceration. He would not be the only Quaker unceremoniously marched out of Woodbrooke, for the Nonconformists, with pacifism as a central tenet of their faith, were in the frontline of anti-war sentiment and protest. Like many, Sudell would combine his faith with a fundamental belief in socialism as the path to a fairer society.

As for millions of others, the First World War changed the course of Sudell's life. As it loomed, he was just on the point of a remarkable change of fortune for a young man born into poverty who found salvation through a love of flowers: 'As a boy I made plants my study. I began gardening in the back garden with a row of sweet peas. I can still remember their delightful fragrance and mixed colours.'[2]

Sudell was born in September 1892 at Newton-with-Scales near Preston, Lancashire, the eldest of four children to George, a hay and straw dealer, and Annie.[3] Leaving school at fourteen years old and with an interest in horticulture, he gained employment as an apprentice gardener, working in the walled kitchen garden and glasshouses, and also learning about ornamental plants and forestry, at the 4-hectare (10 ac) garden of The Larches in nearby Ashton, the property of a local mill owner. He moved into lodgings in the village of Greavestown. Even though the days were long and the work was hard, Sudell showed a passion for self-improvement that would be lifelong and enrolled at the Harris Institute in Preston, which styled itself the Institution for the Diffusion of Useful Knowledge and where he passed Board of Education Certificates in botany, chemistry and geology. Files held at the Royal Botanical Gardens, Kew, show he was employed there for six years, before moving to work with orchids for a Mr W. Duckworth and then with garden contractor William Addison & Co of Lancashire from 1912 to 1914.[4]

Almost eight years as a gardener had given him the confidence to apply for a job at Kew in letters notable for their forthrightness:

'I should like to work in Kew Gardens for about two years to gain experience.' They also evidence that he had begun to enjoy encouraging others towards horticultural endeavours.[5] He tells Kew he is 'requested to give a lecture to our local Gardeners Mutual Improvement Association, this I would like to do ere I leave', before his potential employers had confirmed there was even a vacancy. His persistence was rewarded when he was granted employment at Kew beginning in March 1914 with a reference from the head gardener at The Larches, John Bradshaw, supporting him: 'His work has always been done with that devotion and thoroughness which gives satisfaction and demands respect.'[6] At Kew he made time from his duties to attend lectures in physics, chemistry, soils and manures. His files confirm that Sudell left employment at Kew a year later in March 1915. Effectively fleeing the war and with a career in horticulture seemingly over, he returned to Greavestown and enrolled at Woodbrooke the following year.

In the spring of that year the college newsletter, the *Woodbrooke Chronicle*, carried a list of students who had been brought before the Local Military Service Tribunal – government-appointed committees of dignitaries set up to judge cases – for refusing to sign up to the army. Under Sudell's entry are the words 'Absolute Exemption'. In January 1916 Prime Minister H. H. Asquith's government, against the background of a faltering war effort and a manpower crisis, introduced the Military Services Act, which paved the way for conscription. It did, though, enshrine an exemption for conscientious objection that would clearly excuse Quakers from any combatant service. The local tribunals would be established to adjudicate on those who wanted any exemption from service.

That same month the Society of Friends called their annual gathering, the Yearly Meeting, into a special session to discuss the crisis. While not binding, the meeting strongly supported the view that Quakers should reject the opt-out under the Act in favour of demanding absolute exemption; in other words followers were urged to accept no alternative the tribunal might offer in lieu of military service.[7] Taking this path would leave the conscientious objector (CO) effectively enlisted in the army and, as a soldier, absent without leave, for which he would be arrested and imprisoned. Quakers had, in the decades running up to the conflict, begun debating afresh a fundamental tenet of their faith called the peace testimony, a calling against the act of war and 'the spirit that makes war possible'.[8] When conscription was introduced, many younger Quakers, inspired by the peace testimony discussions, opted to reject exemption in order to become 'martyrs for their faith', sending society the clearest message about the Godlessness of warfare.[9] Many were also attempting to ally their religious beliefs with anti-capitalist ideals through the Socialist Quaker Society. The secular No-Conscription Fellowship (NCF), founded in 1914 by young socialist intellectuals such as Clifford Allen and Fenner Brockway, initially at least also adopted absolute exemption as a policy. The NCF and Quaker groups worked closely together to coordinate their anti-war programmes, and many Quakers were members of the NCF. However, as it became by far the biggest pacifist organization in Britain, with around 10,000 declared members with diverse views and beliefs, the NCF had a harder time holding this line and later began to support members who took alternative options to military service to avoid, or be relieved from, the degradations of prison.

It is important to note that despite the Yearly Meeting debate, there were many practising Quakers who did accept exempted positions with the Non-Combatant Corps, set up under the Act as a unit of the army for conscientious objectors that made members do physical work without going to battle or carrying weapons. Many also served in the Quaker-founded Friends' Ambulance Unit, a volunteer ambulance service that served on the battlefield and on the home front. Sudell was not to be one of these. Both at his tribunal and its inevitable appeal, he was offered exemption from combatant service, and service with the Non-Combatant Corps. Sudell chose the 'martyr' option and refused to cite his faith to gain his exemption. He was handed over to the army and court-martialled. In June 1916 he was sentenced to one year's hard labour at Winson Green prison.[10] This would have included a period of solitary confinement without a mattress on his bed, bread and water rations, and mundane and repetitive work tasks such as sewing mailbags.

Thus began almost three years of defiance from Sudell, which saw him serve three sentences and a total of two years in prison, eight months of which were on furlough. As well as the obvious hardship for Sudell, these years were formative in further developing his political beliefs while maintaining his horticultural interests. This can be illustrated by an option he took, while on furlough from his first sentence, to work with the Vacant Land Cultivation Society (VLCS), a body set up by American philanthropist Joseph Fels before the war to turn idle land in London into allotments for the poor and given a government-backed new lease of life when the conflict started as the need for new sources of fresh food grew. Around the turn of the nineteenth century the provision of allotments had become a political hot potato, especially after the enfranchisement of urban working-class males by the Franchise Act of 1884.

The need to help cripplingly poor rural labourers hit by a decades-long recession in British farming caused by cheaper food imports had led to Acts of Parliament aimed at providing allotments, culminating in the most effective, the 1908 Small Holdings and Allotment Act, which obliged local authorities to provide allotments for the 'labouring population' where they could not be found privately.[11] It is likely that Sudell was born into the middle of this issue, since his father George, as a hay and straw dealer, would undoubtedly have struggled during the agricultural recession, making the need to grow food for him and his burgeoning family vital. This is likely why, in later life, Sudell was a tireless advocate for the allotment movement, serving on the council of the National Allotment Society for many years and becoming chairman of the Surrey Allotment Council when he moved to the county later in life.

Sudell agreed to take on work with the VLCS as an assistant superintendent organizing meetings of plot holders and giving gardening instruction. His motivation was certainly not to ensure potential recruits for the front were well fed and fit, but a lifetime belief in the empowering nature of food self-sufficiency. His horticultural expertise, combined with a dire need to grow fresh food in the capital (even before the war it is estimated 25 people a year died of starvation in the east of the city), meant he was one of the very few absolutist COs given such a non-custodial opportunity. Yet after five months of this work the Home Office ordered him to cease and attend the Wakefield Work Centre, one of several such places set up as custodial quarters, alternatives to prison, for sentenced conscientious objectors where they were also given mundane tasks in the community.

Sudell had already refused to attend the centres and now the Home Office partially relented, allowing him to continue working with the VLCS providing he resided at the London Work Centre in Millman Street. He wrote to the Conscientious Objector Information Bureau (COIB), a body set up by the NCF and Quakers to record the wartime experiences of COs, taking up the story: 'I refused to accept the conditions, pointing out that as a Free Agent I was willing to help organize the production of food – but as an industrial slave never!'[12] This is one of the few first-hand accounts from Sudell of his powerful conviction, combining as it does both a horticultural philosophy – in the letter he describes the VLCS as having 'definite social value' – with the political. He objected not only to war but to what many were beginning to attack as the government's industrial conscription policy: that politicians were using COs and others as a source of cheap labour. Note the defiance about remaining a 'free agent' coming so soon after the traumatic experience of solitary confinement. Sudell's ordeal was reported to Edmund Harvey MP, a prominent Quaker who, in Parliament, had taken up many cases of the treatment of conscientious objectors. In a letter to Harvey, the sculptor and art teacher Christine Gregory, the first woman elected as a member of the Royal Society of British Sculptors, wrote that Sudell's refusal to comply had seen him sent back to prison for another year of hard labour: 'He is an objector to militarization and industrial conscription and believes that the greatest protest against war and its attendant evils is to refuse to be a direct participant in the organization of the country for war purposes whatever the personal consequences of that action may be.'[13]

In a letter written the same day to another Quaker MP, Arnold Rowntree, who represented York and was a member of the chocolate-making family, Gregory gave further details:

> Richard Sudell felt this [the order to reside at a Work Centre] to be incompatible with his principles but was willing and anxious to continue his social service if allowed to do so as a free agent. This course the Home Office refused and communicated with the War Office for his recall to the army. He then resigned from the VLCS, reported himself to the police and is now just commencing his second term of imprisonment (12 months' hard labour) in Dorchester prison.[14]

In early 1917 while in Dorchester, Sudell, probably close to being broken by his second spell in prison, accepted service with the Non-Combatant Corps and was sent to army barracks in Weymouth, Dorset. However, he then had a change of heart and, returning to the 'Absolute Exemption' principle, deserted. On 17 April his flight was recorded in the *Police Gazette*, a weekly Home Office publication alerting the public and the police forces to those wanted for crimes, where he was described as a 23-year-old student. For that desertion, he was again court-martialled in Weymouth in May and given one year's hard labour; and again, for unrecorded reasons, in Weymouth in October of the same year, was handed a two-year hard labour sentence. These were partially served back at Dorchester prison.[15]

Despite the fortitude with which he stuck to his principles, Sudell never wrote about his prison experiences, so it is difficult to gauge how these affected him. For most COs prison regimes were chastening in the extreme, as the experience of Clifford Allen, chairman of the NCF, and soon to be a friend of Sudell, describes: 'This experience has been a greater strain than even I thought. Solitude is a terrifying thing when it is enforced. You cannot stop thinking for an instant. And if you seem to, it is only to listen intently to the beating of your heart drumming in your ears.'[16]

From the introduction of the Act, in January, to July of that year some 750,000 men applied for exemption from conscription during the war in cases that were judged by the local tribunals. The vast majority did so under three of the four exemption criteria, namely ill health, economic hardship or that their existing work was an essential occupation. About 16,500 men chose the fourth criterion, religious or moral objection to war, as the basis for their cases. To put this into perspective, that was about one-third of 1 per cent of the total number of recruits and conscripts who did serve. Of the objectors, around 6,000 of what Thomas C. Kennedy calls 'obdurate objectors' either refused to appear before the tribunal or accept its decision and were sentenced to military or civil imprisonment.[17] Sudell belonged to an even more hardline subset of this group, the roughly 1,300 who were repeatedly imprisoned for their defiance. Of those who went to prison it is estimated that seventy either died behind bars or soon after release because of the treatment they had endured.

After the war Sudell would become friends with a remarkable couple of Quaker Socialist politicians, Dr Alfred and Ada Salter, who transformed the borough of Bermondsey in the interwar years, tackling abject poverty and establishing a Beautification Committee to improve the environment. They were also highly visible pacifists during the war, their office being besieged by a pro-war mob on one occasion. Alfred, who became the long-serving Labour MP for the area, regularly took up the cause of humane treatment for conscientious objectors. Correspondence between Salter and the country squire, poet, philanderer and anti-colonialist Wilfred Scawen Blunt stands as vivid testimony to the often traumatizing experience of COs. It also allows understanding of how steadfast in their beliefs they had to be to withstand society's physical and verbal assault on them. Blunt, who was also opposed to the war, had an astonishing circle of friends in high places including Winston Churchill and Margot Asquith, the wife of H. H. Asquith who was prime minister until the end of 1916.

Salter wrote to his friend Blunt hoping he could wield his influence and help end the brutal regime of the commander of the Wandsworth Detention Centre, a military establishment that held men conscripted into the army after being declined CO status by a tribunal but who were refusing to serve. A Boer War veteran, Lt Col. Reginald Brooke, was the officer in charge and had already ordered one man to be placed in a straitjacket and be force-fed through the nose. Brooke had already replied to Salter's letter of protest over the treatment of a 'Private' Forrester by replying, 'I do not care one atom for public opinion.'[18] In the letter to Blunt, Salter enclosed a written testimony from Forrester about his treatment at the hands of Brooke:

> I told him I was not a soldier and could not obey military orders. The Col was standing near and he thundered up and shouted 'What! You won't obey me?' with a thick accompaniment. I quietly answered, 'I must obey my God, Sir'. 'D—n your God! Take him to the special room.' Four of them then set on me. One of them took me by the back of the neck, nearly choking me, shook me and dragged me

along, while the others punched, thumped and kicked me as hard as they knew how. They banged my head on the floor and the walls and then threw me into a little cell with thick walls and a small skylight. Then they told me to get my boots off but I would not do so and the Sergeant deliberately punched me behind the ears and all of them set on me and bruised me more. They at last cleared out and slammed the door leaving me without boots, coat or braces laying on the floor almost exhausted.[19]

Such treatment of COs in prison and detention barracks was far from uncommon but even the government blanched at this case. Within two weeks of Salter writing his letter to Blunt, the under secretary of state for war, Harold Tennant, was telling the Commons that Brooke had 'ceased to be commandant of the Wandsworth Detention Barracks'.[20] Tennant was the brother of Margot Asquith and thus the prime minister's brother-in-law. Most COs were subject to abuse and physical harm both during the war and afterwards. Politicians and newspapers were vociferous in attacking COs. Tory backbenchers damned the exemption criteria of the Act as a 'slacker's charter' and Lloyd George claimed the public was exasperated by COs 'shrimshaking' at home while others died on the front. In a letter to *The Times*, the vicar of Holy Trinity, Brompton, wrote, 'No honest citizen can tolerate these neurotic curiosities. We have no use for them.'[21] Public opinion was febrile. Thus for many COs career prospects vanished after the war. They were permanently banned from employment with the Civil Service and legal attempts were made to stop them voting in elections for five years: 'For some COs the aftermath was not only disenfranchisement and dishonour but long-term economic deprivation as well.'[22]

There is no evidence that anyone apart from family and close associates knew of Sudell's own war experiences. Sudell's parents were Quakers but that did not mean everyone in the family took the same position on the war as he did. In 1918, while Sudell was incarcerated, his younger brother John died of diphtheria in Edinburgh, aged 22, while serving in the Royal Navy. The government was very slow to release absolutists, especially as many conscripts were still required to serve after victory, with the last of them freed in July 1919. It seems very likely Sudell would have been one of these, having been sent to prison for another two-year sentence of hard labour as late as October 1917. By this time there were signs of a slight thawing in what was admittedly an overwhelmingly hostile public attitude. Some newspapers and politicians did start to question the continued imprisonment of absolutist COs, with Lord Hugh Cecil joining a group of other MPs in writing to *The Times* to warn Lloyd George that changing public opinion would inevitably make continuing punishment of COs as 'impolitic . . . as it has always been wrong'.[23] Over the next two decades the growing awareness of the horrific toll of the 'war to end all wars' did lead to some form of a reappraisal as anti-conflict sentiment grew – and with it at least a grudging acceptance that absolutists such as Sudell were far from 'slackers' but men with staunch faith and firm principles, which, however far from mainstream, were genuinely held.

In 1931 playwright and political activist George Bernard Shaw, who supported COs throughout the war and is likely to have known Sudell, was able to assert, 'As far as the question was one solely of courage, the Conchy [slang for CO] was the hero of the war.'[24] The extent of a wider, interwar, recognition of the human cost of warfare can be judged by the fact that there were 60,000 COs in the Second World War, far exceeding the numbers in the First World War, even though many historians now raise more critical questions about justifications for the latter – a murderous clash of rival empires for some – than the former.

In some ways Roehampton was a perfect place for Sudell to move with Emily, a post office clerk, after the war. The cottage estate was a fresh start for everyone, with tenants coming from various parts of London and beyond with unknown personal histories. While a psychological desire to rebuild lives and look forward, rather than back on five years of terror and extreme hardship, might be expected, it was also virtually certain that almost everyone moving out to new estates like Roehampton would have known one or more of the almost 900,000 British soldiers killed or 1.6 million wounded. Grief was rife and emotions still running high, so it seems likely that Sudell would have remained silent about his wartime experience. Given the strength of his pacifist convictions, as evidenced by testimony both by himself to the COIB and through supporters like Christine Gregory, who was after all asking for his case to be raised in the most public forum in the land, namely Parliament, this might seem strange. But it should be remembered that many soldiers returning from the front also remained silent about their experiences. For some not talking about it helped contain the horrors they had witnessed. Certainly it seems unlikely that, had Sudell's wartime record been widely known, he would have been instantly recognized as a community leader, respected for his horticultural knowledge and easily accepted as the first chairman of the REGS.

While many COs struggled for employment after the war, especially as potential employers almost always asked them what they did in the conflict, it seems likely Sudell realized that returning to an employed horticultural career, such as he had begun at Kew before the outbreak of the conflict, was now shut off to him. Almost immediately he started his own self-employed garden practice in Roehampton. It grew so quickly, on the back of demand for instruction and advice, that he often struggled to fulfil his duties with the REGS. What appears to be true about Sudell in all his post-war activities is that, far from abandoning his beliefs, he determinedly channelled them into garden and landscape philosophy. The skills he possessed, allied to the commitment he had to the cause of a more equal society, were the tools he was best equipped to use to help, in his own way, transform Britain. From the gentle advice he gave his neighbours on how to plant and grow a rose to the battles he would go on to have about the landscaping of a new country, it was the garden and the land through which he would now channel all his energy: 'Beauty is one of the greatest forces in the world, it is the power which can move mountains and in striving after beauty, we are striving after the sublime. Let us then turn to our gardens both to seek freshness of mind and to add beauty to the world.'[25]

Fired by his wartime experience, Sudell was to enter into an astonishingly productive period of his life, convinced of the uplifting power of garden and landscape, which saw him help make a real practical difference to the way many parts of the land looked and felt. He wrote the quotation above in an editorial for the *Guild Gardener*, the magazine he founded for the London Gardens Guild (LGG), a body set up to bring the health benefits of gardens and open spaces to deprived areas of the capital. Here is evidence of the depth of his commitment to a horticultural revolution. Like many others he really did believe in the power of flowers, plants and green spaces to uplift the spirit from the demoralization brought by deprivation. While this philosophy still holds today it is worth remembering just what that deprivation looked like in the interwar years, the sorts of environment from which many of the new tenants of Roehampton had gratefully fled.

Take the borough of Bermondsey, soon to be the subject of a campaign by the Salters to tackle soul-stripping poverty, which was around the turn of the twentieth century one of London's worst slums, and the setting for Jacob's Island in Dickens's *Oliver Twist*. Dr Salter began visiting the dockside borough as a trainee doctor at Guy's Hospital. He found conditions little changed from 1856, when the then medical officer reported that he had visited a family, a husband and wife together with four children, living in one dirty room in the middle of which was a child who had died of measles, laid in a coffin that had not been fastened down and could not be removed because the parish would not conduct single burials with plots so scarce because of the death rate. In 1893, on Salter's rounds, things had hardly changed, as witnessed by this visit to a maternity case:

> It was a cold day but the family were so poor that they had not even a penny to put into the meter for heat. The House was a one-up, one-down with a small scullery and no backyard except for a shut-in paved area, three feet deep. Drying and washing were done in the front court, where, at the other end, there was one standpipe for 25 houses, with the water on for two hours daily – though never on Sundays. There was no place to wash in – no other water to wash with. There was no modern sanitation. There was one water closet for the 25 houses and a cesspool. Queues lined up outside that water closet, men, women and children, every morning before they went to work. Often they stood in the snow and rain waiting their turn. There was no possibility of decency, modesty or health for these people. It was impossible for them to maintain bodily cleanliness. The condition of thousands of homes was the same at that time.[26]

Even by 1923 there had been little improvement for the residents of Bermondsey, particularly around the 4 to 5 hectares (10 or 12 ac) of hovels surrounding Salisbury Street, which Salter described as a 'death trap and fever den' and in which more than 1,000 people lived. The death rate in that area was 50 per cent higher than in the rest of London, with the infant mortality rate nearly double: five times as many children died of measles and three times as many people died of respiratory diseases.[27] The Salter-led borough council would soon demolish these slums and replace them with a garden village, but this pattern of deprivation was repeated in many areas of London. The LGG itself had been founded by Noel Buxton, soon to be a Labour MP and government minister, and the Rev. Rollo Meyer after a visit to the dismal slums of Whitechapel and Spitalfields. As

Buxton described the visit himself: 'people had a family to a room. In one room we visited the inhabitants divided between gardening and poultry farming, the chickens being caged under the beds.'[28] The pair had been shown the slums by social reformer and priest Samuel Barnett who, with his wife Henrietta, established the first university settlement, Toynbee Hall, in Whitechapel in 1884.

Henrietta founded the Hampstead Garden Suburb in 1906, which evidenced how a nascent network of radical social reformers was slowly establishing itself to promote the built environment and landscape as a means of promoting greater societal equality. It had Barry Parker and Raymond Unwin as its architects and was built on Garden City principles. According to Buxton, after the Whitechapel visit a shocked Meyer, a keen amateur horticulturist, suggested that window boxes might help to partially alleviate the misery and the LGG was born. As honorary secretary of the now expanded National Gardens Guild (NGG), Sudell wrote to *The Times* in 1928 announcing a countrywide window box competition with the first prize a handsome £100.[29]

This was the backdrop to the birth of the modern British suburban garden, a context which, in later years, was in danger of being forgotten as they became associated with conformist middle-class Metro-land suburbia or, worse for some critics, the tasteless and garish plots of the working-class council estates. The debates around these gardens took many turns and were subject to interpretations beyond the control of early twentieth-century pioneers and social reformers like Sudell. The egalitarian, health-giving, beautifying nature of the new landscapes and the empowerment that some level of horticultural knowledge gave the newly situated working class were positives that were in danger of fading from the argument. The self-improving ability that poorer citizens had, for the first time, to partially shape and affect their own immediate environment through house and garden was also in danger of disappearing from the story. In their place came class-based snobbishness but also fears that these developments would actually hinder social change, and that the gardens were in fact opiates for the working classes, which would keep them from demanding radical transformation.

Furthermore, by hiding behind the privet hedge these new tenants and homeowners would not only forgo proper community spirit but promote individualism, eschewing the collective political action that would force reform. Lloyd George was clear that part of the reason for his 'Homes fit for heroes' plan, 'even if it cost a hundred million pounds', was to guarantee the stability of the state against Bolshevik-style overthrow. Access to green spaces and gardens had often been considered a safety valve by the ruling classes during periods of unrest and demands from the working class for social justice. For instance, political agitation surrounding the tortuous passage of the 1832 Reform Act, the disappointment of its outcome and the subsequent rise of Chartism prompted an improvement in the provision of parks for the working classes. The Parliamentary Select Committee on the Health of Towns in 1840 reported that more such green spaces were essential not only for the welfare of the poor but for the safety of property and security of the rich.[30]

These new gardens and green spaces were loaded with meaning, and rich in historical, political, social and horticultural narrative. To help us understand this, we first need to journey back deep onto the Roehampton Estate in 1922, as the builders continued their noisy, bustling construction of more homes. The struggle against debris-strewn soil was in the balance and Richard Sudell was beginning his mission. Here, in the literal grassroots, we will find out what he and his neighbours thought of their new opportunities as they spread their colour on the dull claggy soil.

3
Trouble at the Whit Monday Garden Show

It was obvious to Richard Sudell and his allies in the Roehampton Garden Society that the Whit Monday Show, on 21 May 1923, was not going well. Held in the grounds of the demolished Dover House, the event was intended to whet the appetite for the now-established annual summer show, which was to be held over two days at the end of the season. As well as displays of flowers and produce, which would be judged by the REGS committee members, there were attractions for those who were not so green fingered. An Aunt Sally stand, a novelty kiosk selling tat, a coconut shy and other attractions were stationed around the perimeter and there was a hospitality tent that was subsidized for members of the RGS committee.

This was probably where it started to go wrong. A total of £7 worth of beer and spirits was guzzled by certain members of the committee, way over the complimentary allocation that had been set. Not only that but it appeared the Aunt Sally stand had contrived to make a loss. Sudell had worked tirelessly throughout 1922 and the first few months of 1923 to establish the REGS and had then stepped down as chairman to accept a promotion as head of the Roehampton Estate Tenants' Association (RETA), even though his own garden work was taking up so much of his time. The REGS, although starting life independently, became a subsection of the RETA in September 1922. Sudell remained on the REGS committee. His first summer show, in July 1922, had been described as a 'complete success', a triumphant symbol of an estate driven by horticultural purpose, and was attended by several officials from the LCC, who paternalistically nodded approval.[1]

Now he was uncharacteristically angry. The shows were established to showcase gardening skills and encourage others to join in the fun. But they were also to make money to help pay for the activities of the REGS, to subsidize the purchase of seeds and bulbs for residents, to buy shared garden machinery – a lawnmower could cost around £6 in 1923 (around £300 today) – and to help fund the continued lobbying of officials to maintain investment in the green spaces of the estate. This was now in jeopardy.

Who called a special meeting of the REGS ten days after the debacle to begin investigations, and why the crypt at St Margaret's Church was chosen as a venue, is unclear. Up until then a room at the LCC-owned Putney Park House had sufficed. Now someone, perhaps with an acute sense of theatre, had changed the venue.

It is likely the treasurer, Mr Turner, or the former secretary, Mr Robins, blew the whistle on the Whit Monday shenanigans, for at 8 p.m., with soft early summer rain falling outside, they both lined up with Sudell to demand answers. Sitting across from them was the current chairman, W. J. Grose, the current secretary Mr Ball and Mr Hearse, secretary of the local British Legion and committee member. Hearse started off by insisting the Aunt Sally stand had lost nine shillings (around £30 in today's money) because stock and prizes had been stolen. Grose chipped in that clumsy boys had burst too many of the balloons they were blowing up for the novelty stall and that the plastic trumpets on sale had proved defective. They also railed about the 'totally inadequate' drinks allocations. Sudell sternly told them that while they had drunk £7 worth of alcohol it was 'generally accepted' that a £5 limit was adequate for these occasions, although where he had sourced this figure is unclear.

After more of this kind of argument, Robins moved a motion to depose Grose because of the considerable Whit Show losses, but the Sudell faction had overestimated their support. The vote was tied five each with four abstaining. Having failed in his bid to remove Grose, Robins handed in his resignation and was followed by Sudell, Turner and two others.[2] The crypt putsch had been beaten. Turner, who remained insistent that there was financial skulduggery abroad, initially refused to hand over the books and was threatened with legal action. More controversy was to follow at the next REGS meeting in June when it was reported that there was doubt about the forthcoming annual show.

> It is the opinion of the committee that the attitude of the late sec Mr Robins and the late Treasurer Mr Turner, with the connivance of others has been one of delay aimed at the cancellation of the annual flower show ... therefore the committee shall resign en bloc at a special general meeting called on July 31, 1923.[3]

We know the minutiae of this little local drama because the minutes of the REGS are recorded in painstaking detail and in beautiful longhand in ledgers that were found in an old garden shed in Sutton. Rescued by past president Jackie Savage and stored in her attic, there they remained until this author spent a summer's day in 2018 poring over them at her kitchen table. Records like these are the atoms of history, allowing us to understand the millions of daily decisions by millions of people that begin to cluster together to shape their world. And here, in 1923 in Roehampton, within these ledgers, is evidence of a movement. People are carving out space for themselves, forging a new life, contributing a fragment of fabric to a tapestry of social change. The minutes bring long-dead people back to life, show their part in history, their efforts (some of them at least) to improve, brighten and enrich their own lives and, if we go back to visit where they once lived, how that effort still enriches today.

Poster for the second annual REGS summer show, in the *Roehampton Estate Gazette* (August 1923). Note the name of the organizing secretary, who was to become embroiled in a minor financial scandal.

There is no evidence about what actually happened on 31 July. The minute book ends with the second half of its remaining pages still blank. A new book, begun to record the decisions of an REGS meeting in early August straight after the old regime's summer show, has literally turned the page on the immediate past. Richard Sudell is back as chairman and his wife Emily is there too. The venue for the meeting is their home at 65 Huntingfield Road. Sudell control is complete. There is no sign of Grose or Hearse, but Turner and Robins are back. There's final vindication of treasurer Turner's claims. The accounts for the six months up to the actual date of the crypt meeting show a deficit of almost £16 (around £1,000 in today's money), which is high given that members pay a yearly subscription and that outlay for the last half year had been modest. Former secretary Ball owes almost £3; 'he had taken monies without giving regular receipts,' the minutes for a late August meeting unsurprisingly record.[4]

And so it was that RETA, in the form of honorary secretary Mrs F. A. Songhurst, called a special investigative meeting in September concluding 'the responsibility for the sad state of the society's finances (the exhaustion of the profits made in the previous flower show 1922 and on the Whitsun Fete plus the loss of £15/10/2.5) rested with the retired committee, for Mr Ball should have been working under their control.' Songhurst recorded RETA's 'profound dissatisfaction' with the retired committee. The REGS was left penniless (hence Sudell having to type out six hundred individual notices of the AGM, as recounted earlier). Now it also had to sell beanpoles, rakes, forks, spades, watering cans, seeds and hoes that it had bought for the collective use of members of the society.

At least the former committee members Grose, Ball and Hearse would not be taking advantage of the cut-price booze at next year's shows. They were banned for life from the REGS. At the next meeting Sudell again stepped aside to concentrate on RETA and his garden work and proposed J. H. Allen become chairman. Allen and Sudell would become firm friends and later allies in the effort to take the lessons learnt at Roehampton to a national audience.[5]

The 1924 annual show was a total success, as was the following year's effort, with the *Gazette* boasting that the two finally proved that Roehampton was the 'LCC's most progressive estate' and stating that the LGG should be proud of its 'newly fledged infant society'.[6] The magazine had in 1923 celebrated Sudell's election as chairman of RETA, stating he had well earned the honour with his running of the annual shows: 'much of the success that was achieved was directly due to his assistance and advice.' In the same article it praised him for allocating an allotment on one site – Roehampton had three sites – for community instruction and experimentation. There Sudell showed beginners how to grow roses, carnations, wallflowers, delphiniums, lupins and border plants so they could take the knowledge, and the cuttings, back to their own gardens.[7]

The provision of allotments was an issue close to Sudell's heart. While he used one of Roehampton's plots as a training flower nursery for tenants, the importance of growing food was just as important as creating gardens for the enjoyment of residents and neighbourhoods – perhaps more so given the background of the times, with post-war recession and food rationing biting hard. Against this backdrop Sudell's commitment to promoting self-sufficiency in food was total, with many of his instruction books having sections on food growing and showing residents that, even in the smallest of gardens, they could still make space for a spot of tilled earth to grow potatoes or carrots or even plant a small fruit tree.

As so often in his life we find Sudell playing a part in another of the landscape movements of the time, this one perhaps one of the most remarkable, yet unheralded, chapters of twentieth-century British social history. As we have seen, Sudell had joined the VLCS in 1916 on furlough from prison, one of the very few absolutist COs allowed relief from the desperate incarceration they suffered, such was the importance of the new task ahead of him. In some ways the allotment movement was an attempt at a very small reverse of the three-century appropriation by larger landowners and farmers, through both informal methods and Acts of Parliament, of huge swathes of agricultural land and pasture through enclosure. In this systematic land grab, thousands of commoners, cottagers and peasants lost their rights to parish common land for grazing livestock and growing vegetables and, with it, their way of life. They also lost their 'fuel rights', ancient privileges that gave them access to rough land for the purposes of cutting turf, peat and wood for heating their homes and cooking. While debate might surround the necessity of enclosure to advance agricultural practice and make food production more efficient, what is undoubted is that the face of England in particular was changed forever, an agrarian way of life gone, new social classes emerging. The new landless and the increasingly impoverished drifted into the slums of the new towns of the Industrial Revolution, where more deprivation and squalor awaited. Between 1760 and 1801 alone there were some 1,500 individual Acts of Parliament passed enclosing around 1.2 million hectares (almost 3 million acres) of rural land throughout the country, the beginnings of a denial of access to the countryside that we experience to this day. Some of these Acts did offer tiny parcels of land, allotments, reluctantly given by the enriched landowners in exchange for the giving up of fuel rights. These were invariably even smaller and less productive than the land the commoners were losing, but did at least establish a principle of allotments. A combination of the newly emboldened landowners and reluctant government rendered progress towards even a modest scheme to hand the poor land for some form of self-sufficiency painfully slow. Allotment Acts towards the end of the nineteenth century empowered local authorities to provide plots but the legislation was largely toothless. Two years into the First World War, however, with Britain cut off from food supplies, the government finally realized that tough action was needed and under emergency powers given by the Defence of the Realm Act (DORA) local authorities were given the right to exploit unused land, sometimes earmarked for housing or industrial development, for food production.

The VLCS was founded in 1907 by American philanthropist Joseph Fels, who imported the idea from the USA, where thriving projects were under way in a number of cities, most notably New York and Philadelphia. However, until DORA the VLCS found it hard to make progress, with only 140 plot holders gaining land by the outbreak of war. For Fels it was very simple. The war threatened mass unemployment and even starvation. London in particular was dotted with wasteland or space waiting for development that would not be coming in wartime. Fels argued that it could also be improved aesthetically by the installation of colourful allotments. Even two years after the outbreak of war, only eight hundred plot holders had been established in the capital on about 20 hectares (50 ac) as the VLCS's requests for sympathetic treatment from private companies fell on deaf ears.

Under pressure from the VLCS the government was compelled to act. Using its DORA powers, it introduced the Cultivation of Land Order in 1916 giving the Board of Agriculture and local authorities, here mainly the LCC, the power to commandeer land temporarily, without the approval of, or even notice to, landowners. Meanwhile thousands of people had begun to apply for allotments that didn't exist. Matters were not helped when the LCC obstinately refused to exercise its new powers to seize land, even though it had granted the VLCS a licence to operate the scheme. The society described the LCC's actions as a 'deplorable lack of public spirit', recognizing there was a growing agitation from increasingly desperate residents.[8] Eventually power passed down to individual London boroughs where more enlightened politicians in places such as Wandsworth, Woolwich and Lambeth helped speed up the process. Within six months of the Order being passed, the VLCS had grown its number of member plot holders across the country tenfold, from 800 to 8,000, all managed by an increasingly overwhelmed staff. Many of the new gardeners were the wives of serving soldiers. All knew that they might not be able to feed hungry mouths without growing food themselves.

Sudell's horticultural expertise was a godsend to the society. First, he could help teach new plot holders how to ready the most unpromising of soils for growing and guide them as they progressed. Second, he was one of the society's 'advisers' frequently used to counter arguments from landowners, individuals, public and private bodies that land could not be taken because their own 'experts' said it was unsuitable. For Sudell this was almost always nonsense, as the most unpromising sites could yield produce of some kind. He helped the VLCS wrest a 2-hectare (5 ac) unused plot in Putney that was under the control of the – perhaps surprisingly resistant – Board of Agriculture. Lastly Sudell gave the odd lecture on subjects such as 'crops, soil, manures, cultivation, weather, a smattering of chemistry and botany and so on.'[9]

It cannot be overstated how radical this movement was, nor how people who had hitherto grown nothing, never handled a spade or even had a garden took to the allotment with astonishing enthusiasm and eventual skill. It was sometimes a matter of life and death. One example of the remarkable effort put into turning waste into productive land occurred in space next to Latchmere Baths, Battersea. The land had been used by the local authority as a waste tip for many years and rubbish reached down several feet in some places. The local MP had said that not even a 'consumptive cabbage' could grow there. Nevertheless, the land was handed over and twenty prospective plot holders turned up to begin the reclamation work: 'By the first week of March over eighty tons of stones and hardcore, all of which was collected in baskets and wheelbarrows by plot holders, had been removed from the site.'[10] Even then the site appeared unpromising and trenching needed to go 3 metres (10 ft) down to get to decent soil. Work continued and by May the land had been parcelled up and the first green shoots of plant and vegetable growth were showing.

According to Gerald Butcher, senior VLCS official and chronicler of the movement, as well as growing much-needed food 'what the allotment holder has really accomplished has been to beautify not to deface,' a concept whose time, as we shall see, had also come. Potatoes were by far the most popular crop, followed by cabbages, onions, turnips and parsnips, with even the Board of Agriculture estimating that the yield on allotments was 25 per cent greater than that of the farm-grown variety, an incredible performance. Instead of imported meat from Argentina and wheat from Canada or Australia, more and more people were eating potatoes and vegetables from allotments, often plot holders handing surpluses to neighbours. This was important when what was known as the potato queues of

1917 occurred. Supplies from abroad became scarce and prices spiked, leading to huge queues, mainly of women and children, forming at greengrocers often in freezing temperatures and rain. The VLCS claimed that some children had died of pneumonia because of this. However, by July allotment holders across the land were experiencing big yields of potatoes and helped to mitigate the disaster. According to Butcher, 'England must never forget how the allotment holder abolished the potato queue,' and they were even more important when supplies of meat and butter became scarce that year. Allotment vegetables, sometimes sold for a small price, were becoming the staple diet of millions.[11]

It is not known how many allotment plots were allocated in wartime after the government made the process compulsory, but readers of the VLCS journal *Vacant Lots* rose from 2,000 at the end of 1916 to 30,000 by early 1918. By that time it had changed its name to *Allotments and Gardens* and was being produced by the National Union of Allotment Holders, a body the VLCS did much to help set up and which took over the baton after the war. It campaigned for much of the temporary designations of allotment space to be made permanent. The Land Settlement Facilities Act of 1919 increased the right to allotment space of returning servicemen, not just the labouring poor. The rights of allotment holders in England and Wales were strengthened through legislation in 1922, but the most important change came with the Allotments Act of 1925, which established statutory plots that local authorities could not sell off or convert without ministerial consent. These were known as Section 8 Orders.

For Sudell, who would become a council member of the National Allotment Society for decades and, when he eventually moved from London, the chairman of the Surrey Allotment Council, the movement was a perfect conflation of vital practicality and social welfare. Food was cheap and healthy, and there was a reconnection with the land that many urban dwellers had lost, and which promoted a new community spirit. Finally, there was exercise and fresh air in often desperately poor neighbourhoods. Children frequently helped at 'Daddy's plot', giving them much-needed exercise: 'See me on a Sunday morning, shelling peas, my own grown, sitting on my mother's upturned bucket, pipe alight, the missus jumping for joy, kids laughing, dog wagging his tail like a leaf in a gale.'[12] Gardens and allotments cannot be separated in this story. It is worth bearing this in mind when critics of the suburb come into view, as they will.

For two years of his life Sudell did not cease gently encouraging his neighbours on Roehampton to expand their horticultural knowledge. He organized lectures that were well attended, the first, almost as soon as the REGS was formed, by a senior inspector with the Board of Agriculture, N. H. Jenkins. Sudell had arranged the bulk buying from the LGG of lime for soil and sulphate of ammonia to aid the rapid growth of lawns and plants so that residents would not lose heart with their early efforts. He had the LCC stump up cash prizes for the first garden competition in spring 1923, with £5 for winners of best front and back gardens, and £2 for various allotment categories. To obtain the funds Sudell had to recruit fifty entrants, which he easily surpassed.

The winner of the first best front garden competition, a Mr Offaway, went on to claim the prize in the capital-wide contest run by the LGG that year. Subscriptions was another area of focus for Sudell with the £2 annual fee funding bulk buying, lectures, communal equipment and the shows. Building membership up to six hundred in just two years was an astonishing achievement. And it wasn't just the tenants whom he persuaded to part with subscription cash: in June 1922 he signed up theatre impresario Sir Oswald Stoll, who lived in nearby Putney Hill, as a member. The co-founder of the Stoll Moss Group theatre company and owner of Cricklewood film studios had rapidly become a very rich man and was a useful person to have on board. The REGS even had a president, Sir Lawrence Jones, who gave out the prizes at the first annual show. This seems likely to be the 4th Baronet Jones, whose family seat was Cranmer Hall, Norfolk, but who had a home in London too.[13] Sudell was not above employing the upper classes and the monied to further his horticultural cause.

So what did these gardens on Roehampton look like? There is very little photographic evidence of the early versions, although pictures taken a little later in the mid-1920s for the LGG's capital-wide annual gardening competition do give a clue. Much detail can be gained from Sudell himself, who began writing prodigiously for his neighbours, giving them practical guidance and step-by-step advice. These words do give a clear picture of how the gardens on the estate and others like it were beginning to take shape, to burst into colour. It is not clear when Sudell first realized he could write plainly and practically about his passion. Having left school at fourteen he had, while working as a gardener, spent some of his spare time studying for Board of Education certificates in botany, chemistry and geology. There is no hint there that he would go on to be one of the most influential British garden journalists in the early twentieth century, although we have seen he had enjoyed lecturing his fellow Lancastrian gardeners on the subject. Nevertheless, now his words, as well as his actions, began to be keenly followed.

First, he wrote a monthly gardening column in the *Roehampton Estate Gazette*, from its second edition in December 1922 until the end of 1926, two years after he had left the estate, evidence of a commitment to ensure that his former neighbours did not slacken their beautification efforts. Subsequently his writings in the *Gazette* were brought together and expanded upon for his first book, *The Town Gardening Handbook*, effectively the official volume of the LGG. Sudell, whose association with the guild had begun before he moved on to Roehampton, had suggested that such a book could be a vital tool in promoting the spread of gardening on the new LCC estates and elsewhere in the capital. It was published in early 1924, with the secretary of the REGS telling *Gazette* readers it had been written by 'a resident on the estate and undoubtedly an authority on gardening questions. The word PRACTICAL should be written on every page.'[14] The *Gazette* later reported that the book had sold like 'hot cakes and additional supplies are needed'.[15] This first batch of 250 copies had sold out within days of their arrival on the estate.

His first column for the *Gazette* makes it clear that he and his neighbours are only just beginning their journey, with some still wrestling muddy plots left by the builders. 'The first consideration in planning the garden is its aspects. Wherever possible paths should be made to run North and South,' he tells them. 'Make straight wide paths if washing has to be dried.'[16] What followed over the next few years was clear, concise instruction on subjects such as fruit growing in small gardens (the Morello cherry was a Sudell favourite, which appeared in the edition of February 1923); archways for town gardens in May of that year; dealing with greenfly with paraffin in July; hardy shrubs and trees for small gardens in January 1924 and roses the next month and so on.[17] These were difficult times for new gardeners. Nothing came easy to them, starting, as they were, from scratch and with no previous experience. Sudell was always gentle in his writing even though he had firm ideas of how a small garden should look.

However, there were times when even he could not prevent the practicalities of gardening seeming daunting. Take the problem of greenfly. Here is his advice to tenants, at the first sign of the pest, in a column in May 1924: 'Use paraffin emulsion. Mix a double handful of soft soap with half a gallon of water and bring to the boil. Remove from fire and pour into a gill of paraffin. Stir well until a thick emulsion has been forced. Strain off surplus paraffin.' It was perhaps no wonder that some fell at the first hurdle and let the aphids run riot. Despite this, what is clear about the Sudell-inspired gardens that began to emerge is that they were structured and relatively formal, with clear differences between front (or side in some instances) and back gardens, full of bright colour and, importantly, were labour saving. Once they were established, a metaphorical mountain climb for many, they were to be enjoyed and lived in, with work on them restricted to one day a week. Anything else would have been impossible for those working, and now sometimes having to commute to do so, to pay high rents. In the *Handbook*, a copy of which sat on the bookshelf of thousands of new LCC garden suburb tenants, Sudell lays out the distinction between gardens for rest and enjoyment and 'a gardener's garden'; the latter where 'children, animals and games would be tabooed'. Such a place would be, he says, 'an unfriendly garden unworthy of the name'.[18]

Those early Roehampton gardens were to be enjoyed but that did not mean standards could slip. As with most of these estates, pride in the house and garden was encouraged, and sometimes, through the rent book, even enforced. Residents were expected to add their bit to the overall pleasantness of the estate, which meant that their gardens, particularly at the front, had to play a part. For Sudell, who wanted to inspire rather than cajole neighbours to horticultural heights, it was a simple matter of beauty: 'Most of us are glad to appreciate beauty in the world, and it is worth a little trouble if we can add to our quota of it.'[19] The front garden, whose main purpose was ornamental, should bring a smile to the faces of passers-by too. This might even mean, whisper it, the removal of a privet hedge, already becoming ubiquitous in Roehampton and other places, in favour of welcoming *Aucuba* or even standard roses, which, while still giving privacy for the resident, were easier on the eye for the weekend stroller. Pyracantha, with its white flowers and shiny green leaves, could adorn the wall of a house or perhaps some hanging baskets around the door frame, and a small manicured lawn could be bordered with ribbons of pansies. For those with bolder ideas, circular beds could be cut into the lawn for roses or, even more daring, a mixture of *Calceolaria* and snapdragons.

For the back garden it was best to start by designing your plot on paper on the kitchen table on a wet evening and then use wooden pegs to mark out pathways first before situating borders for plants.

Those paths could be made using crazy paving, but it was important to encourage 'charming little plants' such as thyme to grow between the cracks. Sudell borders were triple-layered affairs, heleniums and chrysanthemums at the back with peonies, poppies and spiderworts in the middle and finally edged with thrift, auriculas, pinks and saxifrage. The lawn, 'your outdoor room', should be secluded, with a little shade and a garden seat, near a tree, if possible. Sudell strenuously advised his neighbours to resist boycotting turf in favour of even more labour-saving bricks-and-mortar patios: 'Here in the town we want flowers and plants more than cement and stone.'[20] Next it was important to pay attention to the view from your window so that something of special interest, a dahlia, rose, sundial or archway, catches the eye. Finally, beginners (the vast majority of his readers) were told to avoid mixing up fruit, flowers and vegetables.

In all but the tiniest garden, the last two could be placed in a separate area at the back, perhaps with small fruit trees as the border. What must be remembered about Sudell, particularly when dealing with the criticisms that soon followed over his kind of suburban garden, is that he gave this instruction based on experience not theory. This is why he is a fascinating conduit into this important but overlooked period of landscape history. He knew implicitly what his neighbours could, and couldn't, do with their gardens. Knowledge of the limits of expertise and space he was working with helped him shape the gardens of this period, creating a remarkable tapestry of colour and vitality in a short space of time with enthused citizens swept along with a new passion. Remember that, although from a poor family, he had had ten years of experience of gardening before the war, including on a large country estate that undoubtedly would have had an extravagant planting scheme. He was a specialist in orchids and had trained at Kew. The type of small urban gardens Sudell would be championing in the next decades, both practically and in his writing, was a deliberate choice not a failure of imagination. His motivation was the Garden City-fuelled notion that all had the right to open space and experience of the beauty of nature. It would be pointless and self-defeating to urge his neighbours to take the country house ethos, or even later a modernist approach, and shrink them into their small plots. It would be setting them up for failure and, of course, aesthetically disastrous. This would be forgotten by critics of suburbia and its gardens in the following years.

His gentleness did not mean Sudell, nor the REGS itself, was a soft touch, as we have seen from the crypt episode. Critics' fears of a lack of community spirit on the new estates were largely unfounded, at least on Roehampton. But this sometimes had to be worked at in a way that could be seen as authoritarian from today's perspective, with the LCC, RETA and the REGS all at times appearing to both chide and strongly remind tenants about their responsibilities towards each other. At an REGS committee meeting in November 1923, it was reported that on a tour of the estate it had been noted that weeds were making an unwelcome return both to some allotments and in some front gardens. One can only imagine the trepidation with which the sight of this party was greeted, so fearful were many residents that reports of even minor dereliction might find their way to LCC housing officers: 'The committee took a serious view of the matter and before taking drastic steps would warn offenders through the columns of the *Estate Gazette*.'[21]

The *Gazette*, which was run and edited by tenant members of RETA, was often used in this way, both reminding people how lucky they were to live in such a place but also, adopting a strangely cheery tone, warning how easy it would be for the dream to die. The threat of eviction was never far away, implied in the *Gazette* and sometimes spelt out by LCC inspectors on the doorstep. 'In those days if your garden was not up to scratch, the superintendent in his bowler hat, striped trousers, the umbrella – the treatment – would knock on your door and give you a fortnight to put it right. If not goodbye.'[22] What 'drastic steps' the REGS itself, however, could take over the weeds issue (denial of access to community tools would surely have been retrograde) was never stated. It is worth remembering that this was after all a time in which the LCC was so prescriptive that its tenants' handbook on Becontree warned residents to treat the water closet respectfully: perhaps unlike at their previous homes there was now no need to 'pull the chain with a jerk'.[23]

Nevertheless, the majority of tenants welcomed their new community and the responsibility that came with it, as can be seen in RETA's efforts to take over the lease of Putney Park House from the LCC in 1924. With Sudell now as RETA chairman, a poll of residents was taken that found, by a margin of 376 to 7, that residents were in favour of using the premises as a community club. However, there was less support (197 to 81) for a bar at the club, with fears that many of the men would spend more time propping it up than digging up nettles and creeping buttercup from their gardens. Gardens were certainly seen by temperance Quakers, among others, as a way of keeping men away from the demon drink. Nevertheless, despite some tough negotiations with the LCC – Sudell baulked at £6 a week for rent – Putney Park House was taken over by RETA in March 1924.

Designed in 1838 for a rich merchant by one of the foremost architects of the nineteenth century, Decimus Burton, who also built the Ionic screen and arch at Hyde Park Corner and the Palm House at Kew, it soon became a hive of activity, hosting lectures, classes, sports and meetings. In May it was officially opened by Samuel Samuel, MP for Wandsworth and Putney, at which ceremony, as we have seen, Sudell called for the continuance of the cooperative spirit on the estate to turn it into a 'little garden city'. He had by this time left Roehampton, taking with him the memory of that standing ovation. His legacy and the work of the RGS after him could be summed up thus: 'One set up that has helped to keep the feeling of belonging is the Roehampton Garden Society. It has always held people together very much.'[24]

So from where did the idea come that the new suburbs were places of snobbish one-upmanship, dull conformity and poor taste?

Council estates such as Roehampton were not spared these criticisms. It is true that it was the private estates of speculative builders, such as those in the northwest London ribbon developments of Metro-land, that attracted most flak. Yet in the early twentieth century it wasn't hard to find an artist, writer, town planner or architect who would opine that all new suburbs were tasteless sprawls. They were full of people who sat, smugly satisfied, in their little castles concerned only with their domestic arrangements, untroubled by great ideas or the affairs of the world.[25] Perhaps a small clue from Roehampton is contained in letters written to the LCC as the estate grew throughout the 1920s. As we already know, the Addison Act gave the LCC licence to follow the Tudor Walters Committee recommendations to the full. In 1919 houses were spacious and back gardens given the required 400 square yards. However, as the estate grew and subsequent housing Acts gave less generous subsidy, houses were built to less exacting standards and smaller gardens provided.

As the decade wore on there was also a feeling from some of the early tenants, by now forged into a proud community, that the LCC was not being so rigorous in its selection of new tenants, certainly not to the extent that they themselves had endured. As early as October 1922 RETA swung into action to defend what it thought it had on Roehampton. In a letter to the Council, Mrs Songhurst, the secretary, was asking it to reconsider the project in light of the 'inferior property on the upper part of the estate' now being built. And here was the central fear. 'An inferior type of property will attract a class of tenant comparing unfavourably with that occupying the part of the estate already developed.'[26] Was this the hard evidence of the stupefying selfishness that the new suburbs induced? Were the tenants, many from slums themselves, pulling up the drawbridge on their fellows just three years after moving there, isolating themselves in their semi-rural bucolic paradise? And the knife goes into those, former neighbours perhaps, who might move in next. The difficulty existing in most working-class neighbourhoods was the inability to pay the sorts of 'economic' rent demanded on Roehampton, says the letter. And it isn't finished there.

The next part of the estate to be developed, that abutting Putney Heath, needed 'good class homes', leading to fears the existing site 'must fall tremendously in value if it adjoins a neighbourhood possessing the undesirable features of a poor class locality'.[27] Finally, perhaps, comes one short sentence that offers a smoking gun for all those seeking evidence of the degrading and dull conformity that the new housing landscape was inducing in people, expressed in words that may be seen as dripping with a tragically desperate aspiration to join the middle classes.

> The present tenants who are prepared to settle down here and help in the formation of a healthy and attractive garden suburb will be unwilling to spend time and money to that end if they consider the Council is pursuing a policy which will speedily result in a great lowering of the tone of the estate.[28]

What do we have at work here? Perhaps a willing forgetfulness of many of the tenants' own origins, as if life had only really begun when they moved to Roehampton. A threat too, perhaps, that the estate will disintegrate and adherence to the rules, mores and morals collapse as the new houses are built, the garden suburb dream dying as horrified LCC housing officials look on. And maybe the beginnings of the spirit-sapping mindset that holds its nose at difference, turns away from the unfortunate, closes its curtains to the outside world. In other words, was this the beginning of an imagined middle-class sensibility, the ending of the dream of real radical change in the country, the cementing of the status quo in British society? But the views of the residents, represented by Mrs Songhurst, can be read another way. Isn't this also a call for the best possible living conditions for the many? Having been shown that there is a better way to live, does it not reflect human nature to want to preserve it, to fight to defend it even? And why was it not acceptable for the newly situated working class to want these things, the space, comfort and privacy accepted as a right for centuries by the ruling, landed or mercantile classes and, for the last one hundred years, the middle-class managerial and professional classes?

In one letter, from one estate, hidden away in archives, we have a tiny seed, one of many of course, from which grew the twentieth-century debate concerning the growth of suburbia. A debate, giving a small insight into the psychology of how we live, that continues to this day. For Mrs Songhurst and her fellow tenants this letter represented a fleeting dream, a tantalizing glimpse of escape that the estate might be able to give them. Just three months later reality intervened when she had to write again to the LCC, without acknowledging a certain irony, to request an urgent rent review, 'given the heavy and continuous fall in salaries and wages'.[29] She followed this up by requesting help for a Mr Thompson of Swinburne Road, who was now struggling to pay his £28 annual rent after losing his job as the postwar economic depression began to take hold. Finally, with more than a hint of desperation, a letter at the start of the following year repeated the review request and maintained, 'rents now being charged are out of all proportion to the means of the tenants in view of the general fall of wages.'[30] The LCC summarily dismissed the pleas and some people, including Mr Thompson, did have to leave their new paradise on Roehampton as Britain's two-decade-long economic hangover from the war lingered.

There were now other issues to concern Sudell. He left Roehampton sometime in early May 1924, with his campaign to use horticulture as a vehicle for social change soon to step up a gear. Before he left, he helped plant a line of cherry trees on the estate. Writing in the *Gazette* in August of that year, three months after he had left but still referencing his affinity with the estate, he said, 'I should like to see all our roads planted with cherry trees. Sceptics will laugh but it's done in some places.'[31] This is likely to have been a reference to the London Borough of Bermondsey where an experiment was taking place to plant trees, with the cherry a favourite, in every road in one of London's most deprived communities as well as flowers in every pocket of green space available. It was Sudell's philosophy enacted on a grander scale and it was the work of a couple who have written their own chapter in the capital's social history – one incidentally that is not read often enough – Alfred and Ada Salter. Together with them, and others, Sudell and Emily were to be at the forefront of a garden-inspired revolution.

4
The Birth of Beautification

The address 61 Penrose Street, Walworth, was perhaps an unlikely seedbed for a movement that would stop at nothing short of the transformation of London into a 'capital of gardens'. It was the cramped, slightly shabby, location of the London Garden Settlement in the years immediately after the war.[1] Richard Sudell moved into a room there in 1920 and was joined shortly after by Emily, whom he married in August the same year. They had been living at her family home in Gore Road, Hackney, for a brief period. It was from Penrose Street, sometime early in 1922, that the couple moved to Roehampton. The house was a Victorian terraced property bought by the MP Noel Buxton, who in 1924 would go on to be minister for agriculture in the first Labour government. For this story, though, he was more importantly the founder, with Rev. Horace 'Rollo' Meyer, of the LGG. How Sudell ended up here is unclear but there is little doubt that his work with the VLCS, while on furlough from prison during the war, would have introduced him to a circle of progressives, such as the society's founder, Joseph Fels.

Sudell's politics, war record and horticultural expertise brought him into contact with a network of people like Fels who would make significant contributions to early twentieth-century social and landscape history. He was likely to have met Buxton and Meyer this way. Penrose Street, with its tiny rooms, would be home to a garden version of the Settlement principle. Here middle-class supporters of social reform who were also keen gardeners, admittedly a thin seam of volunteers, would live and mix with the poor of the borough to encourage the growing of flowers and vegetables to aid their health and well-being.

The Settlement Movement might be dismissed as quaint today, patronizing even, but the theory that the middle classes could live in areas of working-class deprivation so that both they and the community could learn from each other was widely supported among progressives and Nonconformist churches. The concept of Settlement was first conceived in the 1860s by radicals such as John Ruskin and Charles Kingsley, idealistic middle-class intellectuals appalled at the conditions in which people lived in inner cities and towns. While one strand of this loose movement diverted into charity work, the Settlement pioneers saw the practical worth of graduates (the early 'missionaries' mostly came from Oxford and Cambridge) moving into deprived areas using education as a means of lifting the horizons of the poor. It was, in effect, the foundation of the principle of social work and was largely promoted and funded by religious organizations and personnel. In 1867 the first such effort was made by an Oxford graduate named Edward Denison, the son of a bishop, who took lodgings in the slum district of Stepney. He befriended his neighbours, offered classes for children and worked to improve housing and sanitation conditions in the area. Two years later, in poor health, Denison had to abandon the project. He died shortly after.[2] Toynbee Hall in Whitechapel is perhaps the most significant existing remnant of the UK movement; although there are still a considerable number of settlements in the United States. The centre is named after Oxford economist Arnold Toynbee who, full of reforming zeal, moved into the Whitechapel slums in 1875, opening a centre for education and undertaking pastoral work under the auspices of Canon Samuel Barnett, the vicar of St Jude's Church. Although he too died early, Canon Barnett together with his wife Henrietta, both Christian socialists, established Toynbee Hall in his honour. It was a university 'Settlement' where a stream of graduates came to live and work and where meetings, classes, advice sessions and discussions were held for the local population. The graduates included future Labour prime minister Clement Attlee and future creator of the welfare state William Beveridge, who undoubtedly used this fieldwork when formulating policy in government.

As we have seen, Henrietta, with support from Samuel, went on to create the Hampstead Garden Suburb inspired by Ebenezer Howard's Garden City movement. Canon Barnett was also to play a part in inspiring the horticultural offshoot of this social work. In the sixteen years up to the turn of the twentieth century a total of 26 settlements were established across London, not all of them based on the 'university' model but led by individual visionaries of either religious or radical political persuasion.[3] Alfred and Ada Salter were active members of another Settlement, in Bermondsey, and would play a big part in the interwar garden story of London. Ada in particular would work with Sudell in a push to take the capital campaign to beautify through horticulture across the nation.

A fusion of social reforming zeal, new aspiration over living environments, growing recognition of the damage done to public health by urbanization and the rehabilitation needs of those who fought in the First World War was fuelling rapid change in Britain. The emergence of the suburbs and their brightly coloured gardens was but one symbol. Governments were either being dragged to reform through fear of unrest or, as in the case of the first, short-lived Labour administration in 1924, were motivated by representing newly enfranchised voters – the Representation of the People Act 1918 tripled the size of the electorate to 21 million – who needed to be satisfied their demands were being met. However, while it is fair to say that policies such as house-building programmes to improve living conditions (both Lloyd George and Labour's first prime minister, Ramsay MacDonald, promoted such projects) were frameworks for change, what is also clear is how much direct action was coming from the ground. In London in particular a network of reformers, radicals, charities, religious leaders and interested benefactors were determined to make a difference as first post-war recession and then in the 1930s the Great Depression took their grip on the country. The lineage from Victorian charity work was clear but it was now allied to what appeared at the time to be almost unstoppable political muscle.

One such example is of course the subject of this book, and here the lessons learned from London's drive to improve its environment through a passion for flowers, plants, fruit and vegetable growing and tree planting are richly illuminating. While a landscape revolution might, looking from today, seem underpowered when set alongside advances in medicine and social welfare, reformers in the interwar years saw no need to draw a distinction. The philosophies of men like Ruskin and William Morris, that an appreciation of beauty in itself had redemptive power and could uplift the spirit, were powering reformers' views on how a society, in the midst of vast inequalities and post-industrial-revolution deprivation and squalor, could help save itself.

Inspired by this swirl of ideas, the Settlement movement and the very visible evidence of society's scars, Buxton and Meyer were perhaps typical of the wealthy and socially conscious class of people who played major roles in philanthropic work in the capital between the wars. These great friends, who met as undergraduates at Trinity College, Cambridge, made quite the pair, with the alchemy of wealth, power, philanthropy, faith and flowers combining to create what was, for decades, a hugely successful movement. Buxton came from a long line of Liberal MPs. Indeed, he was himself a Liberal MP before defecting to Labour in time to serve in the party's first government. His great-grandfather Thomas Fowell Buxton, a Quaker, MP and anti-slavery campaigner, was a partner in the family brewing business, Truman, Hanbury, Buxton and Co. based in Brick Lane, Spitalfields, at one time the second largest brewery in Britain, employing 1,000 people.

The building, still called the Truman Brewery, is today a thriving media and arts quarter, but when Noel Buxton went to work there for a stint of family duty, it was surrounded by abject poverty, which shocked him and spurred him to action. Little had changed since his great-grandfather, who also engaged in anti-poverty work in the district, walked the same streets. Buxton, then, came from a long line of rich and powerful men who took their social duties seriously.[4] Rollo Meyer brought the flowers and the faith to the partnership. An Anglican vicar in bucolic outposts such as the Bedfordshire village of Clophill and Watton-at-Stone in Hertfordshire, he was a passionate amateur horticulturist. At Watton-at-Stone he lived in a large Georgian red-brick rectory with extensive gardens where he began to experiment with hybridizing daffodils and bearded irises. Many, such as the Maiden's Blush daffodil and the Constance iris, named after his daughter, are still available today. His efforts saw him awarded the Royal Horticultural Society's Victoria Medal of Honour (VMH), one of the highest awards the society can give.[5]

Through Meyer, they met Samuel Barnett and in 1895 were taken on a tour of his neighbourhoods. They were horrified by what they saw in the slums of Whitechapel, Stepney and Spitalfields, with overcrowding in virtually every tenement, disease and malnourishment rife and inadequate sanitation. What they also noticed was that, despite the debilitating deprivation, a few residents managed to grow flowers in the tiniest of spaces, backyards and windowsills. It was a pathetic beauty, a clinging on to some kind of hope, that deeply moved them. Meyer suggested that an organized competition could help promote the life-affirming, spirit-uplifting activity of gardening, no matter how small such opportunities might be. He suggested the pair put up prizes and source equipment for a window box competition and so it was that, aided by an enthusiastic local grower, the first such event took place that year in Stepney.[6]

Through Barnett, they also met another Settlement pioneer, Francis Herbert Stead, another Christian socialist, who had established

Inspectors view an inner-city window box in Kensington for the Garden Championships, 1926.

Browning Hall in Walworth Road after being inspired by what he saw happening in Whitechapel. Stead, a Congregationalist minister, was the younger brother of campaigning journalist and editor of the *Pall Mall Gazette*, William Thomas Stead. According to Buxton, Stead was critical to their plan, his 'stimulating intelligence and activity' being described as crucial. The LGG was born and, with a rich seam of Settlement movement progressives to mine, there were plenty of people who shared the belief that flowers, plants, vegetables and green spaces weren't just nice extras but crucial to lift poor people out of their misery. The guild's mission statement was simple and clear: 'To promote the planting and tending of gardens in the industrial districts of London, and to initiate and encourage Garden Shows and Flower Shows.'[7] Just before the war, Buxton took the movement a step further and bought Penrose Street to form the London Garden

Settlement. Later when Penrose Street became both unaffordable and, through the lack of practical volunteers, unviable, Stead gave the LGG space in Walworth Road to conduct its affairs. War brought progress with the LGG to a halt. But post-war, the continuing and desperate need for food self-sufficiency, the huge increase in suburban gardens and the continuing need to improve inner-city environments would see its time come again very soon.

Less than a year after being released from prison, his physical and mental state unknown, Sudell continued his VLCS work on new allotment sites scattered through the capital while also helping to breathe life into Buxton's London Garden Settlement principle. Moving into Penrose Street, Sudell also became secretary of the LGG. His organizational excellence and passion for the uplifting nature of green spaces and gardens would see him excel in roles such as this. But his background and the radicalism of the project he and others were promoting in these interwar years might also have ensured he would rise no further than this operational level in the story of early twentieth-century landscape history. Meanwhile just over 3 kilometres (2 mi.) away in Bermondsey, another deprived area of London, another couple who have unfairly faded from the history of the times were conducting their own mini-revolution. The Sudells would shortly come into the orbit of Alfred and Ada Salter.

In 1910 the Salters' only child, Joyce, died of scarlet fever at the age of eight. They never recovered; Alfred's distinctive loud laugh was not heard in the meeting rooms of Bermondsey for many years. The doctor was more than aware that Joyce's death had come as a consequence of the choices he and Ada had made. A brilliant doctor, trained at nearby Guy's Hospital and with a career at Harley Street his for the taking, Alfred had instead decided to live and set up his practice in one of the most deprived communities in Britain. His surgery soon became the biggest in the country and his determination to treat some of his poorest patients for free was one of the pioneering examples that would lead to the establishment of the National Health

Service. When Salter began his mission, tuberculosis and scarlet fever stalked every street; in 1923 life expectancy was one of the lowest in the country and infant mortality the highest in London.[8] In June 1910 Joyce caught scarlet fever for a third time but now it took its most malignant form. By this time the doctor had become a hugely respected GP in Bermondsey and Joyce was a familiar and much-loved figure, called 'our little ray of sunshine' by patients. So popular were the Salters and so concerned about Joyce's condition were residents that bulletins on her health had to be posted on the front door of the Salter surgery to deal with the numbers of those enquiring after her. Despite the best medical attention available, given willingly by colleagues of her father, Joyce could not be saved. As she reached the end, hundreds of residents, including many of her young friends, gathered in silent vigil outside the house.[9]

The outpouring of grief and love from a community well used to suffering among its own was a powerful tribute to this middle-class family who had come to live among them, to risk with them the often-lethal consequences of their environment. It was recognition that they had made the ultimate sacrifice for a cause in which they believed to the very depths of their being. The rock-hard core of the couple's activism came from the belief they must do God's bidding to help eradicate social injustice, allied to a ferocious work ethic that allowed very little time for anything else. What was almost unique about the Salters is that they spent their entire lives putting their ideas into practice. They would settle for nothing less than creating a socialist arcadia down in the fetid, dockside streets of Bermondsey. London-born Alfred's parents were fundamentalist Plymouth Brethren worshippers from whom he acquired his evangelical passion and a lifelong support for temperance. Unlike them he would adopt a political philosophy that insisted on practical, as well as spiritual, solutions to social injustice. Alfred met Ada at the Bermondsey Settlement, established and led by Methodist preacher John Scott Lidgett. When he took up residence there in September 1898, he was working as a highly regarded research bacteriologist at the Lister Institute, after a glittering early career at Guy's.

Ada, who had arrived the year before, was on the staff, involved with its working girls' clubs helping poor young girls in education, exercise and play. Ada was from a relatively wealthy Methodist family in rural Raunds, Northamptonshire. At that time Alfred had abandoned his religion, developing into a firebrand socialist. They married the following year in Raunds, Ada gently persuading her new husband to return to the religious flock while retaining his revolutionary passion. By 1900 Quaker Socialism had come to seem the perfect fit. The pair then made their life-changing decision. They would continue their work in the community of Bermondsey, eschewing the middle-class comfort their upbringing and education had offered them.

That flowers were an unlikely weapon in the story of the fight against the debilitating effects of abject poverty can be evidenced by the humble window box. They were the only practical way colour could be spread through cramped streets without gardens. When Ada first moved to London from Northamptonshire she did so to work as a sister at the West London Methodist Mission in St Pancras. There she met another remarkable woman, Grace Hannam, another sister with a passion for improving the lives of young women and for flowers. When the Mission collapsed through schism, first Grace and then Ada fled to the Bermondsey Settlement to continue their outreach work. As Grace was moving into her Bermondsey flat to begin her work with the Settlement, taking her wooden window boxes with her from St Pancras, a gathering of curious young children, inured to the presence of infant mortality within their community and unsure what to make of the boxes, drew closer and one shouted, 'there's five cawffins just gone up, five!'[10] One can possibly imagine a similar reaction as Buxton and Meyer launched their competition over in Stepney. Grace made a strong impression on Ada. As the Salters began their move into politics, a term was emerging for the use of horticulture to help combat deprivation. A Grace-inspired Ada was at the forefront of its adoption. It was called beautification.

The Salters quickly embraced local politics with Ada often leading the way, for instance quitting the Liberal Party, over its stance against women candidates, to join the Independent Labour Party (ILP). Alfred followed, setting up the Bermondsey branch of the ILP, and by 1909 they were both serving on Bermondsey Borough Council, Ada as the first ever female councillor for the area and later, in 1922, becoming its first woman Mayor. Alfred for a time also had a seat on the London County Council. The ILP was positioned to the left of Ramsay MacDonald's Labour Party to which it affiliated in 1906, although it left the fold again in 1932, never to return, and gradually withered. In 1922 Alfred became the Labour MP for Bermondsey, a seat he would hold, for all but two years, until retirement in 1945. It was on the borough council, at the grassroots level, that they perhaps did their most innovative work even though some of it, such as flying a red flag with local symbols instead of the Union flag over the town hall, was controversial to say the least.

On Ada Salter's initiative the council established a Beautification Committee in 1920, with herself as chairwoman. The idea was simple. The committee wanted trees in every street and alley and flowers in as many open spaces as possible. Finding space was not easy. Of the borough's estimated 525 hectares (1,300 ac), about 160 hectares (400 ac) consisted of Surrey Docks and its wharves and warehouses, and much of the remaining land was taken by businesses that fed off the cargoes that came in, including the biscuit manufacturers Peek, Frean & Co. Ltd. With little land left for residential use the density of the borough in 1921 was estimated at almost one hundred people per acre.[11] Nevertheless, with the ILP finally taking control of the council in 1922 and remaining its stronghold for the next forty years, efforts driven by the Salters to improve the living conditions of the borough's 120,000 residents were begun in earnest. At their core was the recognition that the prevention of diseases such as TB was better than treatment. People could fight disease if they were fitter, healthier and had access to cleaner air and places to exercise.

Using its newly minted slogan 'Fresh Air and Fun', the Beautification Committee's part in this programme was to identify every area that could be planted with trees, shrubs, tubs, rockeries and even contain fountains and statuary. In addition, a Spring Show in late March and Fruit and Flower Show in the autumn were promoted. The committee began to eye up old churchyards in the borough, one of very few sources of open space, to purchase in order to create flower gardens or children's play areas so that they could have places for health-giving exercise. The plan was to move old gravestones to the periphery of the churchyards and use the land for the benefit of all residents. While most churches agreed to sell pockets of older land to the council, the vicar of St James's held firm. He might have wished he hadn't, for he found himself on the end of Alfred Salter's legendary fiery temper and rhetoric. In full battle cry the doctor railed against the vicar and his church council, calling them 'ignorant and short-sighted Bumbles' who were obstructing 'a great improvement in the neighbourhood'.[12] He got his way. A new church council was elected and transferred the ownership of the old churchyard to the borough council. St James's was to become one of Salter's favourite places in the borough, not least when it became home to England's first covered children's slide. This had been funded by Peek Freans after a director, who had visited St James's to see the new tulips rising where gravestones had once been, also watched as children used a 1-metre (3 ft) stone slab as a makeshift slide.

Under the superintendent of gardens W. H. Johns's team of fourteen gardeners the churchyards became splashes of colour, blooming all year round, moving from early snowdrops, to daffodils, through tulips and hyacinths to geraniums and dahlias. Indeed, at St Mary Magdalen's churchyard two new dwarf dahlias were bred, the salmon-coloured Bermondsey Gem and the yellow Rotherhithe Gem, both receiving recognition from the Royal Horticultural Society. At its first meeting the committee invoked powers that meant it could plant trees in every street, providing no more than two-thirds of residents objected, and set about buying trees, accepting quotes for 831 planes and a similar number of poplars. As it started its work it was estimated the council was responsible for only 376 trees, but seven years later this figure had risen to 6,101 – an incredible achievement given the polluted air in which they were asked to grow.[13] It is worth noting that, as the campaign got under way, the wild cherry, a favourite of the energetic Johns, began to increasingly appear on the streets, bringing a riot of white blossom in the spring. It was this planting campaign that Sudell was probably referring to when he wrote his article on cherry trees for his neighbours in Roehampton.

Two other developments in Bermondsey are testimony to the Salters' total commitment to the philosophy of the Garden City movement. First, the couple were adamant they wanted to tear down at least two-thirds of the houses in the borough and replace them with a cottage estate of wide avenues and detached and semi-detached dwellings. 'A large part of Bermondsey needs pulling down and rebuilding,' wrote Dr Salter in 1928, 'Thousands of dark, wretched and out-of-date hovels, erected 150 or 180 years ago, are totally unfit to house a growing family, and ought to be demolished and replaced by well-lighted and well-planned modern cottage homes.'[14] The scale of the plans was far too ambitious at a time of ongoing economic recession but nevertheless some areas of the borough saw drastic improvement, none more so than the slums surrounding Salisbury Street. This nearly 2-hectare (4 ac) riverside site, where more than 1,000 people lived in unimaginable squalor, had been condemned as unfit for human habitation decades before. Just a few hundred yards from where the Salters lived, infant mortality was 182 per thousand births and diphtheria, TB and scarlet fever were rife. It was undoubtedly there that Joyce had caught her fatal illness.

After a ferocious fight led mainly by Ada against the opposition of the LCC and the government, and a public inquiry by the Ministry of Health, the council finally got its way, helped by the fortuitous timing of the first Labour prime minister, Ramsay MacDonald, taking office. Salisbury Street was demolished and Wilson Grove 'cottage village' was built and officially opened in 1928. It was as much a symbolic victory as anything else, with only 54 cottages built, but it was proof that decent living standards could be achieved for the poor if the political will was there. When finished, Wilson Grove was an astonishing vision to behold as Fenner Brockway MP, a leading ILP figure, co-founder of the No-Conscription Fellowship (NCF) and biographer of Alfred Salter, witnessed on a visit.

> Then the car took a sharp turn and we were in a garden village! There were hedges and silver birches and grass. Among them were neat little cottages built in red and white brick, with gardens brilliant with colour. A climbing red rose framed the doorway of a corner cottage and hollyhocks and chrysanthemums showed above its hedge.[15]

The small village of Hartley in north Kent, about 32 kilometres (20 mi.) from Bermondsey, is perhaps an unlikely location to move to next in this story of garden and landscape revolution. Yet it was here that two important developments took place in the lives of the Salters and the Sudells. The first was the existence in the early 1920s of a thriving smallholding movement in the village, the second was Alfred Salter's discovery, on a walking tour, of Fairby Grange, a manor house that he bought in 1917. Exactly when Richard Sudell first met either of the Salters is uncertain. Alfred was a committee member of the NCF and in 1919, when Sudell was finally released from prison, its chairman. It is entirely possible that this was how they met. Alternatively, while at the London Garden Settlement, Richard's work as secretary of the LGG, in which Ada was extremely active, could have been the origin of the link. Either way, as Quakers, there would have been an immediate bond. As we have already seen, pacifism and horticulture are common threads weaving a whole network of progressives into this story.

In 1924 Richard and Emily moved into this village, first at a house called Prize Poultry Farm. The following year they bought, under Emily's name, a newly built house, a bungalow called Avian on Church Lane. Prize Poultry Farm was owned by a company called Small Owners Ltd, which had bought up the 126-hectare (313 ac) Fairby Farm in 1911 with the aim of parcelling it up into smallholdings with attendant properties. Here owners could grow fruit trees, vegetables and even crops on plots of between 1 and 4 hectares (3 and 10 ac) and where the company itself would offer mutual support, utilizing existing farm buildings, employing a manager and hiring out equipment and horses to the smallholders. As the founder of the company, Leonard Humphrey, explained:

> The offer of the land in small areas attracted applicants of almost every class, some 40 of whom took up holdings of from 3 to 10 acres. All these holders agreed to purchase their holdings, to become small owners, in fact, either by an immediate cash payment, or by means of deferred payments on the annuity system. Ownership is preferred for a number of reasons, but principally in the case of the smallholder because of the value which his own labour, and the natural growth of his fruit trees, adds to the property, a value which is with difficulty realized under a tenancy system.[16]

This was clearly a significant upgrade from Roehampton and, as Humphrey indicated, a change from renting to ownership and with it more luxurious housing and land. That Hartley was an upmarket version of the cottage estates that were being built in London can be evidenced by the fact that two of the company's original board members were Conservatives who saw the smallholding movement as a non-socialist way of expanding landownership.[17] Even here Sudell took any opportunity to continue his garden evangelical work and this time it was the citizens of the small, sleepy north Kent seaside town of Herne Bay who benefited. He contacted a number of newspapers in Kent offering a column and was taken up by the *Herne Bay Press*, for which he wrote weekly advice for two years from 1928. Living in a relatively spacious bungalow in bucolic circumstances did not stop him poking gentle fun at this relatively new style of accommodation in a column in November 1929. He wrote of a new tribe of 'soil tillers', whom he called 'bungalowites', not revealing he was one of them: 'They were people evidently driven by the stress of the times – the noise and congestion – out into the country and there they settle in groups and "streets" reaching far out into the wilds of some erstwhile country lane.'[18] He might have been writing about a rural version of the much-hated London suburb ribbon development, but lest he be thought a hypocrite he quickly described the changes wrought by the emergence of the bungalows and their 'privet hedges and gravel paths' as wonderful 'and the variety to be found in the gardens even more so'.[19] He advised this new tribe to be patient with their gardens because the best were those that developed gradually, and, in typical Sudell style, warned against over-elaborate planting even in something akin to a cottage garden location. It was time to propagate pansies, violas and penstemons under cold frames, he concluded, while planting spring bulbs such as forget-me-nots.

How the Sudells were able to afford this new lifestyle in Hartley is unclear, although there was evidence from Roehampton that Richard's garden practice had become increasingly successful. Avian had been built on former Small Owner land by local landowner and farmer Hedley Symons as interest in the project began to dwindle. It is hard to believe it a coincidence that the Sudells moved to Hartley in the same year that the Salters officially opened Fairby Grange as a centre for social and horticultural work. In 1917 Alfred Salter, with the help of Quaker benefactors, bought the country house, which was surrounded by beautiful formal gardens and 8 hectares (20 ac) of land, after it came up for sale for about £7,500. He had stumbled across it while on one of his long weekend rambles from London a few years earlier.

The house and land, probably the sort of country residence he might have bought for himself if he had pursued a Harley Street career, was surrounded by the smallholdings that had been part of the estate before being broken up. As those Harley Street consultants did for rich patients – namely send them to countryside retreats for recuperation – Salter would also use Fairby as a convalescent home for his patients who could benefit from the rest and fresh air, away from the grime and pollution of Bermondsey. They could stay for free. Later Salter, as the then vice president of the NCF, believing there was a growing need for a rehabilitation centre for COs, extended Fairby's use for this group too. Many left prison seriously underweight and suffering extremely poor health. One of those helped was George Dutch, who went to Fairby suffering from TB. He wrote:

> It was a glorious Spring and Summer and I remained there until October, working for the last few weeks in the gardens, orchards and hayfields. Thanks to good food and care and the fine Kentish air, I was completely cured. It is good to know that our world still produces good and clever men like Alfred Salter.[20]

Typical of his militant pacifism, he also thought it might be used as a summer camp for various boys groups, such as the Young Pioneers, which had been set up by leftists to counter the 'militarism' of the Boy Scouts.[21] In 1923 Fairby and its grounds were donated entirely to the council and, at Ada's insistence, the house would have a new specific purpose as a convalescent home for Bermondsey's working women and new mothers who needed to recuperate after the rigours of giving birth in the slums of London.

As she told the council at the conclusion of her pioneering Mayoral year, the effect on young mothers and their children was instant: 'The appreciation of the mothers of the comfort and change provided by a fortnight's stay at Fairby Grange has been expressed by applications from numbers of them for a further period of stay next year.'[22] She reported that in just the first month of its opening for this purpose Fairby had received 55 mothers, 30 toddlers and 42 babies. Meanwhile back in the borough the council, driven by the Salters, was making astonishing strides in public health provision including establishing the first ever municipal solarium, the Light Treatment Centre, to transmit health-giving vitamin D and thus combat TB, which was causing four hundred deaths a year. Equipped with eight large mercury vapour lamps, two carbon arc lamps, one water-cooled Kromayer lamp and two radiant heat lamps, the solarium was soon being used by thousands of residents, mainly children, every year. In the first year 562 TB cases were treated in almost 18,400 attendances – with immediate effects seen, as new cases of TB fell from 413 in 1922 to 294 in 1927, and deaths declined from 206 to 175.[23]

Gradually from 1923 the grounds around Fairby were converted to grow vegetables that could be eaten by patients but also be transported to Bermondsey. From its establishment in 1920 the Beautification Committee was increasingly attracted to the possibility that Fairby could become its nursery to grow flowers, plants, trees and vegetables for the borough on an industrial scale. Newly appointed in 1923, Superintendent Johns was despatched to consider the use of the land beyond the formal gardens for these purposes. He reported back: 'The acquisition of a site such as to be found at Fairby Grange is necessary for the efficient working and development of Bermondsey Gardens and Open Spaces Department and should result in the production of a greater display of flowering and foliage plants than is at present practical.'[24] By the end of 1923 Johns told the committee he now had fifty flower beds, many in churchyards, more than 1,400 square metres (15,000 sq. ft) of borders and 168 window boxes in his care in Bermondsey.[25] Now, following Johns's report and the employment of a number of gardeners, Fairby became invaluable in this enterprise. It freed the council from the vagaries of the plant and bulb trade, saving considerable sums of money. In total, 3 hectares (8 ac) were given over to propagating flowers, plants and trees for the borough. As an example, from 1 April to July 1924 Fairby provided a total of 2,750 geraniums, 3,530 violas and 3,150 dahlias to Bermondsey.[26]

Three years later, in January 1927, saplings and bulbs to the value of £851 (approximately £50,000 today) were grown in the previous twelve months, and ten years after that Fairby was finally providing all of the borough's needs.[27] It even supplied huge numbers of walnuts to convalescent patients and, to create income, private dealers. A report to the Beautification and Public Amenities Committee in July 1923 reveals the extent of the benefit Bermondsey gained from the horticultural experiment, with a list of produce as follows: 'Spring bedding plants, summer bedding plants, window box plants, renewal of trees and shrubs, supply of turf, cut flowers and shrubs for decoration of town halls, supply of loam and leaf for renewal of soil in window boxes.'[28] Now as a full-time council convalescent home, mini farm and nursery Fairby was officially opened by Labour's health minister John Wheatley in 1924, at the same time the Sudells were also moving into what had become a pioneering village.

There is no documentary evidence to explain why they moved to Hartley, but it would be a remarkable coincidence if the Salters were not involved in some way. It could be that Ada, while working with Sudell, pointed out the opportunities for the couple in Hartley, which might have included horticultural 'consultancy'. It is also not impossible that, as Quakers, there was financial help for them to do so, given that Sudell's secretarial duties at the LGG would not have paid well. Graham Taylor, author of *Ada Salter: Pioneer of Ethical Socialism*, posits that Sudell may have become acquainted with Jane Foote Maxton, who was the last company secretary of Small

Owners Ltd and a successful hotelier in London. As the company was winding up, Maxton bought its remaining assets to farm and live away from London.[29] Taylor thinks the Sudells might have looked after this land for Maxton and, while in situ, Richard could have given advice to the Salters on the prospects of the land around Fairby Grange becoming a full-time Bermondsey nursery. Maxton was the cousin of fellow conscientious objector James Maxton, the leader of the ILP, of which both the Salters were members. Given the Sudells' politics it is entirely possible they were in the party too, especially as they were friends with another leading ILP and pacifist figure, Clifford Allen, although this cannot be verified. Quaker and pacifist networks often led to opportunities for members.

Intriguingly the founders of Small Owners Ltd, Leonard Humphrey and his brother George, also lived in the small Essex village of Coggeshall, which was home to Noel and Lucy Buxton. Lucy, who succeeded her husband as MP for North Norfolk in 1930 when he was appointed to the House of Lords, was to become a key driving force within the LGG. It is also entirely possible that Sudell gave freely of his expert advice to the gardeners of Fairby 'over the garden fence' as they began their mission to beautify Bermondsey. A cash-strapped council finally sold the house in the mid-1950s and it is now a retirement home. Whether through Quakerism, politics, pacifism or the cultivation of beauty through plants and flowers, there was much for the Salters and Sudells to discuss and work on back in 1924. With both couples shuttling between London and leafy Hartley, they were contributing to an explosion of energy, passion and activism in the service of the spirit-lifting power of the flower.

5
Sudell the Flower Evangelist

Why would hundreds of readers go to the intricate effort of wrapping up into a parcel a stick of celery or even three chrysanthemums from their gardens before posting them off in the hope of winning a certificate of merit in a competition? It seems hard to believe but this is what hundreds of Londoners did every month in the mid-1920s as gardening fever swept the capital. The condition in which much of this produce arrived at the offices of the LGG at the Browning Settlement in Walworth Road, and how it could possibly be judged, is not known, but that did not stop the packages arriving from every corner of London. The success led to the staff grumbling about the inconvenience of flowers and vegetables cluttering up the office and comic mutterings about the originator of the scheme who had inflicted this task upon them. Richard Sudell was in the prime of his gardening evangelical life, the eye of a hurricane force of faith, politics, horticultural expertise, journalistic instruction and organizational excellence. It was a combination that had helped him arrive at a time and place when he genuinely believed he was going to join with others to change Britain for the better, starting with its capital.

After moving to Hartley, he continued to build his own practice, supplying gardening advice on contract and increasingly designing plots for some of the owners of the bigger private homes being built by speculative developers. Alongside this he was now involved in the mechanics of the revolution, tirelessly working alongside Emily, in his secretarial position with the LGG and of course still keeping an eye on his former neighbours at Roehampton with his monthly column in the *Gazette*. In 1926 he proposed the launch, and became editor, of the *Guild Gardener*, the LGG's journal. His experience at Roehampton, and indeed giving the odd lecture to Lancastrian growers in his pre-war life, had convinced him of the power of the written word. Simple instruction was a way of proving to the hesitant new gardener that there was nothing to fear from bringing floral beauty into their lives or feeding themselves from the earth outside their back doors. The LGG would make even greater progress, Sudell insisted to its committee, if they had a widely circulated journal that informed, inspired and instructed. Impressed by his commitment, they agreed and the *Guild Gardener* was launched in July 1926, bringing an end to his *Gazette* column. As a later *Gardener* noted in 1937, looking back on its launch: 'The credit for the creation of the journal was Mr Sudell's for he alone of all the officials concerned had the necessary courage and confidence to launch out on such a big venture.'[1] The LGG had made astonishing progress in the post-war years but the *Gardener* did indeed bring its work to a wider audience and was vital in the recruitment of subscription members to the various branch guilds and associated groups, such as the Roehampton Garden Society, which were springing up in the London boroughs under its umbrella.

As we have seen, competition was a vital component of the campaign to promote gardening. Sudell organized contests almost as soon as he moved to Roehampton. The promotion of excellence was viewed as a spur to drive others on, even though suburban neighbourly one-upmanship was sometimes an unforeseen by-product that would later be ridiculed by those opposed to what they saw as the narrowed horizons of those who came to live in these new places. Such views were of no consideration to the garden pioneers who surrounded the LGG. It is perhaps easy to dismiss the postal competition Sudell organized as a quirky little sideshow, until one considers the effort hundreds of people went to every month to have their produce judged. In September 1926 it was the turn of vegetable growers to parcel up either three potatoes or onions to send in. The following month the categories were three parsnips or, more logistically difficult, a bunch of flowers, both to be sent to Walworth Road 'carriage paid'. The prize was 10s 6d of goods that were displayed in the garden advertisements the Sudells brought into the journal to pay for its cost and the certificate of merit. Those who reached the heady heights of ten certificates would receive an LGG Gold Medal.

That Gold Medal was a deliberate echo of the awards handed out at the Royal Horticultural Society's Chelsea Flower Show, which had been launched in 1913 and whose exhibitors were the professionalized garden designers working for big houses or the middle classes. By deliberately naming the prize a Gold Medal, Sudell was telling his entrants that they too deserved the highest praise for their work to beautify their own environs no matter how small. And while the Chelsea Flower Show has become an institution, a world-famous showcase of horticultural excellence, another competition and exhibition in the capital in the interwar years was outstripping it in popularity, providing evidence that the transformation of living environments had real consequences. The astonishing work the LGG had undertaken in the post-war years can be evidenced from the first edition of the *Guild Gardener*. Sudell infused the journal with a pioneering spirit, combining simple instruction with regular calls to horticultural arms with sloganeering that presaged the Government's Second World War campaigns such as Dig for Victory.

The first 34-page edition had the simple screaming headline '10,000 Entered for London Garden Championships' and it told a fascinating story. From the early 1920s onwards the LGG had been running garden competitions in which judges visited homes to appraise gardens overall, and the flowers, vegetables and fruit within them. In 1926 it launched a London-wide version that would be judged by up to 150 professional gardeners. There would be categories for front and back gardens, best society or guild, individual flower displays and, undoubtedly with the backing of committee member Ada Salter, a special category for displays of blooms in vases, which could only be entered by residents of congested areas of the capital. According to the rules, this piece of positive discrimination applied only to areas within 5 kilometres (3 mi.) of London Bridge, which certainly gave the citizens of Bermondsey a chance of success. In an article on the competition Sudell told readers how the entries would be judged: the overall 'culture' of the garden and evidence of thriving flowers, fruit and vegetables would receive 20 points, cleanliness for weeds and pests 5, design, arrangement and difficulties overcome 10, and special features such as statuary, 5. This gave a total

The King's Gardener, Thomas Hay (left), Noel Buxton and President of the RHS, Lord Lambourne, judge a garden for the London Gardens Guild competition, 1926. The householder is not named.

score of 40 points. What was also noteworthy was that two of the judges of some of the garden categories were the President of the RHS, Lord Lambourne, and the King's Gardener and Superintendent of the Royal Parks, Thomas Hay, signalling how successfully the LGG had brought working-class gardening onto the agenda of the Establishment.

Not content with this success, the LGG next decided that winners from across the capital would be showcased in a London Gardens Exhibition to take place at Temple Gardens on the Victoria Embankment over three days from 11 September. The best gardens would be recreated in miniature, to a maximum of 1 by 1.2 metres (3 × 4 ft) for individual gardens, with the local guilds and societies also having the chance to create a 1.8 by 1.2 metre (6 × 4 ft) version of their ideal garden. Competition would again be promoted, with displays being judged and awarded prizes. It worked in much the same way that, upstream in Chelsea, specially designed gardens were on show for the more well-heeled classes. The show was a fantastic success, and the *Gardener*, the following month, reported that huge queues of spectators had formed to enter. When asked by organizers to rest on the grass outside for a while to prevent overcrowding, many refused because they didn't want to risk missing any of the exhibits.[2]

The journal also reported that Sudell's old neighbours at the Roehampton Garden Society had won second prize in the corporate displays by garden societies section. It also noted judges' delight that so many 'splendid roses' were on display, proof that the delicate blooms could still flourish in polluted London. 'They looked clean and healthy,' the report said. The Championship and Exhibition continued throughout the interwar years, with the latter moving eventually to the New Hall premises of the RHS at St Vincent Square via a stint at Lord's Cricket Ground, at the heart of the Establishment indeed. In 1928 the Championship attracted 13,000 entries and had a new category of 'brighter roadway', so that neighbours could enter

Prize-winning Roehampton Estate garden, 1929.

their street. Some 15,000 attended the Exhibition, where among the displays was a recreation of the front garden of a Mr Barnes of Methwold Street, Kensington, who had earlier that year won the Championship first prize and the princely sum of £50. By 1937 the Championship was attracting 50,000 entrants. The garden movement appeared unstoppable.

The LGG leadership at the time read like a who's who of radicals, reformers, wealthy liberals and politicians, all with religion, Settlement principles or socialism, and sometimes a combination of all three, running through their veins: Lucy Buxton was chair in 1927; Richard was organizing secretary and Emily, secretary; while Margaret Stubbs, a campaigner for gardening instruction for prisoners, was treasurer. On the committee was Marjory Allen, wife of politician and NCF leader Clifford, a garden architect and campaigner for inner-city play areas for underprivileged children. Rollo Meyer and Ada Salter were also members. Two years later these left-wing campaigners, having succeeded in turning the LGG into a countrywide movement as the National Gardens Guild (NGG) in January 1928, secured Queen Mary as NGG patron and the wives of George Cadbury and Joseph Fels as vice-patrons.

The Sudells were the organizational backbone of this movement to beautify London and then the rest of the country but, as editor of the *Guild Gardener*, Richard also found his voice. For the next thirty years he would become one of the most widely read garden journalists in the country and he became so because of the iron discipline of his writing. He wrote very simple, almost painfully practical, instructions for people he was extremely careful not to put off from the new and sometimes daunting task of creating a garden. He would gently nudge this new army of beautifiers along with step-by-step guidance, seasonal insight and plainly but lovingly drawn diagrams showing what was possible in small gardens. There was no place here for pacifism or politics. Now editing a widely read journal, however, he could bring to the cause of beauty the passion he had shown for the cause of peace. These beliefs had been forged through his indenture as a teenage gardener in Lancashire, his training at Kew and, following the trauma of his experience during the war, among his neighbours at Roehampton and what he had seen in Bermondsey, Walworth and Hartley: 'Beauty is one of the greatest forces in the world, it is the power which can move mountains and in striving after beauty, we are striving after the sublime. Let us then turn to our gardens both to seek freshness of mind and to add beauty to the world.'[3]

For four years Sudell used his editorship as a pulpit from which to preach his belief in the transformative power of the garden. The fervour he brought to the cause was striking. 'Grow More Flowers!' was the simple headline on the September 1926 edition and inside he outlined the ambition of the LGG. It was simply that London should become known as the 'City of Gardens'. This was a theme to which he constantly returned:

> Though London can boast some lovely gardens it has far too many mean slums and ugly and neglected streets. This sordidness can only be overcome by the creation of a public spirit which will demand a beautiful city. The examples of garden beauty which so many Londoners have already given us, prove beyond doubt that a transformation is possible even around the existing bricks and mortar. The cultivation of the garden rests with the people. I believe that many have a vision of London made beautiful and as this vision spreads the ideal of the London Garden Movement will come ... London a Garden City.[4]

In the edition of August 1926 Sudell took stock of the success of the first all-London Garden Championship, an event he and Emily had played a crucial role in organizing. While many of the great and the good were happy to serve on the LGG committee debating and agreeing policy, much of the actual hard work fell to the Sudells. They had made the Championship a fantastic success. Judging 10,000 entries was an incredible feat. Flushed with this triumph, Sudell's editorial immediately showed his sights were set higher.

> We now breathe again, and take stock and plan another garden attack on them. We mean to clothe every city and town in the land with flowers. This is a task in which every man and woman who cares for beauty can help. Every part of London must have its local Guild or Horticultural Society. Drab Districts will have to adapt to brighter colours.[5]

In the same edition he again turned to the power of beauty, noticing that while there was much progress with back gardens, at the front of the house there was still work to do. Everyone had a duty to work on their front gardens for they added to the improvement of the whole community and were not just for the private enjoyment of the householder: 'We all desire a more beautiful world, a world which will inspire us to do better and nobler things.' Flowers could not only beautify, they could inspire people to enhance their lives. Woe betide anyone who did not share this vision. In October 1926 a medical officer in one of the capital's boroughs had called for action against the large number of front plots in inner-city houses that were being left neglected and had become dumping grounds overrun with weeds. His solution to this potential health hazard was to urge his council to cement over all front gardens that were not being kept up to scratch. Sudell went to war. 'This is a mind without vision, a mental attitude which, if allowed to grow, would soon deprive us of any space whatsoever in our big cities.'[6]

The offices of the LGG were a hive of activity, with the Sudells working all hours. 'The lights of the Guild office were frequently burning at 10 or 11pm.'[7] The launch of the *Gardener*, the organization of competitions, the administration that followed the ever-expanding reach of the LGG across the capital, and the ambition to take this mission across the country created a huge workload for Richard and Emily. The list of London branch guilds in early 1927 included Acton, Bermondsey, Becontree, Charlton, Chelsea, Clapton, the London Civil Service, Croydon, Bromley, East Ham, Fulham, Kensington and Paddington, Islington, Hampstead, Lambeth North, Mitcham and Tooting, St Pancras, Stepney, West Ham and, of course, Roehampton. Many of the gardening competitions run for the Beautification Committee in Bermondsey were organized by Sudell and the LGG. Just as importantly, many of the slogans and calls to arms used in the borough to rally residents to the cause were borrowed from Sudell and the *Guild Gardener*. His influence on the Salters in this area was as profound as theirs on him with their practical delivery of life-improving policies for poverty-stricken residents. As well as organizing competitions, lobbying and promoting gardens, the LGG had to supply these branches with seeds and bulbs to encourage everyone to do their bit with their gardens.

For example, the LGG had a steady supply of bulbs, including tulips from Holland, which it sent out to the branches at cost price. Across Britain only Birmingham had a Guild, which had been established by George Cadbury in 1926, so it was now also time for Sudell to take to the road.

As organizing secretary he had been tireless in touring London, giving speeches to nascent brand guilds about the benefits of joining the movement. He spoke about the beauty of town gardens at the opening meeting of the Chelsea branch in February 1927, for instance. Together with his successor as chairman of the REGS, J. H. Allen, he had succeeded in bringing in the *Daily Express* as sponsor of the Championship and the bishop of London as its patron. He spent much of the next eighteen months touring the country, including one weekend in October 1927 when he visited Liverpool, Blackpool and Sheffield, successfully planting the seed for more guilds to grow. In an editorial at the start of that year Sudell wrote that the movement had 'lit a beacon in Britain that could never be quenched'. Day to day the volume of business increased: 'Today St Pancras joined the Guild, yesterday it was Charlton, tomorrow it will be Chelsea and each tomorrow will bring either new recruits or some district decision to link themselves to the onward march. Enthusiasm has given birth to the movement and enthusiasm will keep it alive.'[8]

Further evidence of Sudell's twin strengths of passion for the cause and organizational excellence could be found at the end of 1926 as the LGG continued its rapid expansion and the NGG was soon to be born. Sudell thought it important that the organization had a proper headquarters branch with a regular meeting place where delegates could gather as its Settlement base was unsuited for the purpose. As a regular visitor to the *Daily Express* offices in Fleet Street, Sudell had stumbled across the LCC-owned Prince Henry's Room at 17 Fleet Street, one of the very few buildings that had survived the Great Fire of London in 1666. Its windows at the rear looked over the Inner Temple Gardens, which Shakespeare had used as a setting for Act II, scene 4 of *Henry VI, Part I*. It was there that Edmund Beaufort, Duke of Somerset, was challenged by Richard Plantagenet to choose between a white rose for York or a red rose for Lancaster, thus sparking the War of the Roses. Delighted committee members were impressed by the number of representatives from around the capital who attended, real evidence of the growing success of the movement. Three months later another example of Sudell-inspired success came at the first NGG conference dinner at Anderton's Hotel in Fleet Street which he had persuaded the *Express*, by now fully aware of the new market for garden-enthused readers, to sponsor. Before sitting down to dinner the 150 guests of London branches and affiliated societies heard the scale of the garden success now sweeping the capital and beyond. Reports told them how there were now fifty societies in London alone; half the mayors of London boroughs were interested in connecting to the LGG or already were. The delegate from Islington reported there were now 240 members in his guild after just a year of existence.

In front of committee members such as Noel and Lucy Buxton, Ada Salter and Marjory Allen, it was now the turn of Sudell to talk about plans for national expansion. As he rose to speak, something surprising happened that may have reminded him of that community meeting room in Roehampton just a few years back. As one, the diners rose to their feet and, as the *Gardener* reported:

> the hall resonated to the strains of 'For He's a Jolly Good Fellow' followed by 'three cheers'. Somewhat disconcerted by this sudden expression of feeling, Mr Sudell nevertheless managed to convey to the meeting his desire that local secretaries and workers should regard themselves as members of a great movement. There was a tendency, he said, to feel that one was fighting a lone fight in the locality but by getting in touch with others working in different places this loneliness was dispelled and one felt inspired to greater efforts.[9]

This was the second time in three years that Sudell had, somewhat bashfully, accepted the approbation of an audience. It might seem remarkable today that such enthusiasm could be generated by a gardener, but it illustrated the excitement caused by a transformation that was taking place in many parts of Britain, the recognition of the hard yards needed to spread horticultural colour across a grey postwar country. It also showed the readiness with which this movement was being taken to the hearts of many across the land and, of course, the part played by this modest man, hitherto unrecognized, in this chapter of British social and landscape history.

For Sudell there was little time to bask in the applause. In 1927 the Prison Gardening Association (PGA) was formed by the NGG and Sudell, somewhat inevitably, became its secretary. Just eight years after his own harrowing experience of life behind bars this was a chance to do something for others experiencing what he had. Sudell and others like him failed to accept any limits on the redemptive powers of gardening. In 1930 he wrote a letter to *The Spectator* appealing for donations to the PGA, which, he said, had had a 'most excellent influence' on the inmates it had worked with. Along with others Sudell had taken part in lectures and, where there was land available, practical instruction in 22 prisons and three Borstal institutions under the VLCS in 1923. One hundred copies of the society's own book on allotment gardening were sent to the Chaplains Inspector of the Prison Service for distribution to the prisons where the lectures had taken place.[10] The idea was seized on by the PGA with Margaret Stubbs to the fore. Her work with women prisoners at Holloway came to the attention of the *Manchester Guardian* in 1930. She told the newspaper:

> They are very friendly and keen about gardening. They have told me that they look out anxiously each morning to see what the weather is like. If there is rain, they know there will be no gardening in the evening. Usually then, I give

them lectures. In one of the plots they grow lettuce, which, I believe, they are allowed to have for tea.[11]

By 1929 the association had fifteen lecturers and instructors regularly visiting inmates for lectures and instruction.

There was still more work to do recruiting more associate groups around the country, for the more people who joined the movement, the more governments and local authorities could be pressured to adopt something akin to Bermondsey's beautification programme. Throughout this time undoubted financial constraints on government spending as the post-war recession continued led to regular debates within NGG leadership about how far it could go in supporting Garden City principles in totality and what compromises it might have to make. With most members from the Left politically, arguments often broke out between members of the Labour Party and those of the more radical affiliate, the ILP, such as the Salters. More practical programmes were beginning to be supported that focused on smaller spheres of influence such as the horticultural education of schoolchildren. In spring 1929 Sudell visited six south London inner-city schools holding LGG-backed flower shows, which displayed daffodils pupils had cultivated at home. He wrote, 'Think what this means, 12,000 of south London's poorest homes, in each of which a daffodil was blooming.'[12] But it wasn't only the poorest of London's inhabitants who received a visit from Sudell. Labour was returned to government in 1929 after its short-lived first period of rule in 1924. Ramsay MacDonald was again prime minister, but as a relatively poor widower it was clear he would not be able to live at 10 Downing Street in the style maintained by some of his predecessors. At that time prime ministers had to fund their own offices and residency in Downing Street. Nevertheless, his eldest daughter, Ishbel, who was constantly at his side, became his hostess at No. 10 and set to work doing her best to beautify her own small area of London. She became hugely popular with the public. Almost as soon as her father was returned to power, she contacted LGG secretary Sudell for advice on what she could do to brighten up No. 10. Sudell had the answer. He visited Ishbel armed with window boxes and bulbs, installing them at front and back and particularly outside her own office as, reported the *Gardener*, 'she was very fond of flowers and her workroom was looking out only on bricks and mortar.' It is perhaps ironic that the modest window box, which had been used to beautify the most squalid inner-city neighbourhoods, was now being installed at Britain's most famous address to do exactly the same.

While others like the Salters were pushing a political programme in Bermondsey that included the health-giving and spirit-lifting power of flowers and trees, Sudell was doing work at a grassroots level that was certainly no less profound. For him the promotion of beauty in small places was equally important, and almost nothing under the sky should be exempt from the influence of the gardener. This included petrol stations, the first of which had been opened by the Automobile Association in Berkshire in 1919 and which were steadily growing in number. For Sudell this post-war growth was in danger of simply being left to market forces without control; at least employing minimum design standards might contribute to the new, emerging, more colourful Britain. Shorn of real power and influence over government planning policy, what he and the NGG could do was promote best practice, and so, reverting to its playbook, a competition was launched. Prizes and trophies for best landscaping 'to drape the average petrol pump in clothes of beauty' were to be offered. Entrants to the Brighter Petrol Station *Daily Express* Gold Cup were exhorted to 'soften the ugliness with grass shrubs, judiciously planted flowers and hanging baskets'.[13] The first winner was Capt. L. F. Peaty's station Coombe Bridge, on the Kingston Bypass, Surrey, with the judges reporting, 'the herbaceous borders and roses were indeed a glorious sight.'

Towards the end of the decade the beautification agenda appeared to be gaining unstoppable momentum. While there were fundamental battles to be fought in the next decade over issues like national planning policy, for now the principle of decent living conditions for Britain's population and the part played by gardens in this appeared to have been accepted at the highest level of politics and by most of the Establishment. Small setbacks such as the failure of the London Garden Settlement paled into insignificance as the NGG spread its influence around the country, Buxton again helping to fund its move to new, more spacious offices in Gower Street in 1928, from where Sudell also ran his own practice, and new members and guilds were joining the cause almost by the day. The London Headquarters branch alone passed 1,000 members in June 1927.

The *Guild Gardener* continued to be used as an effective tool in the recruitment of new members to the guilds that were establishing themselves across the country. But even in its columns there were

Prize-winning Roehampton Estate garden, 1931.

the seeds of a debate over the suburbs that would ignite around Sudell and others in the coming years. His Guild-backed *Town Gardening Handbook* continued to sell strongly, but there were stirrings of a snobbishness about the aspirations of the sorts of people Sudell and others were seeking to inspire. It was almost as if the Establishment accepted progress, but the social order still had to be protected. Gardens should be a balm against agitation for social justice, not a weapon to change the nature of society as some in the NGG believed. The *Daily Express*, a hugely successful newspaper with a mainly lower middle-class audience at the time, had seen a new emerging market for garden-enthused readers and had backed Sudell and the NGG with money and column inches. Nevertheless, when reviewing the *Handbook* it could not resist describing it as 'a book for the people who potter about in their diminutive garden at the weekend'.[14] An earlier advertisement for the *Handbook* again had a quote from the *Express* describing it as 'a homely, charmingly written little book which might easily convert a man who did not know a wallflower from an antirrhinum into an enthusiastic gardener'.[15] The patronization drips from the page and was a small taste of the debate about the suburbs and their gardens that was to ignite in the following years; and in which Sudell, and the instruction he was promoting, would be caught up.

Modernists and landscape architects would begin to push new agendas a world away from the privacy-allowing privet hedge and the rose bush that were being encouraged by the LGG and NGG. What would often be forgotten was the historical context for the growth of these gardens. While they were assumed to be symbolic of a new conservatism, a one-upmanship that destroyed communalism, their roots, for Sudell and others, grew from the demand that all should have what had largely been the preserve of the wealthy: namely open space, healthy fresh air and the spirit-lifting power of the flower, fruit and vegetable. The very first edition of the *Gardener* gave a clue as to the battle lines that would be drawn and the derision that might pour down on suburban garden advocates. In news that might have given both modernists and landscape traditionalists the vapours, an article by George Filby told of a soon-to-come invasion. Filby told Guild readers that rockeries were now fashionable and might even be improved with 'little figure Gnomes with smiling faces and red caps'. And it got worse. For Filby had exciting news about a cargo that was heading its way to Britain: 'A shipment of terra cotta figures is already on its way to these shores which includes all kinds of animals, frogs, birds, rabbits and also old favourites of nursery rhymes, the Babes in the Wood, Red Riding Hood and so on.'[16]

For many the garden gnome and other statuary would be one of the symbols of a tastelessness encouraged by promoters of the suburban garden and the corrupted values that arose within those spaces. Ridicule would be the weapon used against this 'terra cotta' army appearing in gardens and, of course, was employed mainly by those who were wealthy enough never to have experienced the life-affirming boost a garden gave to those who had hitherto hardly dared to dream such things were possible. Sudell himself would take these battles with him into the Institute of Landscape Architects (ILA): an organization, now simply called the Landscape Institute, which he founded, but from whose history books he has been written out. The reasons for this are largely rooted in the work in which he immersed himself in the interwar years. For now, though, in the *Guild Gardener* he was modest enough to mention the ILA's birth but omit his own central role in a body that would take the fight for central planning and the lifting of landscape standards to a new level. He told readers in the March 1930 edition that he welcomed the launch of the ILA as a 'sign of the times. Local Authorities, businesses and private persons have long felt the need for some authority to set the standard in the layout of garden and open spaces.'

Three months later Sudell's name mysteriously disappeared as editor of the *Gardener*, although the secretarial positions he and Emily held were still recorded. In the September and October issues Emily's name vanished as secretary of the NGG and LGG, and the following month all trace of Richard was gone. This masked upheaval in their personal lives. Richard had met would-be horticulturalist Ida Schlittler, the daughter of a wealthy Swiss doctor, in the early part of 1930 and began an affair with her. Divorce papers show Emily petitioned for divorce in August on the grounds that Richard was 'living and habitually committing adultery with Ida Schlittler' at her address in Thames Ditton, Surrey.[17] He had left Emily in Hartley and moved in with Ida in Surrey. Working together at the NGG and LGG was now impossible, and they both resigned. In an editorial in the December edition readers were told it was 'with considerable reluctance that the Execs of the NGG & the LGG have been asked to accept the resignations of Mr and Mrs Sudell from the honorary posts which they have occupied during the past ten years with so marked ability and distinction'. The reasons given were that the 'heavy burdens of personal duties' for Richard meant he found it impossible to devote time to the increasingly heavy workload of the Guild. It was a 'double regret', said the editorial, that Emily had also expressed her wish to resign, though anyone 'knowing the responsibilities and worries attached to the post will realize that she is well deserving of a rest from her strenuous labours of the past ten years'.

> Mrs Sudell by her untiring devotion in her work endeared herself in the hearts of her fellow workers whilst Mr Sudell inspired the whole Movement by his charming personality and his wonderful enthusiasm. In years to come as the Guild grows, we shall probably realise to a greater extent than we do now the real foundation work carried out by these two able pioneers... We know we are expressing the desire of Mr and Mrs Sudell when we say that both of them feel the next way by which members can repay them for all their work so generously given to the Guild is to be staunch and continuous

allegiance to the Movement and this active support on behalf of the ideals for which it stands.[18]

This tribute to them both did not overplay their crucial role in the garden revolution that first conquered London and then spread across the country. Neither should Emily's tireless role in this story be underplayed. She continued to live in Hartley until her death in 1971 at the age of 82 and developed herself into a horticultural journalist. Under the pen name Marguerite James, she still wrote for the *Gardener* before the Second World War and even for a while rivalled her ex-husband in the burgeoning garden book publishing market, authoring *The Family Garden* in 1937 and the following year *How to Make a Garden*. Richard was moving on to more landscape battles, the continued growth of his own landscape practice and, thanks to Ida's wealthy background, a more comfortable bucolic life in Surrey. As for the NGG and LGG, it would never recover its activist fervour, especially after Ada Salter was ousted as chair of the NGG by Lady Seton in 1934. Although Ada stayed on as vice chair, those who supported Lady Seton found the *Guild Gardener* too strident in its support for working-class movements such as the Canning Town Women's Settlement, which was campaigning for slum dwellers to be given gardens, and for unemployed men to be taken on by the government for beautification work. The renaming, proposed by the new conservative leadership of the NGG, of the London Gardens Guild as the London Gardens Society, supported by the publishing voice of the Establishment, *The Times*, was hugely symbolic.

Similarly, with Sudell gone, concerns that the *Gardener*'s leftist tones were putting off advertisers were the smokescreen to turn it into a platform for pure instruction, not political evangelizing. The radicals who made such progress in the years around the First World War would have to find other ways to continue to fight the cause. For people like Alfred and Ada Salter it was politics, for Sudell it was within the newly formed ILA. Here, as debate continued to rage about the transformation of Britain into a land of suburbanites, he would refuse to water down the radicalism of his landscape philosophy while continuing to urge the newly situated working classes to beautify their lives through their gardens. The *Guild Gardener* itself limped on until 1968 and the NGG was wound up as a charitable organization as late as 1992, but it had long ceased to have any meaningful purpose.

6
'Taste is utterly debased'

'If there is one crying demand on most housing estates it is the need for trees and shrubs that will give the necessary degree of exclusion from the world.' So wrote Sudell in his gardening column in the magazine *Ideal Home* in May 1930.[1] We shall shortly see how the boy who left school at fourteen became one of the most widely read gardening writers of the early twentieth century, but for now the quote is illustrative of a debate that was surfacing in the interwar years around the astonishing pace of development of the suburbs. For what was emerging was a division between those who fully supported the right for the many to have decent living conditions and space in which to thrive, and those who feared the expansion that enabled this was out of control and in danger of ruining both England's rural idyll and the shape of its towns and cities forever.

For Sudell and others, the latter argument was one some architects and town planners had the luxury of making. They strongly believed in Britain having central control of its planning to prevent haphazard market-led sprawl and low standards of design; indeed, Sudell would spend the rest of his life arguing for this policy. However, this newly designed Britain had to be for all, and could not be at the expense of improving the lives of vast swathes of the population. There could be no attempt by the middle-class professional to pull up the drawbridge to a green and pleasant land. And why shouldn't the working classes have a small taste of what the landed, country estate dweller and middle-class Victorian suburbanite had enjoyed for ages before them, namely privacy? Indeed, if the Bible promoted the spirituality of the private garden, should it have been surprising that many were desirous of something similar? *Hortus conclusus*, the Latin term for an enclosed or walled garden, referred to the medieval private garden with its suggestions of impenetrability and purity, its derivation from the Old Testament's Song of Songs held to represent the Immaculate Conception. In Renaissance art the Virgin Mary was frequently depicted near or in a walled garden. Owners of eighteenth-century country houses had ha-has constructed to keep unsightly livestock perimeters out of the uninterrupted view of a heavenly landscape from their windows and placed their kitchen gardens and attendant labourers out of sight to the side of the house. Could not everyone else be able to grow shrubs around their small plots to enjoy a few moments of solitude from the strains of everyday life?

> The new [eighteenth-century] owners wanted privacy and seclusion, the chief stock in trade of Capability Brown: the creation of landscaped parks often meant the removal of unsightly cottages and gardens, or, in the classic case of Milton Abbas in Dorset, of a sizeable market town, with a grammar school, alms-houses, shops, four inns and a brewery.[2]

For those who had lived in, or been witness to, the cramped squalor that many experienced in inner cities in the early twentieth century – remember the queues for a single latrine in Whitechapel – the chance for some degree of temporary seclusion would be eagerly seized upon. It was bemusing to many like Sudell that, as the century moved on, this desire for some form of refuge in house or garden became a symbol of narrow-minded conservatism, of curtain-twitching conformity.

Of course, there have been suburbs for as long as there has been urban growth. The vast increases in population during the Victorian era and the increasing industrialization of the country would create opportunity for the better-off to distance themselves from the noisy, dangerously unhealthy source of their new-found wealth. John Ruskin and William Morris both saw the growth of the Victorian town and city as threatening to an ideal of British life. In his novel *The New Machiavelli*, published in 1911, H. G. Wells damned the British suburbs for their 'vast endlessness'.[3] Some figures for London population growth might help to explain why the concentric circles of the suburbs, particularly in London, seemed unstoppable. In 1801 there were 959,000 living in the capital, but by 1921 this had risen to 4,483,000. In 1801 a huge majority of the population lived in the tightly packed inner area, with the outer, defined by places such as Battersea, Chelsea, Lambeth and Paddington, home to only around 64,000.

A little more than a century later these two areas, or rings, were home to almost 3 million, but an astonishing 1,933,000 were living in places beyond this, the aforementioned districts now in effect the inner city. This army of middle-class suburbanites was escaping the capital's squalor. Civil servants, doctors, shopkeepers and teachers were moving into houses built piecemeal by private speculative builders on parcels of land sold by landowners under individual Acts of Parliament. The companies were able to do so through building-society or solicitor-backed mortgages, which enabled them to lease the land and maintain enough capital to move on to the next plot. The vast majority of the new householders rented their properties. Ownership was a twentieth-century phenomenon. Most working-class people remained in inner-city tenements, although the development of the tube and railway network around the capital towards the end of the nineteenth century did allow some movement. One example of this is the Shaftesbury estate off Latchmere Road in Battersea, built between 1872 and 1877 by the Artizans', Labourers' and General Dwellings Company, a philanthropic company established in 1867. This was the earliest example of a working-class cottage estate and a clear ancestor of Roehampton. Company architect Robert Austin designed an estate of 1,000 cottages laid out in tree-lined streets, which attracted better-paid workers and tradespeople paying rents of between 7 and 13 shillings a week. All houses were built with distinctive yellow London stock brick with decorative red and black banding and Gothic ornamentation.[4]

Aside from the odd Shaftesbury estate, the pattern of development was overwhelmingly private housing for the middle classes. In the middle of the century this consisted of large villas or Italianate terraces morphing into a semi-detached style from the 1860s onwards, as can still be seen in Maida Vale, Holloway, Hackney, Highbury, Blackheath and Greenwich. With these came the first signs of front and back gardens, which became the quintessential symbols of suburban house forms.[5] There was much opposition to this growth. Even after a number of late nineteenth-century Acts had tightened restrictions on building, Raymond Unwin, while recognizing the health improvements these new estates brought, added that 'for dreariness and sheer ugliness it is difficult to match anywhere and compared with which many of the old unhealthy slums are, from the point of view of picturesqueness and beauty, infinitely more attractive.'[6] However this was nothing compared to the howls of protest that the real explosion of the suburbs would bring forth in the interwar period and beyond. There was one big difference. This time the new homes would often be constructed for the working classes. It is not too fanciful to ask whether it was the suburbs themselves that were the target for criticism or the people who were now living in them. The birth of this new suburbia and the beginnings of a national garden culture that came with it did, after all, represent one of the biggest social upheavals in twentieth-century British history. Some thought they had much to lose by this encroachment into their utopia.

By 1935 Greater London's population stood at around 8.5 million, double that of just 24 years before. It was estimated that it had been growing by about three-quarters of a million – or, say, the equivalent population size of a provincial city – annually for the past few years. A fifth of the entire nation lived in less than 1 per cent of its land area. And as if to statistically prove the point about the importance of the suburbs, between 1921 and 1937 the population of inner London continued to decline, this time by half a million, while the numbers living in the Greater London conurbation outside this area increased by 1.25 million.[7] The lessons learned during the war about the poor physical shape of many army recruits meant initially there was little coordinated opposition to the sacrifice of the countryside at the fringes of the capital for the new estates. A healthier population was a price worth paying for this continued growth. Before the war less than 5 per cent of all housing was built by the public sector but now that figure skyrocketed under government policies. The principle of local authority supply of decent homes for rent was established: the council house tenant was born.

As well as Roehampton there were other estates built by the LCC that contributed to the population flow from inner to outer London and allowed the planners to create more space for residents, most notably Downham in Lewisham and Becontree in Dagenham. With Becontree eventually housing 120,000 people, it is fair to say the need for scale meant these estates were less varied and more monotonous. Much of the expansion of Greater London was still being driven by private speculative developers feeding off the great advances in transport links that occurred at the same time. The 'ribbon' development that came with it and the 'Stockbroker Tudor' houses that were its main feature did particularly exercise the minds of planners and architects both concerned about unrestrained development and aghast at the garishness of design on display. In truth, though, all of the new suburbia, including the council cottage estates, would be subsumed into the wider debate about the way Britons were living their lives in the early twentieth century. They were damned together. For critics suburbia was after all a mindset, whether you could afford Tudor beams, lily ponds and tennis courts or not. The expansion of the Metropolitan Line and the housing developments that travelled alongside it became a lightning rod for the whole issue. The Metropolitan Railway had begun to buy up tracts of land in Middlesex, Buckinghamshire and Hertfordshire to extend its lines from Baker Street to the northwest taking in Aylesbury in 1892, Uxbridge in 1904, to Watford in 1925 and to Stanmore in 1932. In a faint echo of today's Crossrail project, the company had originally envisaged linking northwest England to London and onwards to Paris but, as this plan foundered on economic reality, an enterprising executive began to eye up the land that surrounded the new lines, envisaging a new life for inner-city dwellers in bucolic Middlesex. The company bought up swathes of adjoining land and now marketed a lifestyle that took residents out of grimy London to a paradise it called Metro-land.

Obviously they would need to commute back to work on the company's trains, but the appeal of a semi-rural lifestyle was an instant hit, with a huge influx of population following in quick time. Middlesex's ancient farmland disappeared under a 30 per cent population growth in the ten years to 1931, Harrow had grown by 275 per cent by 1938 and Wembley by 552 per cent.[8] An expansion in road building – the Watford Bypass and the North Circular Road were both begun in the 1920s – was also under way, allowing more ribbon development. Many of the new residents were now 'home-owners', a rapid rise in mortgages offered by an equally sharp expansion in the number of building societies. This was the uncontrolled explosion of suburbia critics had feared. Few were able to see anything but a stark dividing line between urban and country and most were certainly not prepared to accept that the tree-lined avenues, parks, squares and gardens of the new estates could be seen as a new rurality. The Tudorbethan houses of upper-end Metro-land were an easy target for satire. Architectural historian and cartoonist Osbert Lancaster sketched these wood-panelled paeans to a mythical Golden Age against a backdrop of electricity pylons and planes flying into one of the many new aerodromes that were surrounding London.

Very few defenders were prepared to put their heads above the parapet. The new house dwellers themselves were, of course, largely absent from the debate, perhaps content to sit it out in the privacy of their new back gardens.

This was then the beginning of a dismissal of suburban living that continues to this day, regardless of the fact that most Britons actually live there. A nasty concoction of snobbery, condescension, humour and outrage would be employed by critics to damn this new lifestyle, although fears of unplanned urban sprawl were genuinely held. It wasn't just planners and architects fearful of rampant expansion and the emergence of (in their view) vulgar taste who took part in this debate. It was, and remains, a culture war more generally. Witness poet John Betjeman: analogue multi-media behemoth, chief defender of Victorian architecture and a man whose embourgeoisement made him swing, at high velocity, between sympathy for the little people and dripping condescension towards them. The poet laureate made Metro-land prime-time television in an eponymous 1973 documentary, treating it as a lost land, 'Child of the First War forgotten by the Second', as he described it in the opening scenes. Written in 1951, 'Middlesex', one of his most famous poems, is both a fascinating and rich insight into the growth of Metro-land and something akin to a literary 'safari park tour', a drive-by look through the window at the creatures who live there. Betjeman takes a train journey out to the suburbs with commuter Elaine, going so far as to 'the outskirt's edges, where a few surviving hedges, keep alive our lost Elysium – rural Middlesex again'. Later we learn that Elaine 'the bobby soxer/ Fresh-complexioned with Innoxa/ Gains the garden/ Father's hobby.' Here, beautifully contained in a few lines, is the suburban debate, still raging thirty years after those new estates began to emerge from the rural soil in the immediate aftermath of the First World War. The poem implied a lost paradise, buried under bricks and mortar, a place now where thousands of Elaines and their dads aspire to the middle class, content with a garden as a poor substitute for rural idyll. It is the man of the house who has found himself a little hobby growing petunias and carrots. Is this a good life these people have attained? It is hard to think Betjeman really believes so. In a BBC documentary he made in 1967 called *Contrasts: Marble Arch to Edgware Road*, he went further: 'Dear Middlesex, dear vanished country friend/ Your neighbour, London, killed you in the end.'[9]

Here it is worth pausing to contemplate a riptide of intellectual thought that moved swiftly below the surface of this mass social upheaval, the powerful current of theory that, while eventually turned by the reality of bricks and mortar, still eddies in the pools of debate around the suburbs today. David Matless, in his book *Landscape and Englishness* (1998), calls this thinking preservationist. He describes preservationists as those planners, writers and architects, coalescing around the 1926-founded Council for the Protection of Rural England (CPRE), who called for tight controls on the relationship between the urban and the rural. But with that came an almost violent hatred of the suburb that was dressed up in community theory, politics and even sexuality. At its core was a feeling that the soldiers of the First World War had been fighting for, and dreaming of, an England of rural bliss: a Betjeman landscape of church spires, village green and warm beer. Instead, they had been betrayed by a development free-for-all that was sweeping away, à la Middlesex, all those things that made England unique.

While many insisted they did not want to preserve the countryside in aspic they did hark back to 'old money' landownership where the squire knew his duty to the land and the people who worked for him. Swept away by Victorian laissez-faire and – in the run-up to the First World War – death duties and rising prices, the old estates were now at the mercy of a rampant market and weak politicians. Chief preservationist and Welsh architect Clough Williams-Ellis thought it important that 'educated' people, such as himself, led the debate for all classes of people about what was good and bad in terms of building and planning. Setting aside that he was the architect who plonked the Italianate curiosity of Portmeirion on the Dwyryd estuary in north Wales, Williams-Ellis wanted a rigid planning, centrally controlled system to save the country: 'If there is no master-founder, no co-related plan, we may live to be aghast at what we have made – a hash of our civilization and a desert of our country.'[10] Despite the vaguely totalitarian tone (Williams-Ellis was a member of the ILP) this kind of plaintive language was everywhere as the suburbs continued their march.

Town planner Thomas Sharp was even more emotional than his preservationist colleague when he considered the growth of the new living spaces and the false dream they were selling to the new residents: 'Tradition has broken down. Taste is utterly debased. The town, long since degraded, is now being annihilated by a flabby, shoddy, romantic nature worship. That romantic nature worship is destroying also the object of its adoration, the countryside.'[11] Sharp saw the selling of the Metro-land dream as a return to rural England as utterly false. The suburbs, in fact, were replacing the dramatic contrast of town and country with 'one, drab, revolting neutrality'. Along with others he introduced gender into the debate. In florid terms he described the town as having 'strong masculine virility', and the countryside 'the softer beauty, the richness, the fruitfulness of that mother of men'. And what of the suburb? It represented, Sharp wrote, reaching an almost hysterical crescendo, 'one sterile, hermaphroditic beastliness'. Matless quotes cultural historian Alison Light's assertion that the interwar suburbs fostered a private and domestic 'conservative modernity', and what he interprets as a 'feminized Englishness retreating from expansive and imperial masculinities'.

Preservationists saw the suburb as a privatized space without communal function or spirit. A popular cartoon in the *Daily Express* at the time, 'Strube's Little Man', captured the emasculation of the suburbs perfectly, the small moustachioed hen-pecked character, 'a modest, garden concerned and commonsensical suburban male'.[12] The Little Man was the descendant of Mr Pooter in George and Weedon Grossmith's *Diary of a Nobody*, most of which first appeared in *Punch* and then in a series of popular books. This satire on suburban life frequently portrayed Mr Pooter pottering around his garden tending his flower beds. Could there be anything worse for any self-respecting male suburban dweller than being described as Pooterish or, as the *Collins English Dictionary* has it, 'a type of middle-class person regarded as unimaginative, conventional, self-important etc'? We can all guess what the etceteras are.

In the space of a few years the heroes of the Western Front had been shrunken into their suburban gardens, their dreams of country sold short, creativity and thirst for social change syphoned off into growing petunias and potatoes. Where planners led writers followed. D. H. Lawrence – who else on the subject of reclaiming masculinity – called the new suburban houses 'horrid little red rattraps'.[13] For champion of the working-class male Lawrence, there was little worse than the vulgarity of aspirant middle classes wishing to leave their roots behind. Never one to let consistency trump passionate polemic – in the same essay he had lauded the miners' love of flowers in the backyards of their tiny colliery homes – he had a stab at taking on Sharp and Williams-Ellis in the interwar town-planning game.

> Do Away With it All then ... Plan a nucleus. Fix the Focus. And then put up big buildings, handsome, that sweep to a civic centre. And furnish them with beauty. And make an absolute clean start. Do it place by place. Make a new England. Away with little homes! Away with scrabbling pettiness and paltryness.[14]

Lawrence does not specify whose definition of beauty this would be, although he does praise American cities, which were following the Roman view of citizenship as against the 'silly little individualism' of 'the Englishman's home is his castle'. 'The Englishman still likes to think of himself as a "cottager" – "my home, my garden". But it is puerile.' Fellow champion of the ruled class George Orwell was to give no succour to the newly aspirational, either. His 1939 anti-suburb novel *Coming Up for Air* has its Strube-like protagonist George Bowling living in a 'line of semi-detached torture chambers' and beset by 'a boss twisting his tail and a wife riding him like a nightmare and his kids sucking his blood like leeches'.[15]

As Richard Sudell would discover, there was something worse than being dismissed by critics, and that was being patronized. In the queue of writers lining up to have their say on suburbia, J. B. Priestley, himself brought up in a Bradford suburb, was probably the nearest to a sympathetic supporter the new estates had. In 1927 he wrote of the dilemma posed by new suburbs 'where a desire for beauty wars with our common sympathy. A few more of these houses and this place will no longer charm the eye; a great many more of them and it will be hideous.' His humanity recognized that 'a number of people will have the chance of living decently and in comfort' and that

> people should come first . . . their chunks of happiness or misery are more important than certain delicate satisfactions of our own. We should be content to make the whole country hideous if we know for certain that by doing so we could make all the people in it moderately happy.[16]

Even when some critics attacked the Modern Movement's arrogant dismissal of the suburbanite sensibility and lack of community spirit, it was sometimes hard to view the intervention as helpful. Design writer John Gloag was one of the few who would stick up for this new way of living. He urged Modern Movement supporters to 'travel occasionally in crowded third-class carriages in the bowler-hat hours; and then let them listen to the gardening chatter that seeps under the newspaper barriers that every man erects against a possible neighbour, until he recognizes a garden lover.'[17] It was Strube brought to life. The paternalistic tone of both Priestley and Gloag might even have been more irksome to suburbanites than Betjeman's double-sided observations.

The problem with the debate – apart from the residents themselves being missing from it – was that few 'expert' voices existed to explain the circumstances that gave rise to the need for the new spaces, or support those who actually found living there entirely pleasant. This left the field open to those with the eloquence and passion to essay their pain. What also appeared thin on the ground were alternatives. While many of the protectionists did support Garden City principles, CPRE founder Patrick Abercrombie was among those who lumped such developments into the Sharpian 'hermaphroditic' category in that they were still effectively suburban with all the failure of community that came with it.

It was left to the Le Corbusier-inspired Modern Movement, which by 1930 was in full cry against the spread of suburbia, to posit the answer to the preservationist's dilemma. Step forward Geoffrey Boumphrey, a member along with one J. Betjeman of the Modern Architectural Research (MARS) Group, who had made his feelings plain in a 1935 BBC wireless debate entitled 'Suburbs or Satellites', which gave a fascinating insight into the development of the curious alliance of Modernist/Preservationist thinking. Boumphrey declared, 'the mad building of suburbs must be stopped before it strangles the towns themselves,' arguing that the inner-city dweller who needed the countryside the most was now denied it by an 'inefficient fringe of suburbs' and that, like spreading Japanese knotweed, they even threatened to reach out and swamp adjacent towns and cities. Not only that but the suburban commute, a hellish waste of life itself, had begun to choke the outer cities with traffic. In the broadcast it was left to John Cadbury of the extended chocolate family and a manager of the Bournville Garden Trust to point out that tube trains were the 'best method of cheap travel ever invented'.

Against the negative opinions of most of the programme's witnesses, Cadbury, while concerned with ribbon development, reminded the audience of the real benefit of suburban dwelling. He applauded the achievement of the rapid build of 40,000 houses in Birmingham for nearly a quarter of a million people and admired the way the suburb brought the country into towns: 'I do not call it a waste of land to give a man his own home and garden, where he can feel that it is his own to do with as he wishes and where at least he can have more than enough fresh air around him.' Having received a generally frosty reception from the studio audience, Cadbury succeeded in uniting them in agreement that private gardens were the best and most popular feature of suburban life.[18]

In Boumphrey, an architectural writer, we glimpse both the hatred of the suburban form that characterized those like him and the solutions they were proposing. Along with the CPRE, Boumphrey and others were pressing for a halt to the spread of Greater London – something achieved in 1938 with the establishment of the Green Belt Act – so that the distinction between town and country could be maintained. Such a boundary, Boumphrey maintained, would foster a 'revival of English corporate life'.

> Gone will be the spattering of nasty, pseudo-hygienic little houses, each weakly proclaiming its semi detachment and their place will be taken by groups of dwellings, not ashamed to stand together for the attainment of beauty, symbols of that cooperation by which man has conquered Nature.[19]

So what were these 'groups of dwellings' that would solve the problem of the suburbs and give inner-city residents a new, uplifting lifestyle? In theory if the big houses and landed estates of the Putney Park and Dover House estates on Roehampton were to be preserved as rural spaces where were the residents to be housed in Boumphrey's vision? The answer was to support preservationist geographer Vaughan Cornish's proposal of London as a 'high rise garden city' of steel-framed buildings taking up only one-third of the space. Boumphrey took it even further. London could be 85 per cent open space. Put simply, residents were to be placed in high-rise buildings reaching far into the skies.

> One can imagine the effect of seeing such a city – the acres of green, broken here and there by sheets of water or playing fields, the great trees rising to their full country heights and here and there among them lovely buildings in white and crystal, shining in the clear air. Rebuilt like this, London would sink to a third of its size . . . yet increase its capacity. The country could be brought back to within something like reasonable reach of even this hypertrophied city.[20]

Even if motivated by thoughts of revenge for the snobbishness aimed at the humble suburbs and their residents, the temptation to dismiss such an idea with derision should be resisted. These theorists and planners held the upper hand in the interwar and post-war years. And while the more outlandish of their proposals never saw the light of day, other smaller-scale projects did, making many lives miserable for generations to come. Let's travel back to the high-rise Alton Estate in Roehampton. Remember the one with its tenants now in a 'living hell' with their young having never set foot in nearby Richmond Park? This is exactly what Boumphrey was envisioning. Inspired by Le Corbusier's unrealized Modernist masterplan, Ville Radieuse, and its more limited reality, the Unité d'habitation slab block of flats in Marseille, Alton eventually housed almost 12,000 people. While it provokes despair today, when it was completed in 1959 the international architectural community was still in thrall to Le Corbusier and it remained the object of much admiration.

It is worth returning to one of Alton's designers, Bill Howell, for a clue about the post-Second World War obsession with reaching for the skies. For Howell, who started his career as an LCC architect, and others, this high-rise modern living allowed for open space and did away with the indeterminate, neither country nor city, dreary existence he imagined suburbanites suffered:

> We saw this in terms of the fact that we wouldn't want to go and live there because everything from the bright lights to the art galleries, the continental restaurants, in short 'life', the thing one goes to the city for – it didn't seem to be happening out in the suburbs.[21]

Frankly there was never any worry that Howell, the Marlborough College-educated son of the Attorney-General of Singapore, was going to have to live either 'out' there in the suburbs or in one of the flats in the slab blocks that were so admired on Alton. But being on the wrong side of history as Le Corbusier and his acolytes have so clearly been did not alter the power of their anti-suburban antipathy. It seeped into mainstream debate and remained there even as, one by one, their own skyscraper visions were demolished as unfit for human habitation.

Among modernists, so keen to work with preservationists to preserve the rural idyll, there was never any mention of the gardens that suburbia offered new residents. Any nod to the pleasure that working and relaxing in their own open spaces gave new suburbanites was simply wrapped up in the anti-communal theory that damned them all to hell. The privet hedge was symbolic of the withdrawal of these people to the margins of their own lives. Yet as we have seen in the BBC debate on the suburbs earlier in this chapter, the affection the largely silent residents of the new estates had for their new homes would have been considerably less had they not come with gardens. In the debate Boumphrey had no answer to that. The anti-suburban view, the Sharpian 'flabby nature worship' kind, would have it that the gardens gave an illusion of escape from inner-city life yet were actually destroying Arcadia and pushing it further away from the reach of town-dwellers. For them the countryside was about rugged nature, wild meadows and pastoral bliss, not tea roses planted in diamond-shaped earth amid an immaculate lawn on tiny front garden plots.

That the explosion of suburban gardens contributed to a new riot of colour in Britain between the wars is undeniable. It is estimated that the combination of private and council house building between the wars contributed more than 200,000 hectares (500,000 ac) of new garden.[22] Huge numbers of flowers, vegetables and fruit trees were being planted across the country every weekend in these spaces. Experiments with new breeds, encouraged by Sudell and others, were widespread, and knowledge of seasons and the cycles of life was expanding. Had any of the critics visited Roehampton, for example (they didn't), it would have taken a particularly hard-hearted and dogmatic theorist not to acknowledge some form of a return to the soil that the preservationists believed we had gone to war to fight for. There was clear evidence that this was exactly what was occurring in the allotments and gardens of these new tenants. In truth the gardens were an inconvenient truth for many critics, coming as they were from an architectural and planning background, or for the writers who had either escaped such environments or had no idea about them in the first place. Of course, the gardens themselves had no real champions among the cultural elite, no one to add context to the debate. Landscape architecture and planning was in its infancy abroad. Britain, the land of William Kent, Humphry Repton and Capability Brown, had not even woken up to the new possibilities that an altogether changed country presented to potential new practitioners of a horticultural profession.

Sudell was not a major voice in this debate as it first emerged, and this book does not argue that he was prominent in the theoretical argument that surrounded the suburbs and the new gardening culture they heralded. Yet his brief time on Roehampton reveals

Typical Sudell beds cut into lawn in a garden on the Roehampton Estate, 1930.

exactly why it can be argued that his contribution to garden history rewards study. And, as we shall see, this modest self-taught man recognized before his (now more famous) peers that the potential to seize the opportunity to build a new Britain needed action from landscape architects and gardeners.

But for now, his entire focus was on the practical. In his actions, from buying lawnmowers on the Roehampton estate to his increasing volume of garden journalism, it was the grassroots inspiration of the working classes that was his motivation. And as with his religious and politically motivated colleagues at the LGG the issue was simple. Decent housing and access to fresh air, physical activity and the health and spiritual uplift that come from bringing flowers into people's lives were key. As was giving them the means to grow their own food, which was a basic need for millions of Britons. This was no theoretical debate. Sometimes it was even a matter of life and death. Sudell's deeds and words at this time give us a fascinating insight into early twentieth-century garden and landscape history and the wider social, economic and political context of the times.

As mentioned, the residents of Roehampton, Becontree, Bournville, Letchworth, Hampstead, Metro-land, the Salters' Wilson Grove and other newly built environments found few reasons to complain about their new living spaces. And those estates were of course rapidly changing the face of the country, to the chagrin of many. No exploration of the debate around this issue can be complete without examining the curious intervention of Sir J. M. Richards, who was a hugely unlikely defender of the suburbs but, in his book *The Castles on the Ground*, defend them he did. For 34 years Sir James was the editor of the *Architectural Review*, the leading advocate in Britain for the Modern Movement. His defence of suburbia had fellow architects rushing to explain his lapse, but as he wrote himself: 'On the one hand we have the alleged deficiencies of suburban taste; on the other we have the appeal it holds for ninety out of a hundred Englishmen, an appeal which cannot be explained away as some strange instance of mass aberration.'[23]

Written in 1946 and powered by industrial-strength patronization, the book nevertheless makes the case for the suburbs as collective installations constructed by their new inhabitants and thus worthy of defence. However, had any suburbanite read *Castles*, it is doubtful they would have found much to applaud as Richards stared into his sociological Petri dish. Witness its very opening lines. 'Ewbank'd inside and Atco'd out, the English suburban residence and the garden which is an integral part of it stand trim and lovingly cared for in the mild sunshine.' For the benefit of the younger reader a Ewbank is a mechanical carpet sweeper with which the housewife would obsessively tidy the house, while an Atco is a lawnmower with which the head of the household, the husband, would assume his garden duties outside. There are pages and pages of this stuff. It is hard to resist quoting some more, not just to chortle at the hideous class-bound snobbery of it all but to recognize that this was the tone of the debate of those times. The airwaves were dominated not by grassroots campaigners like Sudell and the Salters and, heaven forbid, certainly not the residents, but by Oxbridge 'thinkers' taking over-educated guesses at what was going on behind the net curtains. Contrasting pre-war Edwardian and Victorian suburbs with the new builds, this time in the north, Richards writes:

> There may be only a number on a gate, or a small oval china plate, instead of a name. Instead of a pillared or half-timbered porch there is a simple brick arch beneath a plain tiled gable and instead of a rack full of walking sticks in the hall a china umbrella stand.[24]

No long country walks with the hounds for these people (from Oswestry or Birmingham, Richards randomly suggests), just the dash through the rain to the station for the morning commute. And there's more like this. In an imagined walk inside one of these houses (it is difficult to believe he would have actually been invited) he finds that the hallway

> smells faintly of furniture polish and somewhat more faintly of the American cloth of which the folding hood of a perambulator is made, a perambulator for which there is really not enough room in the hall, as the visitor will soon discover if he steps too confidently past the foot of the stairs.[25]

Or how about this, when describing residents of the East End of London moving to places like Roehampton: 'The sociabilities of the shared lawn mower and the suburban bowling club replaced the Cockney jovialities of the Mile End Road.'[26] With friends like Richards...

However, we would be wrong to dismiss Richards simply as a by-product of the age, for he makes some interesting design comments about suburbia that had not occurred to his modernist friends. These new spaces in their totality, he wrote, were not a product of dull conformism but a 'series of happy accidents' in which their 'physical nature and the aesthetic qualities are almost wholly the product of the people living there'. In other words, these new residents were creating an environment for themselves, altering their homes, creating their open spaces front and back. Perhaps this is one reason why the professional architect hated them. Richards, unlike his colleagues, was not blind to the importance of gardens. Here he identifies the attraction for residents of the freedom of creating their own open space; a freedom not available in the house itself, built to rigid standards as it obviously was: 'The Englishman's passion for gardening may, it is true, be seen in other places than suburbia, but only here, in exercising this passion, does he create for himself an original world in which nothing is not subject to his determination and control.'[27]

Glossing over the fact that 'determination and control' were what every landscape gardener from Roman times needed to create his (and they were all hims) Arcadia on earth, Richards alights on what Sudell had realized, if in more prosaic language, decades earlier. Namely that these gardens were a refuge from the outside world, not an excuse to show off, peering over the fence to confirm horticultural one-upmanship. The garden was the only place in which, for the first time, the new suburbanites could create their own space and time. It was a freedom of sorts, even if for only a few hours on a Sunday afternoon, from worries over rent payments, the commute to work and the real threat of a return to poverty. While the gardens in council-built estates were the subject of the strictures of the rent book inspector, all interwar versions allowed latitude for creativity even if people like Sudell were on hand to give firm instruction through his books and newspaper columns to an increasingly voracious gardening readership. But the garden was still their own.

For Richards, this garden creativity had been missed by critics. By focusing on what they thought was the hideousness of the sunrise door, the box-like houses on the council estates, the faux historic 'villas' of Metro-land, or even the conformity of the neatly Atco'd lawn, they were too obsessed with the specific. The individual architecture of the houses was beside the point, as indeed was the garden. Suburbia was a collective whole. Residents were evolving their estates by individual actions, contributing to 'a panoramic whole':

> The suburban style is not a style of architecture but the setting of life itself, and its 'taste' is but the local colour the inhabitants gather round themselves in accordance with their peculiar instincts and aspirations. If you take this colour away by teaching them that there are other tastes they ought to prefer, or by means of any other improvements imposed from without, you take away suburbia itself.[28]

While his modernist colleagues tried to digest that message, he had another lesson for them from the Soviet Union. The communist regime had taken Le Corbusier's architectural style to its heart as a symbol of communal modernity, and yet by the 1940s, Richards writes, 'columns and pediments' are back. Not, he insists, because there's something intrinsically wrong with modernist architecture but because 'the Russians are realists and knew that their revolutionary architecture was in danger of becoming too artificial by out-running public preparedness for it.'[29] As usual, revolutionaries see nothing wrong with their visions, it's just that the slow-witted rest of us take time to appreciate the genius. More than eighty years later, public preparedness is not only not catching up, it has quit the race. What remains true of those times is what gardens still mean to us. Sudell, in many ways a simple gardener certainly unqualified to debate Boumphrey on the BBC, understood what the suburbs represented in a way many who were prepared to flex their intellectual muscles did not. It is fitting to bookend this chapter with another Sudell quotation: 'This at once reveals the real purpose of a garden – to give rest and quiet after the turmoil of the day.'[30] As the theoretical debates swirled around suburbia, for Sudell and many of the residents themselves it was all actually pretty simple.

7
'There were little bridges, gnomes and things'

Can a rose be 'political'? Beyond its UK associations with the Labour Party and its civil war connotations, can it contain symbolism and meaning when simply growing in a front garden? In 1924 Richard Sudell wrote *The Town Gardening Handbook*, the official instruction manual for the LGG. It was concerned with giving simple and practical guidance to the new owners of gardens on the LCC council house estates but also to those living in homes constructed by speculative builders. Every neighbourhood could join the gardening crusade. On his travels drumming up new members to join the Guild, Sudell would always keep his eye open for evidence of promising new gardens, both to help develop his own practice and later to illustrate his many books. The *Handbook* was the first volume that would set him on his way to a thirty-year garden journalism career.

In the *Handbook*, themes already familiar to his former neighbours on Roehampton were evident. That front gardens had not only to give householders pleasant privacy but to add to the gaiety of the neighbourhood was clear by page two: 'Most of us are glad to appreciate beauty in the world, and it is worth a little trouble if we can add our quota to it.'[1] It was an observation not much different, except maybe in style, to that the editor of the *Architectural Review*, J. M. Richards, made about the suburb as a whole becoming a living thing, creating its own art. In the *Handbook* Sudell tells of one small

London front garden that caught his eye. It had hanging baskets in the door and window portals, a trellis of jasmine against the wall, a low front hedge of beech and – for Sudell vital – circular plots of earth cut into the tiny lawn in which hybrid tea roses stood proud. Sudell explained that many new front gardens came with privacy-giving high hedges, but the problem was that this made the air in them stationary and unfit for many flowers. However, Sudell told his eager readers, one solution to this was to plant tea roses, which could lift their heads above such shadows for the benefit of residents and passers-by.

The explosion of such roses to cater for the new market meant that by the early 1950s there were seven hundred varieties developed especially for the small suburban garden. Perhaps inevitably they had begun to provoke a horticultural backlash in the years after Sudell began vigorously promoting them. Their porcelain-like blooms were simply too ubiquitous and vulgarly lush. Daffodils had been the centre of a similar pushback as the newer, bigger and brasher blooms, mainly found in suburban gardens, were pitted against more delicate 'old' wilder traditional versions. Now it was the tea rose's turn. Hybrid varieties such as 'Peace' and 'Mrs Sam McGredy' looked gauche next to the semi-wild 'Cardinal de Richelieu' and 'Madame Louise Lévêque', according to the cognoscenti such as educator and florist Constance Spry and Vita Sackville-West, author and creator of the garden at Sissinghurst.[2]

Even the names marked out their difference for the Francophile middle classes. Here was another strand of debate that weaved itself into the early twentieth-century landscape story, pitting the Robinson/Jekyll country house style against the labour-saving regimented and delineated suburban experience. It was a divide with clear social class derivations. And snobbery in the garden has never really gone away. In 1998 writer James Bartholomew wrote his book *Yew and Non-Yew*, the horticultural equivalent of Nancy Mitford's 1954 essay 'The English Aristocracy' on the subject of 'U and

Non-U', spread more widely in the book *Noblesse Oblige* (1956), which attempted to define the ways of speaking that differentiated the upper class and the rest of us. Determinedly upper class herself, Mitford wrote the book as something of a joke, but such were the sensitivities of the aspiring middle classes in the 1950s that it became something of a bible for those wanting to climb the ladder and often made others self-conscious about their 'wrong' use of words. Bartholomew, detecting even in the late 1990s that this level of snobbery still existed in the garden, detailed the painful trials and tribulations of trying to keep up with the 'experts and the aristos'. On the dahlia, for instance, he wrote: 'The Non-Yew gardener thinks they are a wonderful triumph of man and nature combined. The Yew gardener thinks they are a revolting perversion.' When it came to hedges for the Yews, unsurprisingly, yew, beech, holly and hornbeam were in, for the Non-Yew it was the ghastly leylandii or spotted laurel.[3]

Time, money and available space were the constrictions faced by the new interwar suburban gardeners, council tenants and many a Metro-lander alike, which Sudell understood completely. Fuelled by his sense of social justice he had no time for shaming new gardeners into adopting a style wholly unsuited for their new spaces, which he knew could represent a fearful step into the unknown. Gentle encouragement rather than overwhelming instruction was what they needed if they were to contribute to a transformation of the country. He was not interested in gardening one-upmanship. Even the competitions he organized were used as motivational examples of best practice rather than opportunities for boasting. The tea rose was beautiful, adding colour to neighbourhoods and giving a screen of privacy, but also an extremely practical answer to the difficulties of achieving success in these new gardens, particularly in London where the need for hardiness to withstand the shocking levels of air pollution favoured both the rose and privet. Sudell became a popular garden writer – in books, newspaper and magazine columns – because he understood this. But he was up against other garden writers who did not and who induced something akin to anxiety in the new suburbanite. In the interwar period a host of gardening journals and magazines were beginning to appear, to cater for what seemed like an unquenchable thirst for advice and guidance. But the models many of these drew on for illustration and instruction were the labour-heavy cottage garden or even the eighteenth-century manor house. This led to confusion, anxiety and even shame among the new gardeners who had little hope of emulating their gardening predecessors.

Of course, as we know, the suburb and its gardens were not invented after the First World War. But how do we understand the lineage of both the houses and gardens that resulted from this incredible and unparalleled change in the social fabric of Britain in the interwar years? We have seen that the privately owned houses of Metro-land and others referred to a golden era, the tranquillity of the Elizabethan age as represented by the superfluous beams of the Tudorbethan houses along the ribbon developments. In the cottage estates, such as Hampstead and Roehampton, it was a William Morris

A Sudell design for a town rose garden; 'blousy' blooms such as Dorothy Perkins and Betty Uprichard would doubtless have been grown.

Arts and Crafts folksy style that was favoured, while in the bigger LCC estates a more practical consideration caused by size and space nevertheless still built on the 'Englishman's home is his castle' principle. This mishmash of styles drawing on apparently random periods of history could be accepted by the new suburban residents because they had little say in the building of the houses. But what of the gardens, where they were expected to make their mark?

The DNA of the early twentieth-century suburban garden can perhaps be traced back to two traditions. Alison Ravetz detects the nineteenth-century working-class vernacular garden at play, small gardens and allotments giving private pleasure to factory and agricultural workers, just like Lawrence's miners, who developed a high degree of instinctive horticultural skill born of necessity for food and appreciation of beauty through the flower. As we have seen, even in Whitechapel at the turn of the twentieth century the cultivation of flowers, vegetables and the keeping of livestock in the tiniest of spaces became highly skilled. But there was also the influence of the Victorian suburban garden, the villas of the emerging middle and upper middle classes, which themselves drew on the eighteenth-century manor house principle.[4] Here privacy was prized above all else, but the gardens adopted some of the formal landscaping, albeit on a smaller scale, of their predecessors. A proliferation of new plant and flower types in the late nineteenth century, not to mention the availability of cheap glass, helped a Victorian suburban style emerge, with sequential layout of flower beds, sizeable lawn, gravel paths and up into trees for shade. Many of these gardens later came under the influence of William Robinson and Gertrude Jekyll, with their 'natural' school of gardening introducing the herbaceous border and a riot of differing layers of colour and species, the formalism of the manor house style softening, edges blurring and a horticultural impressionism taking hold inspired by the patterns and art of William Morris. These gardens resembled something of a hybrid between manor and country house.

Into this maelstrom of creativity came the new suburban gardener, as we have seen, often arriving in a new paradise to be confronted by a muddy plot of land outside the back door. While Judith Roberts rightly notes the new spaces 'represent one of the greatest opportunities for individual cultural expression of the twentieth century', it did not always feel like that to the 'artists' themselves.[5] There was no end of advice from early twentieth-century gardening journals and magazines that harked back to a 'golden age' of the English tradition, cottage, formal or otherwise. When the new suburbanites first moved in it was to an expectation that the Arts and Crafts cottage garden would hold sway, this small garden style having become favoured before the war. *Homes & Gardens* magazine illustrated this nicely in an article published in 1906. Tudor-style architect, artist and Arts and Crafts advocate M. H. Baillie Scott, who was more often concerned with house design, tried to imagine what the space outside his houses should look like in a way fellow Arts and Crafts architects Parker and Unwin would never dare. It is the cottage garden ideal that Baillie envisages, 'including in its borders roses, lilies and perennial flowers with a background of cabbages, potatoes and other vegetables', although he laments that under the 'specializing influence of modern civilization he finds that the new small garden owners have neither the knowledge nor inclination to grow their own vegetables and flowers'. The suburban gardener must work with nature by growing a wild garden, perhaps with a small orchard underplanted with spring bulbs with shrubs and borders in more advanced cases:

> Keen gardeners can arrange outdoor apartments with straight paths and vistas, a square rose garden centred on a sundial, long perennial borders of delphiniums, phlox, hollyhocks and day lilies in large clumps, not repeated but in a 'well studied arrangement' for colour and summer long bloom, a pergola and trellis for enclosure and mystery, tubs and pots at entrances, a seat 'of good design and solid

structure' placed to view the vista down to the vegetable and orchard plot.[6]

There was plenty more like this. The instruction to imitate stately homes and even public parks in these gardens, particularly the promotion of the herbaceous border, featured in *Country Life*, *The Garden* and *Homes & Gardens* among others, with Gertrude Jekyll writing a thousand articles for the first title alone. The message was clear: a vast array of different flowers and plants could create a dramatic effect through colour, shape and scale. In an article in 1935, *Homes & Gardens* half acknowledged the problem facing new suburbanites but urged them to carry on regardless: 'Though large and impressive gardens are often inclined to be passed over by the amateur as being beyond his scope, they undoubtedly serve as examples of the effects that can be achieved on a smaller scale.' Harry Higgott Thomas weighed in with his unfortunately titled book *The Complete Amateur Garden* in 1924, urging readers to aim for the 'controlled and restrained beauty' with 'wild and natural flowers' contrasted to what he called bolder and more gaudy plants.[7]

For many of the new inhabitants of post-First World War suburbia this torrent of advice must have been akin to being asked to adorn the Sistine Chapel with a paint roller. But many of them attempted to follow it, with both excitement and trepidation about this new opportunity to make a mark. They wanted their gardens to be a space for privacy but also tasteful, with the right planting schemes. It harked back to an English history that, while not their own, might just be buried deep in the subconscious. As garden historian Jane Brown has it, the interwar housing boom was also 'the beginning of popular gardening as one of the great marketing success stories of this century'.[8]

The trouble with all this intense selling of a dream was that it was an illusion, a middle-class horticulturalist idea of perfection foisted on a new gardener without the skills, time or space to implement it.

But for those who did try, their reward was something less than approbation. Barry Parker, one half of the Garden City dream team, noticed some of the gardens on the estates he designed were overloaded. Residents, he insisted, should 'tend towards simplicity and directness... lessening his risk of falling into a vulgarity almost inseparable from superfluity.'[9] The first garden broadcaster, Cecil Henry Middleton, who became so famous and respected he was known simply as Mr Middleton, frowned on 'overtly conspicuous displays'. Incidentally, *Mr Middleton's Gardening Guide*, cashing in on the huge popularity of his BBC broadcasts and first published in 1944, was completely revised and edited by Richard Sudell in 1950, by which time he had become, if not a household, at the very least a potting shed name. Into this minefield stepped Sudell's ex-wife, Emily. Having worked as hard as Richard to promote the benefits of gardens to the working classes of London, she also turned her hand to horticultural journalism, writing under the pen name Marguerite James. In her book *The Family Garden*, published in 1937, she tried to help the befuddled new gardener with a chapter in which she bestowed characteristics on flowers so that chrysanthemums represented 'truth', marigolds 'grief', dahlias 'instability', bluebells 'constancy' and antirrhinums 'presumption'.[10] How this was supposed to help is uncertain, unless it was clear to suburbanites that instability and constancy should not share the same flower bed. What was clear though was that they were prepared to spend available time and money on their gardens, as Rosina Evans, who lived on the LCC Downham estate in southeast London, explained:

> My mother has aspirations which my Dad didn't agree with and she bought a walnut veneer bedroom suite which was like something out of a novel ... my dad was dead against it ... he would have spent any amount of money on the garden and allotment, but the home, oh no![11]

Matthew Hollow's intriguing study of the lengths to which new gardeners went to keep up with the advice handed out by the gardening press focuses on the gardens of the Downham estate. He references the advice handed out by *Homes & Gardens* in March 1927 for a small garden plot. The drawing accompanying the article illustrates the problem, for the magazine's conception of 'small' would have been slightly different from the understanding of the residents of Downham or Roehampton. The magazine's example is, in effect, the Victorian suburban villa, the size of which would have had Metro-landers casting envious glances. On show is a lily pond and archway, the garden divided by trelliswork with different planting schemes creating different effects and sightlines. It is a picture of calm orderliness, a formal nod to the eighteenth century. Hollow then alights on two 1931 pictures, sourced from the London Metropolitan Archive, which show the disastrous consequences of trying to replicate this 'manor house style' in Downham. With front gardens a quarter of the size of the magazine's, the effect is a cacophony. Festooned with flowers and trellis, creating a migraine-inducing assault on the eyes, Hollow describes the result as a claustrophobic environment. What this achieved was the exact opposite of the effect these aspiring working-class residents were hoping for.

The trouble was, in this race to follow the latest guidance, spend money on the new trends in planting and follow the rich by introducing statuary, the results they were unconsciously producing were exposing them to the last thing the aspirational were seeking: ridicule. Downham resident Edna Sevier is quoted by Hollow as remembering 'seeing some gardens up at Woodbank Road ... one was with a little bridge, gnomes and things and that fascinated me.'[12] Meanwhile over in Metro-land the picture was little different:

> In the ribbon development houses of the time ... the mode was for crazy paving, dwarf conifers, weeping trees, gnomes and other tiny ornaments, sundials, very small ponds and

'There were little bridges, gnomes and things'

Prize-winning garden on the Downham Estate, London, 1931, showing the dangers of trying to copy the Victorian villa style as promoted by magazines of the time.

rockeries. To use the word of the time they were 'twee'. 'The half sunburst, a favourite motif of the time, would in fact have been an ideal plan for a front garden.[13]

Ah yes, the garden gnome. He, and it was always a he, has seemed like a long time coming but he's with our narrative now. Originally imported from Germany as matchbox holders, gnomes were first used in the garden by eccentric landowner Sir Charles Isham at his home Lamport Hall in Northamptonshire in 1874. Sir Charles used them to represent 'earth spirits' and they were wildly successful. Just fifty years later, though, transferred to the suburban garden, they had taken on a very different meaning. George Orwell led the charge against 'rock features, concrete bird baths, crazy paving and red plaster elves'. From 'earth spirit' to 'red plaster elves' in less than fifty years was some journey for the little fellows from the Black Forest of

Germany.[14] Set among picturesque country estates they were things of mystery and charm, but reproducing like rabbits across suburbia and exuding a sense of purpose, whether that be fishing, digging or pushing wheelbarrows, they were simply laughably vulgar. Of course it didn't need the middle classes or gardening intelligentsia to point this out. Working-class champions such as Lawrence were happy to dish the dirt too, their pens emanating keenly guided disdain for such botched attempts to climb the social ladder.

Before we leave the garden gnome, grinning with rod in hand on his imaginary riverbank, it is worth referencing a hugely entertaining interpretation of their purpose from Paul Oliver, who together with Ian Davis and Ian Bentley wrote *Dunroamin: The Suburban Semi and Its Enemies*, the first real attempt by academics to explain and understand the popularity of the much-derided communities. Gnomes were, he tells us, phallic symbols with their red pointed caps but more importantly they expressed territoriality, the determination of the suburbanites to settle the land: 'Though their laughing, jovial expressions may seem to invite the visitor, they inhabit the garden in a manner that inhibits any invasion. They face the road as a miniature uniformed army, at ease but watchful; laughter can be an aggressive act.'[15] Beyond the suspicion that Oliver, like many brought up on these estates, might have been mentally scarred as a youngster by these vaguely sinister and unexplained creatures in the garden, here again is the suburban garden as first line of defence, the protector of privacy. So the suburbanite was caught between a rock garden and a hard place. On the one hand a new industry of magazines, plant breeders, lawnmower manufacturers and suchlike were creating a garden frenzy, producing a craving among many new suburbanites to make their mark on their open spaces to bring forth admiring glances from neighbours, to be happy to be upholding the traditions of the English garden, the unlikely heirs of squires and Victorian mercantile entrepreneurs. On the other, as is the fate of all arrivistes, all that actually happened was many of these residents were shot by both sides for their efforts.

'Those tenants who tried to demonstrate their newly achieved sense of respectability by spending their limited earnings on beautifying their gardens often only succeeded in reinforcing their working-class identities in the eyes of those they sought to emulate.'[16]

Something had to give, the chaos could not continue, and in many ways the estates themselves – J. M. Richards's organic whole – began to mitigate the worst effects of the unsuitable country cottage style. As we shall see in the next chapter, Sudell's role as a garden advocate was pivotal in this change even though he defended many of the garden foibles, such as statuary and crazy paving, that had become much loved by the new gardener. Nevertheless, the requirements of the new communities, council or private, began to dictate that – while there was scope for creativity – certain norms must be achieved. A degree of stripped-back formalism, harking back again to the manor house before its country garden evolution, began to emerge as much

A rationalized Sudell design garden in stark contrast to the busy garden on the Downham Estate. The fountain, though, may have been out of reach for some readers.

through practicality as anything else. On Roehampton and other council tenant estates, under the rule of the rent book inspector, front gardens had to add to the overall impression of the estate for the benefit of all and tended to the uniform. On the speculative build estates, however, the front garden, usually much bigger, had to advertise the house itself for potential buyers and thus a degree of individual latitude was allowable. In the back gardens, lawns and simpler flower beds gave way to the vegetable plot and fruit bushes beyond, perhaps being divided by an increasingly popular rockery and, of course, a rose bed. Here domestic innovations that did away with the need for wash houses and outside lavatories meant the back garden could be employed entirely for leisure.

In Metro-land this often led to the abandonment of the vegetable plot for flowers. Sudell, however, remained insistent – his experiences of the hardships of the war and the poverty of inner-city London to the fore – that gardeners should still leave space for a kitchen garden and some fruit trees to the rear. As the Depression of the 1930s continued this indeed happened in many gardens, even Metrolanders finding space again for shallots and potatoes. The reduction of country house chaos in the suburban garden was helped, as Roberts (echoing Richards) argues, by a realization that the collection of roads, paths, boundary fences and buildings was in fact a new landscape. In many ways it began to mitigate itself. Furthermore, the result of this quieting was that 'an ordered formal garden linking the house to its outside space and one plot to another in a structured and predictable way would underline the cohesion of the group without the loss of individual character and privacy.'[17]

The doyen of the country house style, William Robinson, had founded the weekly *The Garden* in 1871, followed by *Gardening Illustrated* in 1879, to propound his horticultural philosophy. Yet the gradual triumph of this collective individualism, the eruptions of planting anarchy beginning to be dampened down, was finally acknowledged by *Gardening Illustrated* in 1930: 'For the layout of the estate has introduced a fresh character of formalism and we may arrive definitely at the conclusion that any serious attempt at natural planning must inevitably be defeated by the boundary fences and by the proximity of formal lines of buildings.'[18] But as gardens can never be free of the symbolism of the past or of politics, this gradual evolution began to take on more profound meaning. For Roberts, for instance, this return to the stable and illustrious past of the Tudor and Elizabethan golden age, as referenced through the more formal late nineteenth-century manor house style, had another effect: to foreground a notion of Englishness. The residents of the new estates, subconsciously or otherwise, did become the heirs to an English tradition and a conservative one at that:

> The formal garden especially was promoted for its distinctly English character free from the corrupting influences of continental forms. In the inter-war period in particular this approach was compatible with the rejection of the architecture of the modern movement and was clearly a part of rebuilding national identity and searching for security after the First World War.[19]

Here, perhaps, is the molten core of the fierce debate that would rage around the subject of how Britain should *look* after 'the war to end all wars'. Liberal intellectuals would favour an outward-looking modernistic reimagining of Britain after the Great War, a fresh start, a place of communal living in striking buildings erasing the tarnish of the past while preserving Albion's rural Elysium. And then there was the quieter response, from the people who no longer talked about what they had seen in the conflict and who sought comfort in a return to a time of peace, comfort and progress: a withdrawal, in this story to behind the privet hedge, if you like.

The modernist steadfast refusal to look back into history and determination to gaze forward to new horizons meant that for many the lure of the suburbs for new residents was almost unfathomable. They were simply speaking a different language. At this stage it is time for a brief diversion to illustrate that the new suburbanite, as Roberts suggests, was indeed part of a definable English lineage. Mocked they may have been, but these new communities gave residents something that had been unavailable to their ancestors – and freely taken for granted by the landed classes – for centuries. The new houses and gardens were, as Sudell often stated, refuges from the 'turmoil of the day'. About 32 kilometres (20 mi.) south as the crow flies from Roehampton is the estate of Albury, hidden away in the Surrey Hills. It was here in 1667 that the polymath, writer, designer and diarist John Evelyn, a founder of the Royal Society, designed a garden for his friend Henry Howard. This was the first Italianate garden in England, inspired by Evelyn's tour of Europe and his experiences visiting an erupting Vesuvius. Nearby he was transfixed by the mysterious power of the tunnel known as the Crypta Neapolitana (c. 37 BCE), which leads from Piedigrotta, on the outskirts of Naples, to Pozzuoli. A Roman burial vault perched above the entrance at Piedigrotta has long been known as Virgil's Tomb. The Albury garden serves almost as a horticultural postcard of Evelyn's journey around Italy and its antiquarian ruins and landscape. From the house a straight-lined vista takes the viewer to a small recreation of the grotto on the horizon, which Evelyn described as a Crypta to honour the Roman poet.[20]

On the journey to the crypt, travelling along a moderate incline, a canal created from the widened and formalized Tillingbourne stream passes through a level dominated by a central fountain and orchards of fruit trees. It journeys further up to vineyards and two niched walled terraces. These are clearly influenced by Evelyn's visit to the antiquarian ruins of the Roman town of Praeneste and run to an unsurpassed 390 metres (1,280 ft) long.[21] Importantly these terraces are bordered by evergreen yew trees, vital to produce the effect of Mediterranean-style perpetual spring. From there the viewer took in the antiquity-referenced Roman Bath and moved on to a water pool, fountain, an exedra and the Crypta at the top. Much of this still remains. But what does this allegory to classical civilization have to do with diamond-shaped rose beds and rockeries of interwar suburbia?

For Evelyn, a man of prodigious learning, the years he spent designing the garden were also the most troubling of his life. A staunch Royalist through the Civil War, the execution of Charles I and the Interregnum, he had disappeared from public life. Even after the Restoration he was unimpressed with what he saw as the frivolities of the new court of Charles II.[22] His garden contained multiple meanings but primarily harks back to a Virgilian concept of a peaceful society based on hard work on the land. The poet's *Georgics* is a clear warning that societal chaos will follow if agriculture is not central to life.[23] The gardens can also be said to reflect Evelyn's belief in the power of Epicurean thought, and particularly that tranquillity away from public life can be found in the garden.[24] The retreat of Epicurus to his paradise garden during the Roman civil war that followed the assassination of Julius Caesar might thus be replaced by the execution of Charles I for Evelyn. For the intellectual and his friend Howard, Albury represented the desire to return to peaceful, ordered times through hard work, and even to reclaim Edenic tranquillity by the process of creating a garden.

For rich men and landed gentry such as these, 60 hectares (150 ac) with a mansion house attached tucked away in the Surrey Hills served as their escape from the turmoil of the times. Dressed up in antiquarian allusion, Albury assumes the mystical space of Elysium. But, at the risk of ridicule, does not this anonymous 48-year-old woman, interviewed in 1998 for a Mass Observation (MO) survey on the importance of suburban gardens, not speak to the same human need?

> I would put up a six-foot fence tomorrow but Dave won't let me because he says it will upset them. Me I don't care,

my opinion is it's my garden and I will do what I want with it. I think the fence will go up simply to give us a bit of privacy, I don't want everyone next door looking at us when we are out having a BBQ or have visitors and I don't like people watching me in my garden, I enjoy doing my garden but I like to do it alone and not watched.[25]

The authors of research into this MO survey are clear. In the last years of the twentieth century the longing for privacy, 'conveyed with equal measures of passion and exasperation', represents an extraordinary longing, an obsession even:

We could interpret this as evidence of the desire to return to Eden, to recreate a harmony that may be missing or lost: gardens are used therapeutically to do just that . . . We suggest therefore that if there is a sacred aesthetic to the British everyday, perhaps it is to be found in the garden.[26]

Almost sixty years earlier an interwar MO survey highlighted the astonishing transformation of Britain, estimating that by 1939 two-thirds of houses in England and Wales had a garden. It found the overwhelming majority of garden city and housing estate dwellings had gardens and, while allotments had dropped 18 per cent because of a post-First World War reclaim of land, this had been more than compensated for by the increase in gardens. While many did struggle to understand the complexity of garden advice, it should not be forgotten that the country was bursting into colour thanks to this patchwork of small gardens, which were also health-giving and allowed families the opportunity to spend time together outdoors. In York in the summer of 1936 a Rowntree report found gardens 'ablaze with colour. It is indeed amazing how soon families, most of whom have never had a garden before, turn the rough land surrounding their new homes into beautiful gardens.'[27] Yet for some writers, even those supportive of the suburbanite experience, the temptation to drip some condescension into the discourse is hard to resist. Jane Brown, focusing on the Metro-land/Dunroamin semi, asks:

> Was it the bleakness of the new estates or the reactionary nature of gardening advice that encouraged so much nostalgia or simply the native urge to return to the land? For the popular semi-detached garden of the early twentieth century became not the twentieth century at all, but of the 17th, an evocation of middle-class paradise in Tudor England.[28]

Brown then attempts to sketch out what this means in practice:

> Along with the candytuft around the sundial, the lawn, the rustic pergola with rose Dorothy Perkins in her shocking pinks masses, phlox, sweet peas, alyssum, and lobelia edgings and the neat Austin 10 outside the garage, together with the coloured-glass galleon in full sail on the front door, thus was glorious Dunroamin' in its prime.[29]

Perhaps it is simply this reader's interpretation, but there does seem to be some Betjeman-style 'cultural safari park' observation going on here.

Even Hollow, clearly sympathetic to the suburbanite dilemma, sees something else at work on the estates: namely working-class residents struggling to live up to the middle-class ideal of their new community as envisioned by local authorities, social reformers and writers. The garden was a space for family life, away from the twin distractions of drinking and gambling. He points to the magazines that showed the new council estate tenants what the rich did with their gardens, creating works of art while allowing the children to gambol on the lawn. He points out that Marguerite James encouraged readers in *The Family Garden* to build a small sandpit and miniature plots for their children, but adds this was difficult for struggling householders who, unlike their middle-class counterparts, had little money; and what they did have had to be spent on growing fruit and vegetables.[30]

While it is true that money on the estates was tight – we have already seen how Roehampton tenants struggled to pay their rents as the 1930s wore on – it can be argued that writers like Hollow, Brown and others are coming at the debate from the wrong end. James's experience working with her husband in inner-city London meant that urging readers on to garden endeavours signified something far more than simply encouraging residents to reflect middle-class mores. Quaker Socialism played a huge part in driving grassroots social change in the interwar years, stressing that open spaces, gardens and children's play were essential tools to improve the health and well-being of thousands of people who, not long before, had lived in unimaginable inner-city squalor. As with the Bermondsey churchyard slide built by the Salters, a small sandpit in a suburban garden was a place where children could exercise and, just as importantly, have fun. For many reformers, it wasn't just desirable. It was vital. Soon Richard Sudell would enter into partnership with Marjory Allen, Lady Allen of Hurtwood, a landscape architect and socialist who, while undoubtedly upper middle class with alarmingly plummy vowels, had an astonishing lifetime mission to create play areas for inner-city children. She saw this as crucial to help free them from the debilitating diseases that stalked them everywhere poverty and deprivation existed.

While Quaker temperance philosophy may have influenced the LCC to be sparing in the provision of public houses in many of its estates, it is worth remembering how this combination of religion and politics made a profound contribution to the incredible social advances made in the short years between the two World Wars. That is not to say that the estates, private and council, were the Land of Milk and Honey for everyone, and of course it is true that the increasing emergence of a Metro-land/Dunroamin lower middle class in those years did not mean that every new estate dweller had been rescued from inner-city hell. However, failure to acknowledge vast social migration in these years, and the reasons for it, risks false interpretations of the new estates as simply places full of twitching curtains and vulgar roses. Strube's Little Man and Mr Pooter come heaving into view. Or worse, you end up with the grotesque misreading that characterizes the modernist thinking of Clough Williams-Ellis, who, in 1929 with his wife Annabel, wrote the book *Octopus* (meaning the spread of the suburbs), which tells of 'mean and petty houses that surely none but mean and petty little souls should inhabit with satisfaction'.[31]

There is overwhelming evidence in Roehampton, Downham and York, in the competitions held all over London and the UK, the work of the Gardens Guilds, the rapid expansion of a gardening industry, the millions who listened to Mr Middleton on the radio and who bought the books and magazines published in this period that, despite the anxiety often induced by living in these new neighbourhoods and the economic uncertainty of the times, this was indeed a mass movement. This was possibly the biggest transformation of land seen since the enclosures. With an estimated 80 per cent of English households taking part in some form of gardening by the outbreak of the Second World War, this was indeed a revolution, not the political one many on the Left were hoping for, but one that lifted the horizons of millions while transforming the look and feel of vast swathes of the country.

This Richard Sudell clearly understood, as we have seen from his editorials with the *Guild Gardener*. But there was no time for rest. There was work to be done. We have seen that Sudell understood the precious gift of seclusion that the garden gave the new suburbanite and he knew that, collectively, this new movement could help beautify the country. But there were more pressing questions. What was the best time to plant a tulip, when should digging of soil be done, what was a half-hardy annual, what was the cheapest way to lay a new path, what flowers thrived best in shade, which carrot type was the most productive? The questions were endless and there was one man in particular, among the many writers who emerged at this time, who was trusted to answer them, earning that trust through his simple, encouraging, practical guidance of millions of new gardeners, whom he brought with him on a mission to change the living environment.

But rather than end on Sudell, perhaps this chapter should leave the last word with the people who are so often missing from this story: the gardeners themselves. For whether they were mistakenly festooning their tiny plots with country house horticultural fripperies or favoured crazy paving and the garden gnome, what is often evidenced from first-hand accounts is incredible joyous enthusiasm and often a quickly learnt skill with which they took to the task. In the early 1990s the charity Age Exchange, which specializes in reminiscence history and arts, decided to interview scores of, now elderly, tenants still living on the LCC cottage estates that sprang up in the interwar years, including Roehampton, Becontree, Downham, Page, Castelnau and Watling. In total thirteen were built in the interwar years. Their tenants' stories of hope and despair, told in the volume *Just Like the Country*, are a treasure trove for historians examining this overlooked story of British migration. What emerges is, on the whole, a pride and excitement about the communities they eventually made. Not surprisingly the garden, as much as the new house, was a key source of this feeling.

Here perhaps we come close to answering the question posed at the start of this chapter about the rose in a sociopolitical context. We have been told how the blousy Dorothy Perkins variety might serve as a symbol of new suburbanite sensibilities, representing a throwback to an Elizabethan era that residents could hardly comprehend. But Joyce Milan, a teenager when she and her parents moved on to the LCC's Page estate in Eltham, south London, in the interwar period, gives the multi-petalled matt pink rambler another meaning. She places it back proudly in the centre of the small garden and, as she does so, tells a story of love and optimism for the future. She is definitely looking forward, not backwards. As with many of Sudell's Roehampton neighbours, when the Milans moved into their new home they found a back garden that was simply a morass of yellow clay left by builders. For them and for thousands of others the challenge was on. A surge of creative energy fuelled by back-breaking evening and weekend labour began, a social movement as inspiring as it would become unheralded:

> My parents set about developing a garden, something they had never known but longed for. Mum was mainly in charge of the operation, and it was remarkable what she achieved over the years. There was a large area of ground, so firstly a crazy paving path was laid made from broken pieces of plaster from the walls of the First World War hutments being demolished. Halfway along, a rustic arch was erected, which later supported huge bunches of Dorothy Perkins roses in the summer. In the right-hand centre was a circular rose-bed with fragrant blooms of every colour.[32]

8
An Unrivalled Influence on a New Nation of Gardeners

It's likely we've all seen a Sudell garden even if we didn't know it at the time. At least we may have witnessed a plot inspired by those interwar years, the birth of small gardens on an almost industrial scale – even if we can't actually be sure their owners were reading from one of Sudell's 47 books or hundreds of newspaper and magazine articles when they created it. I'm old enough to have played in one. My grandfather, who became a municipal landscape gardener after his Second World War service, had one that could have leapt off the pages of any number of early Sudell volumes. It was also where he began to learn his trade. He was guided by the half a dozen books he had on a shelf in the small shed at the top of the garden. Was a Sudell there? It's reasonable to believe it was. My grandfather's progress – he eventually worked on some impressive small-scale council projects in the riverside town of Gravesend, Kent, where he lived – was also the product of trial and error in his garden in which he had to exhibit endless patience. Even in the late 1960s the styles of more than the thirty years before had maintained their grip on suburbia. The modernist designs of John Brookes, 1960s guru of gravel, concrete and glass for the middle classes, found no soil in suburbia in which to flourish. And still do not.

Visitors entered my grandparents' terraced house through a tiny front plot of grass cut with two round circles for roses, a low-lying link fence bordering the pathway. Why my grandfather bothered with this tiny bit of lawn is anyone's guess, but it was important that visitors knew this was a house where things were done properly. But the real triumph was out back, where an explosion of colour awaited in the long and surprisingly wide back garden. Nearest the house was an immaculate lawn, on which my brother and I, both under ten years old, could only play football in the late summer, when the grass he had allowed to grow a little longer shimmered in the sunlight. Later he scuppered our fun by planting a self-created hybrid weeping willow silver birch in the middle of the grass as he became more knowledgeable and bolder in his plantsmanship. On either side of the lawn, borders of coordinated colours from flowers and bedding plants, the names of which I could not tell you, dazzled. And then his pride and joy: a handmade pergola draped in what might have been clematis, I only remember purple, which brought wonderful shade in the summer. A concrete bird table guarded the entrance. And of course beyond this lay the vegetable plots, rows of runner beans and potatoes, and a couple of small fruit trees. Here he spent most of his time hidden away, sitting on the bench by the fence, mulching his compost heap and sometimes mysteriously lighting fires in a brazier. If we were visiting, he might allow us to gaze into the flames on chilly autumn evenings. His own father had a similar garden at his Sussex coast home with a basic flower bed instead of a pergola; after all, a son must attempt to go one better than his father. It goes to show how enduring this small garden tradition was and perhaps still is.

There's a drawing that reminds me of the Gravesend garden in Sudell's book *The Town and Suburban Garden*, published in 1950, when he had a more than 25-year writing career behind him, if you include the *Roehampton Estate Gazette*.[1] All that was missing from my grandfather's garden was the crazy paving and the grass drive leading to the garage at the side of the house in the illustration. These drawings, which are contained in many of the books Sudell authored or edited throughout his life, combine to form a fascinating graphical history of the development of the suburban garden. They help bring the gardens to life, inspiring the gardener to create their own little compartmentalized piece of heaven.

Take one example, from *Practical Gardening and Food Production in Pictures*, written again towards the end of his book-writing life in 1948. The volume claimed to be produced under an 'entirely new principle', namely that all instructions were accompanied by illustrations. The images made up almost half of its pages, the words serving them as long captions. A two-page spread entitled 'How to Adapt Your Garden During Wartime' is typical of the book and in many ways of the advice Sudell gave throughout his career. Although the Second World War was over, rationing was still in place and fresh food hard to come by. Sudell shows the reader how to partially convert a typical suburban garden for vegetable production and even to keep chickens. It represents a familiar theme in Sudell's writings, harking back to his work with the VLCS: that even the smallest of suburban gardens should have some food-producing capability, probably a few fruit trees or a kitchen garden usually divided off from the lawned area and placed at the back of the garden. But more than that, the text is simply and concisely written, and the layout of the spread is beautiful to gaze upon. Book art academic Susan Johanknecht likens it to a 'mediaeval manuscript' and praises its 'spot the difference' drawings, which show how 'rose arches disappear in wartime, herbaceous beds shift to cabbage and an Anderson shelter appears "inconspicuously" near a newly created chicken run ... Located where the domestic meets the political, and painfully practical, this double spread is probably a complete work in itself.'[2]

As we have seen, Sudell's garden journalism career started in 1922 with the *Gazette*, which he continued to write for two years after he left to join the LGG mission, and took off when the latter published the *Town Gardening Handbook* in 1924. This had to be reprinted, such was the demand from residents of Roehampton and elsewhere

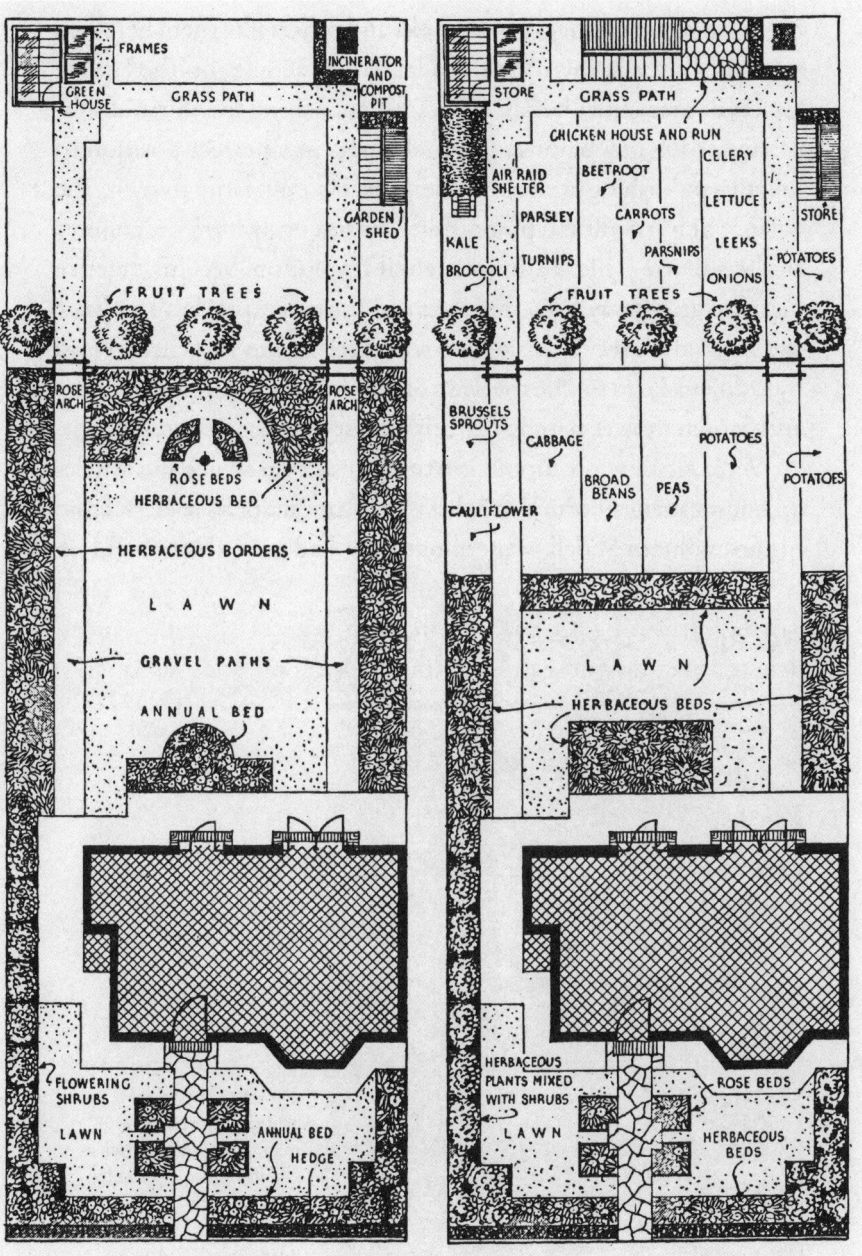

Before-and-after Sudell drawing of a suburban garden converted to grow more food and even to house chickens in an age of rationing.

for its beginners advice. These books and others like them heralded the shift of garden writing from laudatory articles on the landed estates in magazines before the war to quenching the thirst of suburbanites for new knowledge. Sudell was in a perfect position to join this publishing explosion: 'Suburbia is coming into its own. The balance of horticultural power shifts continuously from the country to the suburb . . . it is a fundamental revolution.'[3] As his practice began to grow away from the estate and the success of the *Handbook* was noticed, he secured a column with *Ideal Home*, launched in 1919 by Odhams Press to ride the wave of new interest in suburban house and garden. It was, perhaps, the first lifestyle magazine in Britain.

Ideal Home was a curious mixture of practical advice and articles on houses, many of which were beyond the means of its readers. From his first column Sudell wrote about what had proved successful on

Cover of the launch edition of *Ideal Home* magazine with Sudell as garden editor (January 1928), which combined features on aspirational homes with Sudell's practical gardening advice.

'Metro-Land', an example of the poster series published by the Metropolitan Railway over a period of seventeen years (1915–32).

Artist's impressions (above and opposite) of Sudell's planned garden at Dolphin Square in a 1937 brochure for prospective tenants.

Dover House Estate with cottage garden design and privet hedge, 2021.

Tranquillity in the garden at Dolphin Square.

Chequerboard design at the City of London Cemetery and Crematorium Memorial Garden.

One of two thriving allotments of the Roehampton Garden Society.

Resident Helen McKinnon's white flower bed at Dover House.

Highcliffe neighbourhood on Alton Estate.

Dover House conservation area.

Roehampton. In 'Making a New Garden' he writes of the importance of screening from adjacent gardens using Lombardy poplars with yew and holly hedge in between, the poplars to be removed within five years as the other shrubs grew.[4] As we have seen, Sudell's embrace of small gardens, which gave relief from the 'turmoil of the day' or 'exclusion from the world', was a typical leitmotif of his philosophy, a style in the crosshairs of the modernists who detested the privatizing spaces symbolized by suburbia. It could be argued that Sudell's lived experience and understanding of what these new houses and gardens meant to the suburban dweller gave him insight that the theorists could not muster. Here though were the roots of a divide between those concerned with the practical – the inch-by-inch spread of gardening culture – and those who wanted to promote visions of the future, of how open spaces could look if the firm grip of the past was loosened. Sudell found himself in the former camp, for which his reward was to be written out of the landscape history books. The air around the modernist debate was too rarefied for a man who left school at fourteen and who learnt his trade as he collected blisters while actually working in the gardens.

As his career progressed, however, refusing to let his background hold him back, he began to fight for a garden philosophy, powered by his increasingly strident views on social justice, that brought him into conflict with some of those who joined him in a crusade. Sudell was the founder of the ILA, the first attempt to professionalize landscape architecture and put it at the forefront of the rebuild and reimagining of Britain. As we shall also see, the people who joined him on the project – Jellicoe, Colvin, Mawson, even Barry Parker – have endured because they are said to have brought 'art' to the home and garden. Sudell, who one might mischievously call the patron saint of crazy paving, was so closely associated with the suburban garden that he suffered reputationally as these spaces became the source of professional embarrassment and ridicule. It must be remembered that despite the changes sweeping across Britain it was still a class-bound society. Where you were born, where you went to school, what your father did and how you spoke still counted for (too) much. A passionate Lancastrian with little formal education would have discovered this in the committee rooms he sat and argued in over the next decades.

Ideal Home illustrated this tension as it sought to address the issue of how to coordinate the increasing number of modernist houses, beyond the reach of most suburbanite readers' pockets, with a tradition of garden design that still had both feet in the 'olde world'. A Sudell column in 1929, 'New Ideas for Garden Design', addressed this issue.[5] Close reading of the column, and indeed much of his other writings for the magazine, reveals the dilemma. The article's standfirst does indeed mention that a 'modernist spirit has extended to the garden', and the piece itself begins by stating that in 'these days of greater culture and wider knowledge all things need revision'. And yet after the first few paragraphs Sudell is back to what he and perhaps his readers know best. Ever the plantsman, he quickly returns to species of shrub to consider 'dense tufts of rock plants among stones' and mixed borders.[6] Three months later any hint of 'modernism' is decisively forgotten when, in an article on creating elm chairs, Sudell offers the advice that readers could 'introduce, for example, a rabbit or a squirrel at a corner of crazy paving'.[7]

Yet this is not to say that Sudell was behind the times. What he was acutely aware of, as he had learnt on Roehampton, was that the improving nature of gardens and the environment they created could only be achieved by taking gardeners with him, nudging people along to experimenting with new blooms, shrubs and features. He was cognizant of the readership of *Ideal Home*. Few lived in the type of houses it featured. Readers of both gawped in wonder at the properties on show. It was fantasy. But with gardens there wasn't the luxury of daydreaming about climbing the housing ladder. The gardens would not take care of themselves; readers needed to make their mark. Unlike the houses they moved into, the garden could at least be individualistic, allowing some degree of creativity. The garden columns in the magazine had then to serve a real, not illusory, purpose. This appears not to have occurred to the landscape architectural vanguard with which Sudell was increasingly mixing.

His troubles on this front are succinctly essayed in the foreword to his own book, perhaps his seminal text, *Landscape Gardening*, published in 1933. In his foreword, President of the Royal Horticultural Society's Conference on Landscape Design Sir William Lawrence opines: 'Crazy pavement is bad enough, but intolerable when stuck over little plants and looking like galantine.'[8] By page 114 Sudell is showing his readers how to lay just such a path, leaving spaces for plants and adding that 'crazy paving can form a charming semi-formal pathway,' as he had written in the *Gazette* to his small-garden neighbours. Crazy paving almost stood as a symbol for a connection Sudell had with suburban gardeners that, it could be argued, some of his fellows at the ILA and RHS did not.

However, it would be a mistake to suggest Sudell's gardens were not in themselves modern, in that they spoke of a style suited to the new times and, as such, are rich in historical meaning. A strict formalism characterized Sudell's approach to gardens in his instruction, writing and books. Order and compartmentalization were important, hence the ubiquity of crazy paving, which added to the rigour of the garden, necessitating straight lines and delineated spaces. This was the labour-saving garden, undoubtedly beautiful but, importantly, achievable. In his *Ideal Home* articles, while other writers had readers longing for the unattainable small country house or state-of-the-art kitchen, Sudell showed that self-improvement and beauty were possible in the garden. In one article, describing how holidays in any hilly district reveal 'undreamt loveliness', with their combination of stone, grass, soil and flower, he urges readers that they too can recreate such a vision in their own gardens, the smallest of banks serving as a rock garden in 'Nature's own sweet way'. But conscious as always of his readers' lives, he adds: 'To plant a rock garden so that excessive labour is unnecessary, avoid rare Alpines, especially the diminutive ones, which are usually choked with weeds.'[9]

Sudell was a passionate hill and mountain walker, taking time to study the region's geology and its wild plants as he journeyed. Bringing the beauty of those landscapes into the suburban garden was something he was particularly keen on, the subject cropping up in numerous articles. While many of his colleagues would undoubtedly have looked aghast at suggestions that a representation of wild nature could be crammed into the gardens of Dunroamin, Sudell had no such worries. For one thing the gardens would not only be beautiful but would save hard-pressed residents undue time and effort. Sudell started working for *Ideal Home* in 1928, was first by-lined as gardening editor in 1935, and finished in 1958, although by then he had been reduced to a very small 'gardener's diary' column. His articles are a mixture of the prosaic – 'Webb's standard carrot, a stump rooted kind, is a remarkable cropper'[10] – and the occasionally poetic, as in 'the priority of the white Madonna lily never shows to better advantage in the garden then when it is associated with the towering cathedral spires of delphiniums.'[11]

Sudell understood only too well that a house and garden must work in harmony. In May 1930 he told readers that near the home 'formality of design is essential. Every outlook should present a picture to the eye and the main lines of the garden should lead to objects of intrinsic beauty.'[12] Later he told readers, 'every home window and doorway should frame its own garden picture.'[13] What Sudell was doing in *Ideal Home* was not unique. A plethora of magazines, including *Popular Gardening*, which was first published before the war, *Garden Work for Amateurs*, *Amateur Gardening* and *Homes & Gardens*, were dispensing practical garden advice to a voracious new market. Yet as Sudell began to develop his garden business away from Roehampton he also expanded his audience. His work with Odhams Press made him the perfect fit to take the role of gardening editor on the left-wing mass-circulation *Daily Herald*, relaunched in 1930 with the *Ideal Home* publisher taking over a 51 per cent stake from the Trades Union Congress and ready to serve a new market that arose with the increasing popularity of the Labour Party as an emerging alternative to the Conservatives. Its readership was almost exclusively working class. His move to the *Herald* also illuminates how Sudell connected two networks of people who played a part in the interwar landscape story.

As he joined in 1930 he briefly worked with Clifford Allen, who was a director of the newspaper from 1925 before leaving in the year Sudell started his columns. Allen, like Sudell, had been imprisoned three times as a conscientious objector during the First World War and we have already encountered his harrowing experience. Allen was chairman of the NCF, a staunch pacifist and the chairman of the ILP. Surprisingly supporting Ramsay MacDonald's national government in 1931, to the chagrin of the bulk of the Labour Party membership, the prime minister awarded him a peerage and as Lord Allen of Hurtwood he continued to support the administration from the House of Lords. Allen never recovered from ill health induced by his prison experiences, including TB, and died in 1939 at the age of 49. His wife Marjory, Lady Allen, was also known to Sudell through their work together on the LGG. The three shared a leftist philosophy that, in the case of Richard and Marjory, percolated into gardens. Both saw the benefits of open spaces and play for deprived youth, Marjory devoting her life to the welfare of children, designing playgrounds in inner cities and campaigning for legislation that eventually became the 1948 Children's Act, which established a comprehensive childcare service.

The year Sudell joined the *Herald* was fantastically busy. Not only was he building his own landscape practice, dealing with the fallout of his divorce from Emily and writing prodigiously, he was also helping Marjory develop a rooftop garden at Selfridges in London, perhaps an unlikely venue for the two socialists. Just as importantly, the ILA had been formed the year before with Marjory made its first

Fellow in 1930. It is important to remember this political background both when considering the debate over the merit of interwar suburban gardens and the arguments that would ebb and flow within the institute itself over the coming years. Sudell and Allen were decidedly from the political wing of the ILA, a body which was to see itself as anything but in the following decades. The organization contained the second network of people that came into Sudell's orbit, those landscape architects mentioned above who did not share the same philosophy as Sudell and Allen but whose legacy continues today. And yet when the *Herald*'s circulation rose in 1933 to become the biggest in the world, Sudell's influence had, in the space of a decade, expanded from 2,000 readers a month on the Roehampton estate to 2 million across Britain every week. This was an audience the aforementioned landscape architects could only dream of.

The *Herald* articles effectively mirrored those of *Ideal Home* and the *Estate Gazette*, concerning themselves with small urban gardens, what to plant and when, and what would look the best without undue effort: 'Sooner or later in most gardens the problem arises of how best to reduce the amount of necessary labour.'[14] Perhaps unsurprisingly, crazy paving was one solution mentioned in the same article. What was noteworthy about this article was that Sudell understood the anxiety that could be induced in his readers by a lack of time to look after their gardens properly. It was important that they didn't give up when faced with the pressure of time and money. He describes a small back garden he had seen that was covered by crazy paving and had no time-consuming lawn: 'The crannies had, however, been carefully planted with various cushion-like plants such as Arenaria balearica, creeping Thymes, Sedums of many kinds, Mossy Saxifrages and dwarf pinks. Round the wall of the garden a number of evergreen climbers were growing – honeysuckles, golden ivy, winter jasmine and so on.' It was, Sudell told his readers, 'an ideal rest room for the summer months'. Here then is the heart of his philosophy. Without a trace of snobbery, he consistently urges readers not to feel shame about being unable to create works of garden art. A small garden with some sweet-smelling flowers and shrubs was better than none at all and even spending a few hours every week carrying out a bit of weeding would bring benefits to the resident and help to beautify a neighbourhood. He even suggests a small corner of a garden could be left wild, with primulas, foxgloves and others returning every year for the small outlay of a little weeding and growth control now and again.

Sudell continued to write for the *Herald* until the late 1950s, as indeed he did for *Ideal Home*. In May 1933 he asked his readers, 'Is your garden a real home garden or just a glorified allotment?' It was obviously a loaded question, for although he continued to insist until the end of his writing days that all gardens must bring forth produce to feed the family, he also thought it important, as the article says, that members of the household 'should be able to linger there, to rest or read, and take their meals in the open air'.[15] Garden furniture was important, and close to that reposeful area scented plants should add to the air of relaxation: 'Stocks and tobacco flowers, or some of the climbing roses that combine fragrance with beauty – Albertine or Mrs Herbert Stevens – are happy suggestions for beds near a seat.' In August 1931 he introduced readers to the dreaded damping off that many beginners experienced when experimenting with seedlings. If they couldn't afford a cold frame to be ventilated on sunny days, cedar chippings surrounding the seedling pots could help, with the resin from the wood acting as an antiseptic. This is more evidence that Sudell was consistently concerned that his new working-class gardeners should not be disheartened by failure.

The *Herald* often asked Sudell for his opinion in articles that fell outside of his gardening column, none more strangely than in December 1938 when, under a '*Herald* Debate' headline, the subject of the rising threat of Hitler was raised. A Gloucester vicar had suggested in a letter to the newspaper that had the Führer married and then worked in a garden of his own for twelve months his warlike tendencies would have been cured. A panel of 'experts' were asked to support or oppose the idea, with one opining that Hitler would not have been Hitler if he were the sort to dig a garden – which was, after all, hard work – and that his actions were more the result of a cruel childhood. Sudell, billed as the paper's garden expert, came last. It must have been a strange assignment for him, on the cusp of another World War and having been jailed for his pacifism during the last one, although it is doubtful that many at the *Herald* knew this. Sudell agreed with the vicar, making the point that 'there are no monuments to great gardeners, but there are plenty to men who led others to death,' showing that his pacifism had not dimmed in the slightest: 'A man who is ambitious is no trouble to the world or to himself once he takes to gardening. Nature sets enough problems to solve and gives enough outlet to the most ambitious. It is perhaps the world's tragedy that Hitler never dug and dug in his garden.'[16] It was a bizarre, only semi-serious article with Sudell giving unwitting support to the notion that gardens were opiates mitigating against social change, even if on this occasion everyone could agree that was a positive outcome.

This garden 'evangelist' seized every opportunity he could to promote the uplifting nature of open space and flowers. In 1939 he was employed to write information on a number of flowers for the hugely popular W. D & H. O. Wills cigarette cards series. It may seem ironic today that he was promoting the health-giving nature of flowers on such a platform, but it was estimated at the time that more than half of over-sixteens smoked in 1940 in a population of 48 million people, with the figure rising to two-thirds of men. Beautifully illustrated in full colour, the cigarette cards, begun by Wills in 1888, were a hugely successful marketing tool, creating an almost fanatical following of collectors. They could also be bought separately from newsagents at a penny each. As well as Wills, hundreds of other cigarette manufacturers such as John Player had joined in by the early 1900s, producing cards on subjects such as transport, racehorses,

Kings and Queens, footballers, merchant ships and flowers. Yet Wills's early adoption of cigarette cards helped the company remain the leading brand of the day.[17] This was a huge audience for Sudell, and his full set of fifty garden flowers included Ageratum, Begonia, Alyssum Anchusa and Zinnia. The latter, Sudell told smokers, needed 'a sunny position and rich soil'. A full set can still be purchased on eBay for around £5.

By the mid-1930s, with a combined audience of *Daily Herald* and *Ideal Home* readers, and even smokers, Richard Sudell had an influence among the new gardening classes unrivalled by those in the ILA mentioned above. His productive partnership with Odhams Press – he with the expertise and the journalism, it with an ever-growing market to feed – led to the publication of a large number of Sudell-authored books.[18] This was an astonishing workload: his garden practice, journalism, authorship, membership of horticultural bodies and, as we shall see, his founding role in the ILA and the battles therein, all combining in a flurry of activity, instruction, practice and advocacy in the service of landscape architecture and gardens.

His personal life added to the maelstrom. In 1930 he set up home with Ida Schlittler, whom he married the following year against the wishes of her forceful father, Professor Emil Schlittler, an ear, nose and throat specialist in Basel, who tried regularly to lure her back to Switzerland to pursue a medical career. He even tried to get her sectioned to prevent the wedding. Nevertheless Ida, who was fifteen years younger than Richard, was not cut off from the family wealth and Sudell was suddenly catapulted into a different life. Ida, determined to pursue a horticultural career in the land of the gardener after studying in the field in her home country, had set herself up in a large rented detached house in Ember Lane, Thames Ditton, Surrey, which Sudell visited during their affair. After marriage in 1931 they moved, again mostly using Ida's money, to the even more bucolic address of Durford Cottage, Sandy Lane, Cobham, which ironically already contained a cottage garden teeming with Jekyll-style beds of wild garden flowers. Over the years Sudell added a sunken pond, cultivated a huge bank of rhododendron along the western boundary and built a tennis court. It even had its own strip of Oxshott Woods.

The couple would have three daughters: Anne born in 1931, Dorothy in 1932 and Erica in 1935. Dorothy eventually made her life in Australia, marrying actor, broadcaster and politician Ray Sherry. She described her upbringing at Durford as 'very stable and ... rather privileged'.[19] Dorothy remembered that her father's practice and her mother's inheritance led to a comfortable lifestyle. But during the war the area was sometimes bombed by German planes on their way to and from raids on London. When war was announced the girls had been playing in the garden. Their father came out and led them inside: 'I shall never forget the look of sadness and apprehension on his face as he explained that we must always come inside

Sudell and Ida on the beach during a holiday in Rottingdean, East Sussex, 1931.

Sudell and Ida pictured enjoying the view over Devil's Dyke on the South Downs while on holiday. The caption reads: 'Memories of Cricket, Music, and Fresh Air.'

whenever we heard the sirens and get under the stairs until the all-clear sounded.'[20] She later knew her father was a CO and that he had been 'pretty badly treated' while in prison for his beliefs. Eventually the whole family had to be evacuated to Berkshire. 'We all piled into my father's little car, plus the dog and the cat, and with the chicken coop strapped to the roof.'[21] Ida had a thick Germanic accent and was considered a 'foreigner', which would not have made it easy for the family during a time of heightened tensions. Nevertheless, after the war the family returned to Durford Cottage and normal life resumed. Sudell had come a long way from 65 Huntingfield Road, Roehampton, in a short space of time. It was at Durford that he began to seriously expand his own garden practice, with Ida as his hired hand; he also began including a wider range of gardens in his writing. Town gardens didn't disappear, but it was noticeable that larger works did begin to find space in his later work.

Richard and Ida on holiday with daughters Anne (left) and Dorothy, 1931.

By the time of the publication of *Landscape Gardening*, Sudell, as well as Lawrence, was able to call on some heavy-hitting colleagues to contribute chapters, including Thomas Mawson and Brenda Colvin. *Landscape Gardening* was also the first time Sudell dared to venture beyond the painfully practical, and the book was also more rounded. Reflecting his own enhanced circumstances, large formal gardens were showcased as well as summer houses, statuary and tennis courts. These were well beyond the means of those on the Roehampton estate or his *Herald* readers. The book showcased an emerging Sudell theme of how gardeners and landscape architects could come together to improve the country. For the first time he includes publicly what he and many in the ILA had begun to argue, namely that the beautification of Britain should take in housing estates, factories, hotels, golf courses, roads and even petrol stations.[22] The latter of course had been the subject of competitions run by the NGG.

In his preface Sudell talks about wanting to show his readers the principles that underlie good garden design and 'the modern tendencies at work' in garden design, including 'a drift towards simplification and specialization. Rationalization perhaps!' He succinctly identifies social changes that were leading to the break-up of old post-war landed estates and how what replaced them must be the work of the landscape architect: 'Not only have scientific inventions revolutionized the appearance of architecture, a fact which alone would necessitate the creation of a new style in garden design, but changes in the social order are having an even more far-reaching effect in the matter of gardens.'[23]

Later he expands on the need for simplicity: 'Our gardens suffer from a surfeit of good and indifferent things... in designing a garden the keynote should be simplicity. This means good taste in selecting plants and material and a determination on the part of the designer to avoid overcrowding both of architectural features and of trees and shrubs.'[24] This was a clear message to the wild garden country house advocates seeking to transplant their theories into suburbia. Many of the illustrations reveal country houses surrounded by at

Sudell's bucolic residence Durford Cottage certainly did not have a suburban-style garden although the house itself had mock Tudor beams.

least a hectare (2–3 ac) of land, not unlike Durford Cottage. A dairy farm spectacularly converted into a formal garden and even Hampton Court's sunken garden are called upon to show the new Sudell reader with obviously more time and money what they might achieve. Town gardens are not forgotten but are tucked away at the back of the book, with a Sudell-designed rectangular plot appearing on page 369. Crazy paving dominates over two small strips of turf, borders of perennials and shrubs are sketched in, a statue is tucked away in an alcove of box with a bench as the focal point at the top of the garden. Straight lines are everywhere. Make the paths straight and wide, says Sudell, keep walls and fences low where possible so flowers, especially roses, can benefit from free-flowing air and the quiet and secluded lawn. Finally, he adds, 'the views from the windows and from the street should each have something of special interest to catch the eye – a Standard Rose, a sundial, an archway or a fine shrub.'[25] Sudell is temporarily back on familiar territory. The book carries an introduction to the history of the English garden by Mawson, and chapters on international design, including one by fellow ILA member Colvin on American gardens. Sudell authors sections giving planting advice and year-round 'what-to-do' lists for the amateur gardener. Each chapter ends with a list of potential flowers and plants for a particular garden type, some running to several pages. The section on dwarf conifers and shrubs for rock gardens, for instance, runs to more than two hundred varieties. We are a long way from the *Town Gardening Handbook* here.

While continuing with his journalism Sudell wanted to take some of the thinking within *Landscape Gardening* a step further, this time combining landscape architecture with political theory. Despite living in leafy contentment in Cobham, he had not abandoned his political zeal and had begun to amass the scars of battle within the ILA, today renamed the Landscape Institute, over the direction it should be taking. Predictably Sudell's file at the Landscape Institute archive at the Museum of English Rural Life, University of

Reading, is thin compared to those of his more illustrious colleagues, but in his folder a yellowing sheet of paper speaks of thwarted ambition. In his own neat handwriting it starts with a quote from Oliver Goldsmith's 1770 poem 'The Deserted Village': 'Ill fares the land, to hastening ills a prey/ Where wealth accumulates and men decay.' This is a fitting reminder that Sudell had not lost his political principles and proof that they were often grounded in definitions of landscape. Goldsmith's cry against the enclosure of common land that was driving peasants from their homes, the resulting rural depopulation, the accumulation of excessive wealth and the creation of large, landscaped gardens, served to illustrate this perfectly. These two lines were to be quoted beneath the title of a new book he wanted to write called *Towards a New Britain*. In the middle of yet another bloody conflict, the Second World War, Sudell was certain that radical change was needed in Britain both politically – to prevent the cycle of young working-class men being sent off to die in foreign lands – and in its definition of landscape. *Towards a New Britain* would be his mobilizing work, a rallying call that would set out how the landscape of the post-war country should look. It would be a properly planned and designed nation with open spaces serving the majority, wresting power for the decisions on these issues from what he called 'the present ruling class'.[26]

The book's proposed subtitle, 'Planning the Countryside, Village, Town and City in the Modern Landscape', summed up the scope of Sudell's ambition. The first section, entitled 'Things As They Are', would describe good and bad examples of current practice in planning but even include commons, mountains, rivers and parks and how these were being managed. The second section, 'Things As They Might Be', would have started with a call for a national planning policy, examining the interrelations between town and country with industry and agriculture and 'sources of wealth'. It would end with a proposal for a National Planning Board 'with the power to initiate and direct local and national effort', and an explanation about how all this was to be financed. Here Sudell was echoing calls in the early 1930s for a national planning policy led by town planners such as Patrick Abercrombie, who demanded action to ensure new development was in harmony with its settings while conserving the existing rural landscape to prevent its disfigurement from encroaching new builds.[27]

It is not known if he ever started writing the book but certainly it was never published, the only evidence of intent being the single sheet in the archive. The reason for this is unclear. Sudell's radicalism might not have found favour among all in the ILA if he were looking for sponsors and it is uncertain that publishers would have taken the risk of selling such a challenging and potentially uncommercial text, not least from a man who had hitherto made a success of telling gardeners when to plant their carrots and hyacinths. The failed enterprise perhaps also stands as a symbol of Sudell's forlorn struggle to establish himself as a primary voice in the emerging discipline of landscape architecture. Such high-minded books were perhaps not for an uneducated son of a hay dealer with a radical pacifist persuasion and a criminal record to boot.

Evidence of Sudell's other network and his political radicalism emerges in a letter he wrote to Geoffrey Jellicoe, at the time president of the ILA, outlining his plans for the book and telling him he wanted socialist MP George Hicks, at the time parliamentary secretary to the Ministry of Works and Buildings in the wartime coalition government, to write the foreword: 'I know George Hicks slightly but have not yet approached him in connection with my book.'[28] Hicks was a former bricklayer and trade unionist who had been a founding member of the Socialist Party of Great Britain in 1904. He had been prominent in the London building trades lockout of 1914 as workers were punished by employers for a series of earlier strikes over wages and workplace conditions and was a supporter of syndicalism at the time. He was elected Labour MP for Woolwich East in 1931. Had it been published it could be argued that *Towards a New Britain* might have gained Sudell contemporary recognition as a noteworthy contributor to the early twentieth-century debate about how Britain was being shaped, ebbed and flowed.

As it was, Sudell's championing of working-class gardening made him prey to sniffy criticism from within the ILA. His journalism skills made him the obvious candidate to edit the ILA's house journal *Landscape and Garden* from its foundation in 1934 and into the 1950s, with a brief pause for the war. Anyone looking for clues to the differing worldviews and landscape influences within the organization might look no further than the first edition. While Geoffrey Jellicoe writes of the eighteenth-century garden theatre at Herrenhausen, Hanover, in contrast Sudell contributes an article, 'Design in the Town Garden', that challenges garden architects to think of designs to fit a 'back yard', advising on small water features and even lead statuary: '"One little leaden lad" can, as the years pass, acquire something of the companionship that most of us recognize in an old loved tree.' The sound of teeth gnashing among some of Sudell's modernist colleagues can perhaps be heard almost a century later.

As a coup de grâce straight after this article, an anonymous review of his book *Landscape Gardening* reveals what he is up against and wearily opines, 'it is a pity that there are so few [pictures] obtainable showing the possibilities of newer materials such as glass and concrete which might replace the thatch and stone crazy paving to which we are all too accustomed.'[29] Even years later Sudell's contribution to early twentieth-century garden and landscape history was being dismissed. While recounting his memories of the ILA, the Cambridge-educated Peter Youngman, who landscaped Milton Keynes in the 1960s, described *Landscape Gardening* as an 'utterly useless book'.[30] Such vindictiveness may have been founded on horticultural considerations, but it is equally likely that Sudell's appeal to the amateur gardener and what were imagined to be 'conservative' suburban tastes was also at play. The opinions of Youngman and others like him ensured that the man who was the driving force behind the organization that, in the first half and middle of the last century, led the fight for a properly considered newly landscaped Britain, not to mention helping many new landscape architects successfully launch their careers, was airbrushed from its history books.

9
'A new Britain must arise on better lines than the old'

The London Gardens Guild had, in the late 1920s, moved from its Walworth Road offices to a more salubrious address at 9 Gower Street, Bloomsbury, a stone's throw from the British Museum. The LGG gave Sudell a small office to use for his own garden practice at the top of the three-storey building. It was here on a freezing night at 7 p.m. on 20 February 1929 (the coldest February since 1895) that a group of men climbed the wooden stairs to discuss the effective professionalization of landscape architecture. Sudell had called the meeting and understandably assumed control of proceedings. For some in the room this could not be allowed to continue. Geoffrey Jellicoe takes up the story and reveals what Sudell was up against: 'Sudell was in the chair, and it was decided to found the Institute. Gilbert Jenkins whispered in my ear "we must get Sudell out of the chair, and we must get Thomas Mawson in".'[1] That Sudell's place as a key driving force in the birth of a professionalized landscape architecture has been overlooked can perhaps be partially explained by the quote above.

Gilbert Jenkins, the son of a rich marble merchant from Torquay, was a minor landscape architect who travelled on the coat-tails of W. H. Romaine-Walker. While he was responsible for designing buildings such as extensions to the Tate Gallery and His Majesty's Theatre in the Haymarket, London, Romaine-Walker's most well-known landscaping design is probably the Arts and Crafts garden at

Great Fosters in Surrey, on which Jenkins assisted. ILA member and professor of landscape architecture Brian Hackett later remembered, 'There was also a man called Gilbert Jenkins who I don't think practised much landscape but seemed very keen on coming to Council meetings and giving wise advice.'[2] Jenkins whispered his intrigue into the ear of Jellicoe, presumably hoping it would be the latter who would take the action, surrounded by emerging landscape designers such as George Dillistone, Oliver Hill and Edward White. They were all there thanks to the drive of Richard Sudell. While many of the figures who climbed the stairs went on to make names for themselves in landscape architecture, developing successful practices and creating landmark work, Sudell, in that particular field, did not. Removed as the chairman at the end of that year, it was not until 1955 that he was eventually made president of the organization.

Possible reasons for this have their roots in the very beginnings of the institute itself. Jellicoe recognized that it was Sudell who had taken the 'initiative' to bring together people who could begin to have a collective voice on the landscape of Britain.[3] After the war, Sudell became an associate of the RHS, his work at Kew earlier introducing him to the organization, which brought him into contact with people like White, Dillistone and Mawson. That Sudell was vocal in urging his fellow horticulturalists and architects to seize their chance can be evidenced from October 1928 when the RHS hosted the International Exhibition of Garden Design and Conference on Garden Planning. Exhibitors in the British group included Brenda Colvin, Percy Cane, Edwin Lutyens and Stanley Hart.[4] Hart and Sudell, who were friends and colleagues, thought the British section lacked unity of purpose compared to their foreign counterparts, particularly those from Italy, Spain and France. This was compounded two years later when the RHS held its exhibition of landscape designs and photographs in London. Sudell was stunned by the beautiful work that landscape architects were producing in Norway and commented thus: 'If we set a high value on our craft and resolutely determine that it shall claim its rightful position in the creative arts of the world, then this can be accomplished, but every individual must play his part.'[5]

It was Sudell who took the initiative, placing a notice in the *Gardener's Chronicle* inviting people to attend the February meeting at his office of what he called the Society of Garden Architects.[6] Under the title 'Proposed Society of Garden Architects', the small advertisement ended, 'All those desirous of receiving an invitation should write to the convenor, Mr Richard Sudell, at the above address enclosing a stamped and addressed envelope.' Sudell evidently did well enough at the February meeting for another follow-up to take place at the Chelsea Flower Show in the spring. Here it was agreed that the body be renamed the British Association of Garden Architects and also that Sudell would be chairman: clearly Jenkins had more work to do to oust him.[7] At and after Chelsea more established names such as Prentice Mawson and Barry Parker had rallied to Sudell's call, now architects and planners joining horticulturalists, bringing more kudos and existing professionalism.

At some time between Chelsea and its first full council meeting in December that year, Jenkins had gathered enough support for the coup and Sudell had been told he would have to stand aside, although by which of the conspirators it is not known. At the December meeting Mawson was indeed elected as first president and the name was changed to the Institute of Landscape Architects before the year was out:

> At the next meeting we proposed that although Sudell had done splendidly in starting the thing off, an Institute must have a great name to get it launched and Sudell was extraordinarily gracious and resigned from the chair and Thomas Mawson, in name only, became President because of the prestige of his name. Our small group grew.[8]

Removing 'garden' from the title was a clear statement of intent and undoubtedly wrested control from the plantsman and horticulturalist. There was a sense that the mission was too important to be left to mere gardeners, both because of what it wanted to achieve and perhaps, as Jellicoe alludes to above, who it had to influence. As fellow founder member Brenda Colvin later said, 'Most of the people who started the institute were only doing private gardens, you must remember... If we had called it Landscape Gardeners, it would have taken us much longer to arrive at the full scope the profession has today – if we had arrived at all.'[9] The founder members of the ILA were listed as Sudell, Marjory Allen, Geoffrey Jellicoe, Edward Prentice Mawson (elder son of Thomas), Edward White, Gilbert Jenkins, George Dillistone, Brenda Colvin, Stanley Hart, J. E. Grant White, Giffard Woolley and Arthur Cobb.

Certainly Thomas Mawson was a name and, by 1928, an Establishment figure. He ran a landscape and town planning practice that spread to North America and Europe, particularly Greece, where he was awarded the Order of the Saviour for his work on the replanning of the fire-destroyed city of Salonika. He was president of the Town Planning Institute in 1923 and a founder member of the Royal Fine Art Commission, alongside Edwin Lutyens, the following year.[10] Although described by one critic as an 'ego in search of a crown' with as many failures as successes, he clearly held the reputation that many in the newly formed institute thought they needed to compete for the ear of government alongside more established bodies.[11]

Of course, the term 'landscape architect' was not invented in 1930. It had come in and out of fashion throughout the nineteenth century, with Jellicoe himself even arguing that the cave paintings of Lascaux, France, created around 30,000 BCE were examples of the first landscapes conceived by man. The eighteenth-century landscape designer Humphry Repton had been described as an architect by John Claudius Loudon, but its use in Britain had certainly disappeared by the end of the nineteenth century. Mawson himself had called for a revival of the term as early as 1911, but it was only after the First World War, with Europe lying in ruins, that many began to believe there was an urgent need to position landscape alongside the built environment as having equal billing in the rebuilding and reimagining of entire countries. The title had to be reinstated, the seriousness of the 'art', which went way beyond a horticultural knowledge of planting seasons, had to be established. Soon after the ILA was formed Sudell lost his friend and ally Stanley Hart, who resigned because the first constitution, echoing the principle of the already established Royal Institute of British Architects (RIBA), forbade members from making money from the gardening or building trade by selling specific products from commercial companies or turning a profit in a sale. In effect they could only act as consultants on projects in which they did not have a financial interest. This was supposed to keep the ILA 'pure' but also denied some landscape gardeners, not nearly as wealthy as architects, access to a decent living. That constitution, which had been largely written by Jenkins, used the word 'Art', with a capital A, numerous times as the ILA sought to elevate its practice. Clause Two of the constitution stated: 'The Institute shall be formed to promote the study and general advancement of the Art of Landscape Architecture ... and to serve as a medium of friendly intercourse between the members and others practising or interested in the Art.' This mission would be supported, according to the constitution, by establishing a headquarters, arranging lectures, promoting the publication of a journal, arranging exhibitions, founding a library, educating the public in the 'Art of Landscape Architecture', securing the establishment of training centres, organizing visits to good examples of landscape architecture, and holding conferences with other societies who could assist in promoting the 'Art of Landscape Architecture'.[12]

While Mawson became a figurehead for the new institute, Sudell, who was made a vice president and a fellow of the new body, did not retire from the fray. He took the constitution to heart, spending the rest of his professional life working across all those fronts to convince the public they must take the landscape around them seriously. Beauty would not come naturally. It had to be worked on for the good of all, promoted, otherwise a laissez-faire approach – with land at the mercy of market forces – would destroy the vision of a peaceful egalitarian nation living in harmonious environments. It was heady stuff, which some might have considered the ideals of a dreamer, but Sudell was referencing his own rural childhood: garden training from the age of fourteen, Bournville, Roehampton and the Garden Settlement philosophy. Primarily he continued to lobby for the institute to take a robust line in the promotion of good landscape architecture, design and planning.

What Sudell had recognized – but for which he seems to have received little credit – was that, by 'professionalizing', the institute would be well placed to gain work from a public sector charged with rebuilding. Indeed it quickly transpired that local councils and other public bodies *did* come to the institute for recommendations of member practices that could design new sports facilities, parks, estates, cemeteries, road landscapes and even aerodromes. In the early years these ranged from the London Electricity Company seeking the rehabilitation of several sports grounds it owned, to street scaping for the Borough of South Shields, to work on the gardens of the Imperial Hotel, Torquay. Typical of Sudell's industry in the Roehampton years, the institute archives sketch out his uncompromising drive to ensure Britain's landscape was transformed in a utilitarian manner. In correspondence mainly with new president Geoffrey Jellicoe in the 1940s, Sudell repeatedly states his belief that landscape architecture should be at the centre of reconstruction, wresting power away from vested interests: 'The present ruling class will never radically change Britain and we shall have to find new and more virile leaders if we are really going to get things done.'[13]

Sir Geoffrey Jellicoe was one of the twentieth century's greatest landscape architects. Often working with his wife Susan, he created

'A new Britain must arise on better lines than the old'

Richard Sudell (front row, third from left) next to Geoffrey Jellicoe (to his left) at a meeting of the Institute of Landscape Architects and the Town Planning Institute, 1934.

award-winning iconic works such as the garden at Cliveden, Hemel Hempstead's Water Gardens, the RHS Wisley garden canal and the Kennedy Memorial Park at Runnymede, among many schemes. He was also a successful book writer himself, authoring seminal texts on landscape architecture including *The Landscape of Man* and *The Oxford Companion to Gardens*, whose intellectual heft far outweighed anything Sudell published. He was also the ILA's longest-serving president, holding the seat from 1939 to 1949, understanding perhaps better than anyone else the task faced by the organization. 'It is only in the present century that the collective landscape has emerged as a social necessity.'[14] Many books have been written about him and this is obviously not one of them. Though from a completely different background from Sudell – middle-class, trained in architecture, student of classicism, expert on Italian Renaissance gardens, university lecturer – the battles they had are hugely illustrative of this period in British landscape history.

Jellicoe's gentle character made it unlikely he would have been the one firing the bullet to remove Sudell from the chair. However, the disagreements the pair had were often sharp despite being always conducted with the utmost of decorum. Sudell, perhaps frustrated, despite his own mild-mannered nature, at his demotion, had a vision for how the organization should press its case. As we have seen, his left-wing politics, honed with the LGG, often came to the fore. It was certain that Jellicoe and many others in the architectural camp were not fuelled by experiences of the many injustices of early twentieth-century inner cities, not least because they had not seen them at close quarters. Sudell also believed that the ILA needed to take a more hardline stance in its campaign to convince the government that rebuilding Britain should not be left to the market but needed central planning. Having seen the erosion of a dream of greater social equality and a more democratic access to land as the 1930s wore on, he now found himself living through another conflict despite believing the first was 'the war to end all wars'. The country could not afford to make the same mistakes as last time; change should be deep-rooted and permanent. So, while this time spared conscription because of his age (he was 47 in 1939), he focused his energies on trying to influence policy in the only realm of public life he could: landscape.

Jellicoe did not disagree with Sudell that the ILA had to broaden its influence, with an attendant increase in workload for its small band of officers. Jellicoe visited the USA and Canada in 1942 as president, and was impressed with the scope and ambition of the American Society of Landscape Architects. He and Sudell were on the same side in the attempt to bring the wider landscape under the influence of the body. However, both were also concerned that the ILA maintain the promotion of good garden design as well as seeking a stake in larger public projects. According to Jellicoe, abandoning the latter would be like 'excluding poetry from a course on English Literature'.

There was a difference in tone and emphasis between the two, however, with Sudell wanting to push the organization further to seize its chance and urging more radicalism. Jellicoe, as the long-term president who had to steer the ship, was more diplomatic and perhaps more empathetic to those of 'the ruling class' with whom the still small organization had to negotiate. This divide can be illustrated by a disagreement Sudell had with Jellicoe even as the Luftwaffe bombs rained down on London, causing him to evacuate his own office in Bloomsbury, which suffered severe damage in December 1940. Sudell foresaw that the country would witness an explosion of commercial flights after the war, with an attendant increase in the number of aerodromes. The astonishing progress of aircraft technology during the war, which allowed the Luftwaffe to bomb central London and the RAF to lay waste to whole towns and cities in Germany, would supercharge the post-war aviation industry.

The Air Ministry had built aerodromes on approximately 200,000 hectares (half a million acres) of land, particularly around London, 'and in a small island like ours you can imagine the effect of this large number of aerodromes upon the landscape'.[15] Sudell wanted the ILA to establish a subcommittee to draw up guidelines for the landscaping of the permanent new aerodromes that he believed would follow. As we shall learn, he had already designed the landscape that surrounded pioneering aircraft manufacturer de Havilland's new state-of-the-art headquarters at Hatfield in 1933, so he understood something of what he was talking about. Sudell wanted to start by working with the LCC to draw up planning guidelines for the aerodromes that were beginning to ring London. For Sudell this was effectively following the ILA constitution, widening the influence of the landscape architect beyond the confines of gardens. He had also seen the work the American Society of Landscape Architects had conducted in this field. It had produced what amounted to a manifesto for aerodrome landscaping, which, Sudell told Jellicoe, could be repeated on this side of the Atlantic at a cost between £500 and £1,000. 'I would undertake to see 2 or 3 of my clients who are constructors of aerodromes and manufacturers of aeroplanes', among whom he would certainly have included de Havilland.[16]

Jellicoe effectively found himself caught in the crossfire when the LCC's chief architect, John Forshaw, whose cooperation was needed, refused, citing his all-consuming work preparing for the County of London Plan. Unbeknown to Sudell, Jellicoe dropped the project after talking to Forshaw, incidentally also a member of the ILA, a decision Sudell described as 'undemocratic'. Jellicoe wrote to Sudell, telling him that setting up such an enterprise would be a 'tremendous undertaking . . . We cannot afford to undertake such an important work. When I write this, I feel you must think I have already joined the ranks of the pompous.'[17] The last sentence reveals Jellicoe's nervousness that he would be perceived as an Establishment figure without the campaigning zeal of his colleague. In truth, though, Sudell's plan was impractical at the time, even if such work was one of the activities in which the ILA had pledged to involve itself, in its own constitution.

Sudell wrote back reminding the president of this. 'But we are an Institute of LANDSCAPE ARCHITECTS. The design and treatment of open-air spaces is our job and a vital process is in operation which is rapidly changing the landscape of these Islands.'[18] Jellicoe responded with a letter that reveals his high estimation of Sudell, but also hints that other frustrations are at play: 'My dear Sudell, I know what you feel but I should like to talk with you as to the real reasons. Can I give you a ring during the week, and possibly you would come and have a cup of tea.'[19] Sudell was not one to bear grudges and continued his work on aerodromes, becoming the first chair of the ILA's committee set up after the Forshaw debacle. Even with his wings clipped he sought to influence individual aerodromes to lift their horizons when it came to landscaping. That year he also met Lord Sempill, a former chairman of National Flying Services, the government-subsidized company set up to create and manage aerodromes and flying clubs around the country, but which had collapsed before the war. Nevertheless Semphill, a distinguished record-breaking pilot who served with the Royal Flying Corps and the Navy during the First World War, still had huge influence on the nascent aviation industry from his seat in the House of Lords. Sudell met him to press the government to back proper landscaping on airfields.

Neither Sudell nor anyone else, except Winston Churchill and other government figures, could have known that Sempill was a fascist sympathizer who had been selling aviation secrets to the Japanese right up to the attack on Pearl Harbor. This was only revealed when intelligence records were released by the Public Record Office in 1998, having been covered up by Churchill.

It is impossible to know what the frustrations Jellicoe references might have been about, but one cause might have been that Sudell was certainly finding his influence on the body he had done as much as anyone to bring to life extremely limited. Although he was editor of the ILA's *Landscape and Garden*, we should remember he was not made president until 1955, with Jenkins taking up the position a full twenty years before him and even town planner Thomas Sharp, the scourge of suburbia, assuming the title four years before one of its founders. It could be argued that this reflected some colleagues' views of the level of his 'Art' and perhaps his politics. On the latter he certainly did not hide his convictions. He had earlier objected to Jellicoe's plan to make Sir John Reith the president of the institute, on the grounds that he was not a landscape architect, and possibly also because of his role as a bogeyman of the Left at the time: Reith had coached Prime Minister Stanley Baldwin to make a national broadcast about the General Strike in 1926, but refused to allow Labour leader Ramsay MacDonald to do likewise.

This might have been harsh on Reith – in the background the government ruled out the MacDonald broadcast – but he was eyed with suspicion by socialists from that point on. In an earlier letter Sudell offered this opinion: 'Personally I do not like Sir John Reith.'[20] Jellicoe tried again the following year, but Sudell remained steadfast and urged Jellicoe to appoint his friend Lady Allen instead. Jellicoe remained anxious to obtain Sudell's approval, pointing out that Reith had the gravitas to raise the profile of the ILA because the former BBC Director-General, he said, would grow into the role and was a figure of national standing. 'People do not take it [the ILA] really seriously,' he added, proving how far the organization had to travel before it could wield real influence. In the end a compromise was found in which he agreed to go with the majority decision as long as his letter was read out at the meeting to choose the next president. In the end Reith chose not to take the post and, after leaving the BBC, became chairman of Imperial Airways.

Sudell's desire for social change through post-war reconstruction was often palpable: 'With cities going down like ninepins – if we can manage to live through it – it is our job to see that the new Britain arises on better lines than the old.'[21] Sudell's file at the Landscape Institute archive gives a glimpse of a restless energy, cajoling and advocating members to press their case particularly for a key role in the rebuilding of Britain after the Second World War. His new-found relative wealth after marriage to Ida did not quench Sudell's thirst for change. He urged the organization to draw up a list of experts to speak at a conference he wanted to hold, 'so that the ILA can be fully equipped with the necessary knowledge to play its part in post-war reconstruction'.[22] These experts would talk for five minutes each on a specialist subject. He suggested Brenda Colvin speak on private gardens, Edward White on municipal gardens, George Dillistone on forestry, Lady Allen on flat gardens, Edward Prentice Mawson on coastal towns, and himself on aerodromes. Later in the war he pressed his case for a 'Design in Landscape' tour of twelve provincial cities, with the same speakers as proposed for the conference, to explain to the public what could be done after the war with 'gardens, parks, sports grounds and open spaces generally'. The places to be visited by this travelling band of landscape evangelicals were to include Edinburgh, Manchester, Hull, Belfast, Maidstone and London.[23] While the conference did take place in 1942, there is no record that the tour occurred. As with the aerodrome subcommittee proposal, Sudell often had plenty of forward-thinking views but not always the power base to see them enacted. Despite the occasional setback, Sudell continued to make his arguments, sending the ILA his definition of landscape architecture – 'the Art and Science of design applied to open air spaces for human use and enjoyment. Any area open to the sky is a potential field for the work of the Landscape Architect' – and expressing concern when others tried to move into what he considered a specialist field.[24] Shortly after the end of the war, Sudell was dismayed to learn that the Roads Beautifying Association, established in 1928 by the then minister of transport, Lord Mount Temple, had offered the government advice on how a new network of roads across the country should look: 'The RBA are not in a position to implement their offer of free advice since they employ no Landscape Architect.'[25]

What was remarkable about the strength of Sudell's opinion at this time was that it came against a backdrop of brutal war, when many were struggling to stay alive, let alone start thinking about post-war reconstruction and planning. The members of the ILA were scattered to the four corners of Britain in the war effort, with very little time for theoretical debates. Coming closest to looking to the future was Brenda Colvin, who was in Somerset training girls to replace serving men in work on private gardens, thus opening up the profession for them in the years to come. Jellicoe, Edward White and Sudell himself had had offices destroyed by bombs, the latter's a small room he had taken in Bloomsbury Street. Even the bucolic Durford Cottage in Surrey was not safe, as bombs destroyed the house next door and Sudell and Ida evacuated the children to a house near Faringdon in Berkshire (now in Oxfordshire). However, in a letter published in *Landscape Architecture Magazine*, the journal of the American Society of Landscape Architects, Sudell was still eyeing the horizon as the bombs rained down. The government's new Ministry of Building and Reconstruction under his old bête noire, now Lord Reith, was toothless, he told his American readers, and the political ideas for the future were not 'straightened out'. This was perhaps an overly harsh analysis since Britain was but three years into the conflict. There was some cause for optimism, though, given that there was now acceptance that pre-war housing was inadequate. Talk of a post-war National Land Board to properly plan and utilize land, which would require some sort of hoped-for nationalization, was a good sign. People were returning to the self-made and to handicraft, as promoted by William Morris, rather than the 'mass article', which also made Sudell optimistic. Landscape architecture, he said, would be more in demand than ever when the conflict was over: 'It is a curious thing that many persons whom you would least expect are concerned about planning a better world. If it were not for the tragedy of it all, the destruction of all our worn-out towns and cities would be to the good.'[26]

Clearly Sudell was not the only person making these points. Issues of reconstruction and national planning were key battles for the ILA during and after the Second World War, with Jellicoe remaining particularly forthright: 'We are now at the beginning of the struggle between the old and the new. It is the work of the landscape architect to adjust the differences and lead the way in creative design.'[27] Yet Sudell was often in the background, advocating and proposing, taking the lessons learnt from his experience of an earlier war and its aftermath and applying them to this conflict. Sudell's skill as a garden journalist saw him appointed editor of the ILA journal *Landscape and Garden* from its first edition in 1934. He ceased in 1941 when Jellicoe briefly edited a truncated version, the *War-Time Journal*, and returned in 1946 when it was renamed the *Journal of the Institute of Landscape Architects*. As we have seen, the first edition set the template for the journal under Sudell. Maud Haworth Booth writes on sixteenth-century Gravetye Manor, Brenda Colvin on the relation of plant form to architecture, Madeline Agar on the rose in garden decoration, E. P. Mawson on the function of the landscape architect and, of course, Sudell on town gardens. The breadth of the content showcased perfectly the range of work Sudell and his fellows at the ILA considered within the remit of landscape architects. In the first editorial the journal does not forget the amateur gardener, with a message perhaps not unfamiliar to the members of the Roehampton Estate Garden Society. Calling for proper planning of towns and cities, the gardener is reminded that they must play their part too and ask themselves, 'does my share of the picture add to its charm? . . . Privacy, as the modern Landscape Architect can easily prove, is not incompatible with a beauty that is shared by others.'[28]

The ILA conference of 1942, which Sudell had proposed, was reported on in the *War-Time Journal*. Sudell used his five minutes to touch on aerodromes but also on a subject close to his heart: the need for landscape architecture courses at universities and, as a horticulturist, the necessity that every student should understand plants, trees and shrubs. Many ILA members were skilled designers and architects but had little horticultural knowledge. He urged upon those considering the establishment of training centres the 'need for thoroughness in training students in the practical use of plant material'. Yet he went on to stress that education should not be 'overweighted' with detail such that 'the precious gift in design and creation is prevented from its natural expression'.[29] In his presidential address in October 1955, which was covered in the journal, Sudell returned to these themes. The profession in Britain itself, however, had begun to be absorbed within local authorities and their parks departments, having retreated from the battle to exert its influence in the private sector. Undaunted, Sudell insisted the fight was still to be won to ensure public gardens, children's playgrounds and even allotments were brought back to the centre of the country's cities;

the wealth released from what he pointedly called 'wasteful war production' flowing into reconstruction. Sudell again called for landscape architects to involve themselves in 'missionary' work down in the roots of communities just as he himself had done three decades before.[30]

At this point the ILA was creating connections with both the Town Planning Institute (TPI) and the Council for the Protection of Rural England (CPRE). In 1933 the ILA had been invited to the former's annual conference and summer school, whose theme was 'Landscape in Relation to Town and Country Planning'. Thomas Sharp had been president of the TPI in 1945 and followed it up by taking the same position with the ILA five years later. But the relationship with the CPRE is most interesting. Gradually all three bodies began to merge their policies on house building, reflecting the CPRE position that urban and rural must remain separate by planning law. Any idealistic Garden City philosophy that residents seeking decent housing and a new life away from inner-city deprivation could have a taste of both was seen by many as a dangerous fallacy. As we have seen, polemicist Sharp was particularly adamant that the two were separate entities. Proving what a broad church the ILA had become after the Second World War, another scourge of the suburbs, Clough Williams-Ellis, also became a member. All this placed Garden City advocate Sudell in a dilemma. As editor of *Landscape and Garden* it was his job to reflect the positions of the ILA and it was noticeable that several editorials began to suggest great landscapes were under threat from encroaching development. One even suggested drawing up a list of notable gardens and landscapes earmarked for protection.

In 1943 Sudell started on this project, enlisting Christopher Hussey, editor of *Country Life*, to help get it under way and then sending out to members around Britain to suggest additions. It appears to have been completed at some point, but when an attempt to revive it was made in 1952 Sudell had to confess that he had searched everywhere for the 'red folder' but could not find it. This was perhaps unsurprising, with his Gower Street office having been bombed and new offices established first in Surrey and then in 1952 in Ludgate Hill, London. The journal also pointed out that an LCC survey had revealed that 2,225 hectares (5,500 ac) of land had been lost in 1930 alone and another 1,215 hectares (3,000 ac) in 1933. The Restriction of Ribbon Development Act in 1935 did prevent houses being erected on some arterial and major roads out of towns and cities, but Sudell would undoubtedly have found himself conflicted in pushing a line that came close to calling for the end of all new suburbs. It should also be remembered that the two other organizations dwarfed the ILA in size. From a handful of founding members in 1930 it was still only claiming nine hundred members by its fortieth birthday in 1969 and 1,500 in 1978, a year after it was renamed the Landscape Institute.[31] The circulation of *Landscape and Garden* was unrecorded but would have been unlikely to spread the word beyond a small circle of members. Jellicoe, however, when editing the *Wartime Journal* in 1941, did praise his friend for 'his unremitting work of so many years, work which has made the quarterly publications eagerly sought by lovers of gardens and the countryside, thus widely extending the knowledge of our institute and its aims'.[32]

Sudell's position in the gardening wing of the ILA meant he was often called upon to contribute to the less glamorous but still important parts of its work. Few had the grounding in horticulture that he did. While the ILA had important lobbying work to do, it was also concerned with setting best practice for landscape architects developing new projects. Despite her emerging brilliance as a landscape architect, Brenda Colvin often found herself in secretarial positions on the ILA, with Sudell once noting that 'Miss Colvin will take notes' for the General Purposes Committee. She sought his final sign-off for the ILA's Topsoil Report to go to the Ministry of Agriculture. Sudell took this responsibility extremely seriously. Later in life he would give speeches on cemeteries and even, not long before his death, was passionate about the rehabilitation of landscapes around former quarries and collieries. These were, after all, significant pieces of landscape that needed to be beautified. The removal or levelling of spoil banks and subsequent planting and landscaping could create places of wonder out of dereliction, he told his audience at a government conference.

The ILA's legacy is both difficult and easy to assess. From today's perspective its calls for a coherent, nationally planned, professionalized approach to the landscaping of Britain have been a manifest failure, the free-for-all non-interventionist piecemeal approach of the last fifty years creating a nation of vastly different tone and feel beyond perhaps its national parks and uniform high streets. Certainly today the Landscape Institute's activities seem more directed at education and networking rather than campaigning. In recent years it has faced growing criticism around stagnant membership numbers and a perceived failure to actively promote the art of landscape architecture. However, while the CPRE influenced the direction the ILA increasingly followed and this appeared to sound the death knell for Garden City thinking, it was not finished quite yet. Ironically Forshaw's *Greater London Plan*, which he wrote with Patrick Abercrombie, also a member of the ILA, heralded what might be considered the offspring of the Garden City. This was the New Town.

Forshaw and Abercrombie insisted that 1.6 hectares (4 ac) per 1,000 population should be devoted to open space and upheld the importance of clean air, a sentiment that would have been heartily supported by Sudell, stressing that the battle against vermin and disease should be critical to the planning of post-war Britain.[33] For Sudell, though, it must have been disheartening that this was still a pressing need thirty years after his own campaigning. Nevertheless, what is clear from Forshaw and Abercrombie's membership of the ILA is that gardeners, planners and architects were at least coalescing after the war around some sort of egalitarian principle. As Sylvia Crowe, who succeeded Sudell as president, said, the ILA had brought influential people from allied professions into its orbit, 'who realized we had a contribution to make, something to marry to their work.'[34] Incidentally Crowe, when looking back on her time with the ILA, created an unlikely pairing in its key founder and its first president: 'I preferred informal gardens to the more formal designs of Mawson and Sudell.'[35] During Crowe's period as president, the ILA moved offices and was temporarily offered space at Sudell's own offices while the new headquarters was prepared. 'In moving to our new premises we shall not forget the debt of gratitude we owe to our past President.'[36] While Crowe was undoubtedly sincere, it is questionable whether the ILA ever really understood the magnitude of Sudell's contribution to its causes.

The Second World War was clearly an opportunity for proponents of national planning. The war effort had necessitated a command economy and state intervention, which had huge popular support. Some 200,000 houses and hundreds of factories had been destroyed by German bombs, and the need for a coordinated rebuild was clear. New Towns – Stevenage was the first in 1946 – were a product of this thinking. The Report of the Committee on the New Towns in the same year, a government body chaired by Lord Reith, recommended the close collaboration of planners with landscape architects. Indeed Jellicoe at Hemel Hempstead, Crowe at Harlow and Colvin at East Kilbride made significant and long-lasting contributions to these communities. Research by Elain Harwood, an architectural historian with English Heritage, however, casts doubt on the effect landscape architects had on the large-scale built environment projects, setting aside New Towns, that emerged after the Second World War. More often, she found, it was architects themselves, disconnected from the ILA, who were solely responsible for the landscaping of their own projects. She details numerous examples, small and large, where landscape architects were absent. Chief among these is the Golden Lane Estate in London, built in two stages between 1953 and 1963. Here architects Chamberlin, Powell and Bon built a

Le Corbusier-influenced high-rise estate of more than five hundred homes, with a high population density but with about 50 per cent geometric open spaces. Its highest block also had a roof garden. Said Geoffrey Powell: 'There is no attempt at the informal in these courts. We regard the whole scheme as urban. We have no desire to make the project look like a garden suburb.'[37] This feels like the beginning of the end of the Garden City dream, certainly in London, and Powell's words perhaps signify that the landscape architect was, by the mid-1950s, becoming superfluous to this kind of project.

Harwood adds the example of the Alton Estate in Roehampton to hammer the final nail into the coffin. She praises Alton West (the estate is divided into East and West), which was designed by, among others, Bill Howell. It was, she says, 'remarkable' with its 'sweeping contours' and she comments on the 'added drama' of 'its five great slabs slammed sideways into the slope'. Leaving aside what we know of the miserable living conditions it has created for its residents, Howell and his colleagues employed no landscape architect in the design and construction of the project. What is clear is the brutalist, Le Corbusier-influenced style was holding sway in many places in the mid-twentieth century, sweeping away the garden suburb philosophy. The optimism of the ILA, as expressed by Crowe, appears misplaced. As we have seen, these new projects were actually following the example of the vernacular builds of Metro-land and Dunroamin in excluding landscape architects from involvement. Harwood concludes that while Jellicoe, Crowe and their ILA colleagues did influence the design of a vast range of projects, including motorways, power stations, rebuilt industrial schemes and work for public bodies, she had expected to find many examples of multidisciplinary work in this post-Second World War period on architectural-led schemes but, in fact, failed to. Harwood says in her research she 'expected to unearth a host of unrecognized talented landscape architects: I did not expect that their names would already be so well known in another field.'[38]

There was an obvious problem confronting any landscape architect wanting to join the modernist bandwagon in the post-war years. In architectural terms modernism dominated new-build projects such as schools, civic centres and even some New Towns, even if these were often pale imitations of the grand visions expressed by some in the movement. However, no sufficient interpretation of what a modernist landscape should look like was available. As ILA member Brenda Colvin noted, 'Architecture is dealing with new materials as well as new needs, whereas the natural materials of landscape (land and vegetation) and the basic human needs which landscape fulfils are ageless.'[39] One man who did push for a modernist interpretation outside was Christopher Tunnard, who wrote *Gardens in the Modern Landscape* in 1938. He called for landscapers to find new ideas that looked to the future, not to the past, to meet the needs of 'contemporary living'. But as garden historian David Jacques points out, the writer's idea of such living 'envisaged an idealized lifestyle that probably only a very few of Tunnard's acquaintances – for example his clients in Surrey – were lucky enough to partake in fully at the time.'[40] Jacques points out that some of the photographs Tunnard used to illustrate his book included householders, mainly from abroad, reclining in chairs, lounging by the pool or sailing, and children playing in sizeable sandpits.

Defining what such a landscape should look like became problematic, with even Tunnard admitting he had been over-optimistic in calling for sweeping change. Any attempts that were carried out became too functional and decorative. One Arts and Crafts landscape architect dismissed the entire idea of a modernist garden: 'The few examples where any serious effort has been made are of such severity, or of such grotesqueness, as to have little resemblance to anything we should recognize as a garden.'[41] While the Modern Movement would appear to be a landscape dead-end, the ILA did serve as a forum for new ideas and thinking. Jellicoe himself suggested it was art and art history that should be referenced for new approaches to the garden. In a speech to the ILA he said his purpose was to 'stimulate a study of painting and to see whether it is possible for the landscape architect to reach the heights the painters do, not only on the drawing board but in the field'.[42] Some, such as Crowe, went even higher for inspiration: the harmony of the cosmos. She saw the special role of the artist, in this case the landscape architect, as exploring 'the relationship between our minds and the universe' and then translating them into the physical world: gardens. She thought that 'underlying all the greatest gardens are the certain principles of composition which remain unchanged because they are rooted in the natural laws of the universe.'[43] Influenced by Freud and Jung, she believed the unconscious understood the natural form and rhythm of landscape from early dawnings and by stripping away intellect that connection with the land could be re-established. Colvin herself believed that beauty derived from unconsciousness's recognition of harmony and that the landscape architect had simply to achieve an equilibrium between man and environment. There was no space here for the ideology of the Modern Movement. Meanwhile, despite the theorizing of some ILA thinkers, a form of modernism was spreading, dictating the way people lived and worked, with the landscape architect largely sidelined. The question remains about why the building projects referenced here failed so spectacularly to ignite the passions of residents as opposed to their architects or have, for the most part, become modern-day architectural pariahs. The debate might also consider whether the involvement of talented visionary landscape artists like Jellicoe, Crowe and Colvin might have helped soften the brutalism of these builds and given those residents a chance of living decent lives in them.

Sudell was largely absent from the intellectual landscape debate. His was a practical and political focus, but he did showcase his versatility by landscaping de Havilland's new Art Deco headquarters at Hatfield and, as we shall see, he did get one chance at landscaping one large-scale housing development when he was commissioned to create the courtyard garden at Dolphin Square, Pimlico, London. Instead he dedicated himself to continuing the fight for the professionalization of landscape architecture, his own practice and his work helping to turn interwar and post-war Britain into a nation of gardeners. It is true that Sudell did not have the high-profile reputation built on the back of landmark work that many of his colleagues had, yet in 1984, almost twenty years after his death, Sudell's pioneering career was still being dismissed. At a lecture and discussion on the life and works of Thomas Mawson, the man who replaced him in 1928, Sudell was waspishly described as 'not really of a very high order' by chairman Peter Youngman, a past president himself of the ILA and the man who had already damned *Landscape Gardening* as 'utterly useless'.[44] But in word and deed, Sudell arguably rises above such considerations and deserves reinstatement in the story of early twentieth-century garden and landscape history.

In his presidential speech Sudell looked forward to the next 25 years of landscape architecture, combining his grassroots knowledge of the human relationship with land and a utopian vision of how far that relationship might take society – even if, for many, it was already becoming clear it might remain a dream: 'So far we have only touched the fringe of landscape beauty in relation to human environment. We shall in the future create towns and cities of undreamt beauty and purpose. I foresee a noble architecture arising amidst a landscape fashioned to meet the desires and aspirations of man.'[45]

10
The Landscape Architect Struggles to Make a Mark

In July 1956 two balding men, one tall and upright and the other slight and bespectacled, hurried their way through the summer drizzle for an important meeting at the Ministry of Transport and Civil Aviation in Whitehall. They walked with a determination to put into practice their belief that the rebuilding of Britain had to be properly planned and more importantly landscaped, a one-off chance to create a modern nation by employing the highest design principles. For Richard Sudell and Geoffrey Jellicoe there could be no greater contemporary test of the worth of landscape architecture, at least in the eyes of the 'ruling class', than involvement in the construction of Britain's first motorway, the M1. The London to Yorkshire stretch opened to the public in November 1959. With the ILA pressing its case that every project 'open to the air' should be influenced by professionalized landscape architecture this was a major challenge. As Marjory Allen had told the ILA in 1942, landscape architecture had to be established as a 'new national service' with central and local government fully signed up to the role it could have in the quality design of open spaces. The building of the M1, as car ownership soared in the late 1950s, was seen as symbolic of a modern and exciting new Britain, finally throwing off the yoke of post-war depression. To get this right was important.

And yet by the late 1950s there was growing doubt that the ILA or the profession itself had come anywhere near to establishing itself as an automatic choice for inclusion on such projects. We have already seen how architects had elbowed out landscapers in the design of big private projects, and even the speculative developers of Metroland and Dunroamin had seen no need for costly experts to tell them how to lay out their new estates and ribbon developments. While they were winning contracts to work on new factories, aerodromes, reservoirs, power stations and some housing estates, Jellicoe in particular was aware that there was much work to do to get a seat at the top table of national reconstruction. Brenda Colvin knew this too. In her presidential address in 1951 she had warned: 'The profession of Landscape Architecture has yet to reach the point where it is felt to be indispensable in its own field.'[1] With the M1, the largest single public project since the end of the Second World War, the signs were not good.

We know that Sudell had been irked by the establishment of the Road Beautifying Association (RBA), which had been advising local councils on roadside planting since 1928. The key to his irritation was that, although they may have included horticulturalists like himself, the RBA was concerned with planting schemes, not the overall design picture. This was clear evidence of Sudell's own evolution from a fourteen-year-old apprentice gardener to a fully fledged landscape architect. Colvin had already sounded the alarm in 1939, attacking the 'pathetic lack of vision' the country was showing when it came to road design, with engineers effectively content to lay the tarmac and have others prettify the roadside.[2] While not naming the RBA, she clearly had them in her sights. What Colvin, Jellicoe, Sudell, Sylvia Crowe and others wanted to see was comprehensive design on these new roads, recognizing the dominance they would have over the countryside but wanting them fitted to the contours and existing features of the landscape. Drivers should be presented with a new, interesting vista as they travelled. Put simply, planting up verges was largely a waste of time as motorists sped past without noticing. With a sideswipe that England had become too 'garden city minded' by indulging in too much detail, she wanted roads to open up the natural landscape to people who might hitherto have had little access to it:

> Travelling at anything over 30 miles per hour, the details of the flower and leaf count for very little, form and mass, light and shadow are the materials we must make use of, and these are also the requirements from the point of view of the more distant observer to the countryside.³

Movement was the key to this new landscape, which called for a new depth of composition when designing roads. Jellicoe urged landscape architects to look for lessons on this front in England's great Repton- and Brown-designed picturesque parks and suggested even landscape painting held clues. He alighted on a nineteenth-century watercolour by Norwich artist John Crome, called *The Shadowed Road*, which portrayed a country road winding past trees, a cottage and distant horizons, full of light and shade. Jellicoe suggested even this bucolic scene could be translated into a modern road-landscaping scheme.⁴ On a more prosaic but certainly more practical front, Sudell had suggested to Jellicoe towards the end of the Second World War that, to advance the ILA's case for central involvement in these projects, it begin to put together 'contrasting photographs' of well-planned roads and poor examples to press its case. For the latter he proposed they use a road they would both have known well, given its proximity to Kew: 'the Great West Road at Hounslow. It is a shocker.'⁵

At the Ministry meeting, Sudell and Jellicoe put their arguments forward and recommended a range of ILA members, no doubt Colvin and Crowe among them, who would be more than capable of being appointed landscape architectural consultants to the grand project. It is difficult to ascertain when they realized their arguments were falling on stony ground. Also in the meeting were leading officials of the M1 consulting engineer company Sir Owen Williams and Partners and civil servants concerned primarily with transport matters. Sir Owen, who was not present at the meeting, was an engineer and self-taught architect who had designed the first Wembley Stadium in the early 1920s and, perhaps ominously, would go on to design Gravelly Hill Interchange in Birmingham, more often known as Spaghetti Junction, two years later. The project did have a Landscape Advisory Committee, on which sat an independent, Clough Williams-Ellis, and Crowe as the ILA representative. However, it had a narrow, superficial remit and was not even in the Whitehall room for the meeting. Those who were there listened patiently but were keen to cut to the chase of the price to be charged for the services of an ILA-affiliated landscape architectural practice. It was a clear indication that cost would be key for the first big transnational project the country had seen since the war.

Sudell and Jellicoe were told they would get a response, and didn't have to wait long to find out what it was. A landscape architect in addition to other consultants on the project would be too expensive, they were told. To add insult to injury, the consultant engineers simply employed two foresters instead. In the winter of 1959 more than 72,000 trees, mainly alder, ash, common oak, Scots pine and Spanish chestnut, were planted together with 4,700 shrubs.[6] One need only imagine Sudell's reaction to the decision, but he was not alone. Angry letters flooded in to the government and the newspapers from the Royal Fine Art Commission (Jellicoe was a member) and RIBA as well as the ILA. While the ministry did eventually appoint a landscape architect in 1961, it was too late for the first two main stretches of the road.

Predictably, once finished the reaction to the new road among the creative sector was uniformly negative. There was a clear contrast to be found here between a country that had lost the war and a supposedly triumphant nation. Germany's post-war reconstruction had begun to be compared favourably with Britain's on several fronts, leading to the oft-reported joke wondering who the actual victors in the conflict had been. The autobahns were marvelled at by many British architects and landscape architects, with Crowe quick to compare the M1 unfavourably with the Ulm to Baden-Baden route. For Crowe the autobahns revealed 'a fluid plasticity' with 'smooth transition between road and countryside with the route shaping itself to the contours of the existing landscape', while the M1 was bedevilled with harsh, angular lines and constructions that 'act as a jarring element divorcing road from landscape'. It was all 'negative interruptions and disruptions'.[7] Crowe was joined by a host of other eminent architects, critics and designers, many of whom alighted on the brutalist reinforced concrete bridges of the M1 compared to those of the autobahns. John Betjeman, writing in the *Daily Telegraph*, described the landscaping and bridges as 'matters of lasting regret'.[8] Even though a landscape architect was employed for later stretches it can be argued this was too late. The chance to create memorable landscapes as envisaged by Jellicoe, Colvin and Crowe had gone, and possibly with it the profession's chances to influence a national planning policy.

While the Second World War may well have created an appetite for central command economy controls, this dream began to die under successive Town and Country Planning Acts, which devolved planning policy to local authorities. Over the years powers have been successively watered down so that developers with deeper pockets and ready for the fight can increasingly steamroller their projects into existence. Landscape architecture increasingly went two ways: private and public projects either built or destroyed the reputations of landscape architects both in the UK and abroad, but for the most successful business flourished, perhaps diluting a sense of unified purpose and reforming zeal that characterized the war years and the immediate aftermath. In addition, many local authorities began to employ their own landscape teams, working on sports fields, playgrounds, local parks and walkways. While these could beautify individual cities and towns, adding to the satisfaction of residents and serving as a lure for inward investment, it was hardly guaranteed to promote national minimum standards, particularly with the desire to do so rapidly evaporating from within the central government. For Sudell and others the lifelong dream had effectively died even if he and the ILA continued to advocate for the highest standards of good landscape architecture and showcase the best British design could offer. On this front there was still one area where the individual landscape artist could make a mark by creating new vistas for projects arising from scratch from the earth: New Towns.

In many ways Jellicoe's work for Hemel Hempstead was indicative of a problem often faced by landscape architects. That is, they were more often used to adorn new-built environments rather than being in on the plan from the beginning, from the ground up. In 1947 Hemel in Hertfordshire, a small market town, was chosen by the government to be the third New Town, communities to be built to meet housing needs after the Second World War. Jellicoe was originally asked to propose plans for the entire development based on his concept of a 'town in the park' with generous health-giving open spaces. To his huge disappointment Jellicoe suffered another defeat by Whitehall when in 1949 the Ministry of Town and Country Planning opted for a more modest proposal prepared by Hemel Hempstead District Council. The initial negative response from the market town residents might not have helped, although progress on the more conservative version still met with protest from existing residents. Although also a trained architect with an impressive track record, for Jellicoe and others at the ILA this was proof, if it were needed, that too often architect and landscape architect were not seen as an equal partnership. There were notable exceptions but often building came first and landscape afterward. Despite Jellicoe's disappointment he was persuaded to return to have another look and revive some of his ideas after some persuasion by chairman of the Hemel Development Corporation, Henry Wells, who felt the emerging town centre was lacking adventure.[9]

Today Jellicoe's Water Gardens are much admired and cherished by local residents. Completed in 1962 the works canalized the River Gade, transforming an area of watercress beds, ironworks, allotments and orchards. Inspired by artist Paul Klee, Jellicoe transferred the Gade into a serpent with a lake for a head, its fountain the eye, and a curving tail stretching through a series of weirs each designed to make a different sound as water cascaded, bringing the serpent to life. An ornamental rose garden sat on the creature's back, shrub planting representing its scales. A sculpture, called *Rock and Roll*, of two dancers gliding across the lake, which Jellicoe said was frozen at the point in which the girl was flung out ready to be coiled back into her partner again, was commissioned.[10] The fact that these were not ballet dancers but rock and rollers hinted at new beginnings for the community in the 1960s. Later Jellicoe described the Water Gardens as one of his most enjoyable projects and in 2010 they were placed on English Heritage's register of Parks and Gardens of Special Historic Interest as an important example of twentieth-century urban design. It is impossible to imagine how his entire plan for the New Town might have been eventually received, but for landscape architecture it was another withdrawal from the national planning battlefield despite the success of many individual projects, like the Water Gardens.

The New Towns were in many ways the last hurrah of the Garden City movement and its leader Ebenezer Howard. But it was a significant concluding chapter. It seemed for a while the philosophy he had promoted, that of building new communities complete with integral leisure and work opportunities ringed by preserved green land and rural idyll, had been accepted by the post-Second World War government in its entirety. His First Garden City Ltd company, which with its own financial resources built the garden city of Letchworth in 1909 and Welwyn in 1920, had morphed into the Town and Country Planning Association (TCPA). It had gained a driven acolyte of Howard's called Fredrick Osborn, who took up the cause of New Towns with passion. In the interwar years and beyond, the TCPA did establish links with the ILA and the CPRE, although with such a diverse range of individuals supporting different visions of the future, agreement was often difficult and joint lobbying ineffective. Nevertheless, there were two complementary driving forces that finally saw the passing of the New Towns Act in 1946 and the Town and Country Planning Act in 1947, paving the way for new construction. The first was the TCPA's view that new communities, as well as providing bright fresh beginnings for residents, could also halt the outward sprawl of London and help protect the Green Belt around it. The Green Belt Act of 1938 had established the principle but placed the onus on hard-pressed local authorities to enforce this with mixed results.

New Towns would also stop the establishment of dormitory towns around London and the misery of (what many thought to be) the pointless and time-wasting commute into the capital, by creating contained communities with their own employment opportunities.[11] The second driver was that leading town planner Patrick Abercrombie had, with LCC chief architect John Forshaw – he who upset Sudell with his aerodrome committee veto – produced the County of London Plan in 1944, which Abercrombie updated a year later into his *Greater London Plan*. Both were members of the ILA. Primarily the plan addressed the impact of the war on the capital, not least the Blitz, which had destroyed 50,000 inner-city homes and damaged 2 million more. The widespread destruction created the opportunity for a new, properly planned restart with better housing, more space and a healthier environment in which inner-city residents could live. Together with a strenuously enforced Green Belt around the capital, this would mean more than 1 million existing residents would have to be displaced and moved elsewhere. The New Town's time had come. In total 27 were built from 1947, starting with Stevenage and including Hemel, Bracknell and Milton Keynes not far from London. Peterlee in County Durham, Cwmbran in Wales and Livingston in Scotland were some of those established elsewhere in the country. In addition, existing towns such as Peterborough and Northampton were expanded as New Towns.

ILA members were involved in the development of New Towns, with some degree of success. Not only that but they also succeeded in establishing some landscape principles that were enshrined in legislative guidelines, even if they were not always followed in the years to come. The New Towns Acts, starting in 1946, were the result of a Parliamentary committee set up to examine the issue and led by Sudell's old enemy Lord Reith. ILA members Sylvia Crowe, Brenda Colvin and James Adams submitted written evidence. They covered large-scale planning issues such as site selection and the relationships of a New Town to its surrounding countryside, as well as more detailed design elements such as playgrounds, appearance of houses, private gardens and even cafes. They advised that 'the town must be so cited [*sic*] in relation to the existing topographical features that it lies naturally within the landscape, the trees and contours forming a background to the buildings, and the flow of the land, in conjunction with the surrounding views and landmarks.'[12]

Crowe's remarkable 26-year association with the landscape of Harlow is perhaps the standout example of how a landscape architect could influence the shaping of a place, and not just its open space. Beginning at the same time Jellicoe got to work at Hemel, her longevity on the project crucially allowed her to influence the open and built environment as it evolved, in a way he could not. Like Jellicoe she talked of her role as creating Harlow as a 'New Town in the Landscape' rather than the other way around, insisting it should reflect and harmonize with its surroundings. In turn her detailed planning of the landscape informed the masterplan of Harlow architect and town planner Sir Frederick Gibberd, rather than being seen as a nice add-on. Unlike Jellicoe, Crowe did not channel or culvert existing open water but incorporated them into open spaces and parks. The crowning glory is her 66-hectare (164 ac) Harlow Town

Park, which was opened in phases from 1957 to 1988 with both natural and designed features. The latter include a water garden where retained spring-fed watercress beds were incorporated into formal pools and cascades.[13]

It could be argued that Crowe's sixty-year career has had a more lasting effect on the British landscapes than that of almost anyone else. Her work included reservoirs such as Rutland Water, nuclear power stations, power transmission lines and crematoria, hospitals, sewage farms, Harlow, motorway intersections and USAF bases including Greenham Common. She was landscape consultant to Britain's Forestry Commission and to the Central Electricity Generating Board, but still found time to design gardens for private houses, parish churches and Oxford colleges, as well as writing seminal books on landscape architecture.[14] In terms of the quantity and quality of her work on the wider landscape of Britain, it is not too unfair on Sudell to state that she was a significant upgrade; it was in his work with the emerging gardeners of the country as well as his beliefs, the politics of landscape if you like, that his real success lay.

Peter Youngman, whose uncharitable views on Sudell we have already encountered, was another involved with New Towns. He worked on the masterplan for Cumbernauld New Town in North Lanarkshire, Scotland, insisting on designing a forest that still helps protect the windswept site from North Atlantic gales. In the 1960s he executed a similar plan for Milton Keynes with notable success. His insistence that an American-style grid of horizontal and vertical distributor roads be abandoned changed the feel of the town. After walking the site Youngman gained an appreciation of its slowly unwinding undulations and persuaded the planning team to convert the rectilinear grid into a curvaceous mesh, flowing with the landscape.[15] As with Cumbernauld, he also argued, successfully, for a town forest to absorb the highways: 'In an urban context what is striking about Milton Keynes is the extent of the landscaping within this civic centre and the degree to which it is integrated with the wider urban environment.'[16] Thomas Sharp in Crawley and, briefly, Clough Williams-Ellis in Stevenage were also ILA members who were involved, in some form, with New Towns. It was arguably the high-water mark of landscape architecture's influence on environment. That is at least if you overlook, as many frequently do, the impact Sudell and others had on the spread of millions of colourful hectares of newly established twentieth-century suburban gardens. With the arguable exception of Crowe at Harlow, the landscaper was rarely an equal partner with the architect planner in the project even if their principles had been enshrined in the New Town legislation. More often than not the chairmen of the Development Corporations that oversaw the building of New Towns, with one eye on the purse strings, were little different from the mandarins of Whitehall.

One year after the M1 meeting, Sudell was finally made president of the ILA, an astonishingly tardy recognition of his immense contribution to the cause of landscape and garden. By then Sudell knew the game was up, as far as the complete architectural and landscape reimagining of post-war Britain was concerned. Now in his sixties, he had a growing practice and a reasonably comfortable personal life. It was time to admit the socialist utopia such as that envisioned by the Salters in Bermondsey was never to be realized. Instead, Sudell retreated to what had really been his strength throughout: the practical. If he was not the champion of big ideas, he could be the inch-by-inch promoter of progress that had made him so successful in a few short years on Roehampton. While the last chapter ended with a flight of rhetoric from his presidential speech in 1955, what was notable in his address was its return to basics, the administration of small-step change. Delivered at the General Meeting of the ILA on 20 October, it began with, as Jellicoe had already noted, an extremely gracious acknowledgement that Mawson was 'appropriate' as the body's first president.

Sudell had to admit that the ILA had 'made steady if not spectacular progress' in its mission to enlighten on the uplifting nature of good landscape. The speech was really one to be expected from the president of a professional body. It certainly had no hint of the revolutionary organization for change that Sudell had originally imagined it could be and which he had advocated for in his letters to Jellicoe. He described how work was ongoing to have landscape architecture taught at universities, the ILA helping to fund such courses at London and Durham, with a special mention for Reading for its early cooperation with the ILA on education. There was the recognition that landscape architects were being subsumed into local authorities, with the painful reflection that even there they did not have the positions to have enough influence on coherent design. Instead, private practice, like his, was now engaged in commercial work such as factory landscaping, mineral works and, despite the M1 defeat, minor roadways. Ever the optimist, though, Sudell urges his audience to consider other opportunities in this field: 'I am sure there is a need for consultant landscape architects in connection with the new atomic plants that are now being planned in various parts of the country.'[17]

Private work landscaping big gardens on estates was rapidly diminishing as tax burdens on the minor gentry grew, but there was still much to do within urban spaces. Although New Towns were still being constructed, the full Garden City philosophy was in danger of being diluted. Not all New Towns were as successful as Harlow and Milton Keynes and not all employed ILA members even for open-space work. In his speech Sudell turned his attention to Modern Movement-inspired rebuilding. He noted that big city slum clearance was making way for projects that built 'tall blocks of flats, horizontal blocks, with some cottages in the form of mixed development'. Here the battle was on to ensure public gardens, children's playgrounds and even 'a few private gardens and allotments for such persons who care to cultivate them'. As we have seen, this was already a forlorn hope, with landscape architects excluded from most of these developments: 'It would be a great pity if the opportunity were lost when we are rebuilding our big cities to bring back landscape into our towns.'[18]

As we have seen, Modern Movement advocates like Bill Howell, with their belief that huge swathes of land could be reclaimed if homes rose into the sky, thought this too, although these open spaces were to be communal not private. The reality was already very different. Despite this Sudell wanted his audience to remain positive, as indeed any good president should. Two World Wars had blighted the land but now 'if mankind can agree to settle their differences without the resource of force a tremendous liberation of energy will be set free for positive construction and development.' Each member needed to be a 'missionary' when this happened, just as he had been, and in 25 years' time he saw no reason why progress could not be made. He quoted Greek philosophy to illustrate many of the views he had expressed before in the *Guild Gardener* and to fellow tenants on Roehampton: 'The love of man rises upon the stepping stones, from beautiful bodies to beautiful institutions to beautiful ideas until it attains to the idea of absolute beauty and at last knows what the essence of beauty is; this is the life man should live.'[19]

The gradual retreat of landscape architecture into small individual impacts was an unlikely background to convince his audience they could have a major role in bringing to life the beauty for which the Greeks had striven. Sudell must have known this, especially as by now his practice was sometimes involved in the minor landscaping of the grounds around gasholders in Essex. In 1961 at the age of 69, and five years after he and Jellicoe lost the battle of the M1 at that Whitehall meeting, he ceased his ILA activities, writing to its secretary, 'I have a strong feeling that younger members should be given an opportunity of running the Institute.' He donated a number of his books to the ILA library.

In many ways the hopes of the Left began to disappear after the post-Second World War reforming government of Attlee gave way to the returning Churchill in 1951. Another Labour government did not take power until the Harold Wilson administration thirteen years later. In that intervening period progressive dreams of a centrally planned, uplifting new environment for Britain – with the government working with the private sector to rebuild Britain – were disappearing over the horizon, much like the brutal M1 on its straight line north. In the first half of the twentieth century, however, a leftist, sometime pacifist, network originating around the First World War did reach into a number of spheres of influence including politics, business and even gardens. Up until the late 1940s Sudell clung on to the hope that Britain could be changed along more egalitarian lines against 'the present ruling class'.

We have seen how he was acquainted with many politicians who, like him, either came from the Left or whose pacifism stemmed from their religious beliefs. Founder of the ILP and the NCF, Clifford Allen, was one such contact, as was wartime minister George Hicks. Into this mix came another absolutist CO, Arthur Creech Jones, who became secretary of state for the colonies in 1946 under Clement Attlee. Creech Jones, a senior trade unionist, had refused to serve in the forces and had been jailed from 1916 until, like Sudell, he was one of the last to be released in 1919.[20] The pair, while not friends, were aware of each other. As with many COs, Creech Jones was unable to resume his career in the Civil Service after being released, so dedicated himself to trade unionism and Labour politics instead. Not surprisingly as a member of a radical reforming government, Jones was an anti-colonialist, believing in eventual self-government for all British dominions.

In the late 1940s, trouble was flaring in British Guiana, the colony on the northeast edge of the South American mainland. The country, a colony since 1814, was the size of Britain but had a population of only half a million, most of whom lived on the coastal strips away from the dense forest that covered about 90 per cent of the country and in which its indigenous people, who made up just 4 per cent of the population, lived. Gold, diamonds and bauxite were mined there, but the inhabited part of the country was in effect a large-scale sugar plantation dominated by four big British companies. Africans, descendants of those who were victims of the slave trade, and East Indians transported from another British colony and signed up as indentured labour made up about 75 per cent of the population and in effect the plantation workforce. The British white community, the managerial class, made up less than 1 per cent of the population.[21]

Such were the conditions on the plantations that sporadically, through the first half of the twentieth century, riots against oppressive working environments and poor wages had broken out. The most severe of these was probably the Ruimveldt Riots of 1905, when stevedores at the dock of the capital, Georgetown, struck and were joined by workers from other industries, primarily the sugar cane plantations. In 1939 a confrontation between police and workers at the Leonora Plantation near Georgetown saw four people killed and many more injured.[22] Then, on 16 June 1948, the events of what has become known in the modern-day country as the Enmore Martyrs Day occurred. Five sugar plant workers lost their lives in clashes with the police at the Enmore sugar plant in East Coast Demerara. This followed an industry-wide strike, organized by a newly formed and more radical union, against new labour-intensive practices of cutting and collecting the cane that had been introduced three years earlier.

As workers at Enmore tried to re-enter their factory to confront strike-breaking labourers brought in by the plant's owners, the police opened fire, killing five and injuring fourteen others.[23] In the House of Commons Creech Jones insisted the police had been attacked by a mob, wielding cutlasses, lead piping and sticks, even though the MP asking the question insisted the workers were unarmed. 'They were obliged, I understand, to fire in self-defence,' Creech Jones told Parliament.[24] Nevertheless against a backdrop of increasing tensions and new political agitation in the colony and the Labour government's increasing nervousness about the treatment of its own subjects, he also announced a Commission would be sent to examine the background of conditions on the plantations. Privately Jones knew measures had to be taken to prevent events escalating. Economist Professor John Archibald Venn, president of Queens' College, Cambridge, and son of the creator of the Venn Diagram, was chosen to lead the two-man mission to the colony. Perhaps rather surprisingly Creech Jones also asked a fellow pacifist and political traveller to go too: Richard Sudell.

By 1948 Sudell was ensconced in what appeared to be domestic bliss with Ida, Anne, Dorothy and Erica at leafy Durford Cottage. His moderately successful practice and an inheritance Ida had received meant life was relatively comfortable. He had not abandoned his principles though, as evidenced by his ongoing struggles to have the ILA take a more radical stance on some issues. Neither he and certainly not Venn were prepared for what they found when they visited British Guiana on their fact-finding mission. The country was a prime exhibit of pure imperialism, complete with a sham democracy. The country was treated with high-handed colonial disregard by the UK government, with four big British sugar plantation owners governing the economy, and thus determining the living standards of inhabitants, acting almost as mini-East India Companies. Booker McConnell Ltd controlled 75 per cent of the lucrative sugar cane industry, leading many to jokingly call the country Booker's Guiana. The company went on to sponsor the Booker Prize for literature.

Although slavery in British colonies had been abolished in 1833, in reality there was little difference in conditions for the people who lived in British Guiana. While the companies made huge profits to be shipped back to the mother country and had already been paid handsome reparations from the British government for the loss of their slaves, wages and living conditions for workers were shockingly poor. Even the Colonial Officer reported that housing conditions, 'leave much to be desired'. Few people could afford a healthy diet on the wages they were paid, and education was virtually non-existent. Employment on the sugar plantation was often on a piecework basis and was back-breakingly tough. In the 1950s workers could expect to earn at most $2 a day.[25] It was subsistence living at best.

Into this picture had come a new party led by a charismatic man who gave the colonial powers plenty to fear. Now widely regarded in Guyana as the 'Father of the Nation', Cheddi Jagan was the son of indentured Indians and was brought up in rural poverty. Fiercely intelligent, his family scraped together enough money to send him to study dentistry in the USA so that he could escape the deprivation they had experienced. Returning to the colony, Jagan became convinced that throwing off the yoke of British colonialism was the only way to free the people from the shackles of poverty and desperate inequality. He co-founded the Political Affairs Committee (PAC) in 1946 and was elected to the Legislative Assembly, the colonial administrative body on which some were elected but others, mainly sugar company officials, were nominated. In 1950 he founded the People's Progressive Party (PPP) to push for independence.

It was enough to convince both Winston Churchill, then Leader of the Opposition, and the Truman Administration, always alert to agitation in its 'backyard', that he was a dangerous Communist with links to the Soviet Union. There was no evidence at all for this. In 1948, when the Venn Commission visited, Jagan was an extremely impressive witness, presenting a fifteen-page submission densely packed with facts and figures and persuasively argued.[26] He showed that the sugar companies owned vast tracts of land but had at least 30 per cent of the total lying idle, unwilling to turn it over to the people to farm themselves and even start their own sugar cane production. Land reform was vital to help people lift themselves out of poverty, but it was clear that the big four sugar companies were deliberately standing in the way of progress. They wanted instead a flexible and low-paid workforce to create their huge profits, which immediately went abroad rather than be reinvested to develop the country.

A new union, the GIWU, which was agitating for more pay and rights for workers, had not been recognized by employers, Jagan told the Commission, who favoured existing and supine workers' organizations. Jagan eschewed firebrand calls for social reform in his report, concentrating on the practical and the factual in a way that hugely impressed Dr Venn and Sudell.

The Venn Commission's eventual report and recommendations did reflect the desperate need for reform and some of the arguments of Jagan and others like him. But it went further, calling for huge government intervention in the colony to promote more equality, opportunity and health and educational support. It proposed that the British government grant British Guiana a subsidy of £1 for every ton of sugar produced so that sweeping social improvements could be made. The government should also take over the sugar cane industry's poorly observed responsibility for decent housing, education and health care. Four new state hospitals should be paid for by the British government, it said, as well as new schools being built on every estate. Children under fourteen years old should be at school, not at work on the estates, and the sugar companies themselves should provide canteens, showers, community centres, a crèche and – Sudell favourites – sports grounds at the plantations and factories, and playgrounds elsewhere. The report even called for the end of the use of workers to clear irrigation canals, which were often infested with alligators, and said a contributory pension scheme should be introduced by sugar cane companies. It also called for an investigation into use of dormant land owned by the companies by individual farmers and communities. Unsurprisingly it was greeted with fury by the companies themselves and in truth the government was nervous at the high cost of such social reform.

The price to be paid for not acting was further social unrest and bloodshed. Sudell's philosophy of using open space for the good of the most, not the few, was certainly evident in the final report.[27] Indeed in his 1955 presidential address he referenced his visit to

British Guiana and told members the ILA's major opportunity in the years to come would be in the colonies. He said there were forty colonies and protectorates 'all crying out for landscape architects'. Indeed, a member had recently been appointed as parks administrator in the capital, Georgetown: 'He will have an opportunity for designing tropical landscapes with a luxuriance of plant material undreamt of in this country.' But mindful of the colonialist horrors he had seen seven years earlier and careful not to suggest a horticultural imperialism, he warned that while initially British architects could lead the way, the training of local people, perhaps at universities in Britain, to continue the work was the longer-term priority.

When Sudell gave that speech he must have been aware how much of a long shot this ambition was, given his experience seven years before. Progressives of all kinds were in retreat in Britain and its colonies. With the 1940s giving way to the Cold War-dominated 1950s, disappointment and defeat were regularly replacing hope. For the people of British Guiana, Jagan, Venn and Sudell, the chance of improved living conditions and justice for all foundered on Churchillian fears of a Communist threat. After Churchill remarkably returned to power in 1951, the Venn Report was to gather dust in Whitehall. The man who coined the phrase 'Iron Curtain' was not going to stand for a 'socialist' reform of British Guiana. Indeed in 1953, after Jagan's PPP had been successful in gaining power in the first elections under universal suffrage in British Guiana, Churchill ordered the military to seize control in the country, suspended the constitution and placed Jagan under severe restrictions of movement. He was unable to leave Georgetown and spent time in prison when he tried to do so.

Despite this naked intervention in the democratic process, the PPP won two further elections in 1957 and 1961, leading Britain and the United States, via the CIA, to gerrymander future elections to keep Jagan from power. Although the country, newly named Guyana, finally gained independence in 1966, covert CIA activity around elections ensured the PPP did not gain power, with Jagan as president, until 1992. This was 39 years after he was removed from office by the British.[28] Never a diary or memoir writer, it can only be imagined how Sudell, who had given almost a year of his life to the project, felt about the failure of the Venn mission. It was another retreat along the road he had hoped would lead to social justice and fairness. Improved living conditions, whether through suburban gardens for the British poor or land to grow crops for the colonial worker, were the foundations on which all society should be built. Events in Britain in the second half of the twentieth century and the dashing of reforms in British Guiana showed Sudell how far any of this was from being realized.

11
'An important and influential figure'

In 2019, more than half a century after his death, Richard Sudell's name was cited by campaigners in a battle against the development plans of a giant U.S.-based real estate investment company. It was a fight he would have enjoyed, on the side of powerless tenants who feared losing the homes they had lived in for decades. It was also the first stirrings of a reappraisal of his reputation. By then long forgotten and hardly regarded, his work unrecorded, at the centre of the fight was one of the last remaining – and certainly the largest – of his garden works. Seemingly out of the blue in 1937 he was commissioned to design the courtyard garden of what was to be the largest block of flats in Europe: Dolphin Square in Pimlico, London. Typically, there is no surviving record to explain how he came to design such a prestigious showpiece garden in the centre of the capital, a stone's throw from the Thames. But that he did led to a decision by residents, garden historians and the pressure group The Twentieth Century Society (C20), forming as the Dolphin Square Preservation Society, to attempt to revive his reputation both as a tactic to beat the development plans but also as a recognition that the courtyard garden was a quintessential example of the landscape of the times and that Sudell was one of its foremost practitioners. Mustering a compelling case, the campaigners, including many of the elderly residents who had lived there for decades, had a major breakthrough when the public body charged by the government with preserving the historical environment, Historic England, decided to register Dolphin as a landmark of historic interest with this description: 'One of a limited number of schemes known to survive by Richard Sudell, an important and influential figure in the development of mid-C20 landscape design, and a pioneering theorist, writer, and advocate of the profession.'[1]

The decision represents a significant enhancement of Sudell's legacy and is certainly the first time an official evaluation of his contribution to interwar garden and landscape history recognizes its worth. We have seen how Sudell was often sniffily dismissed by contemporaries because of his association with suburbia, and even Historic England's intervention did not stop one proponent of the 2019 plan describing the garden as 'not really that remarkable' to this author. The courtyard garden at Dolphin Square is both the largest project on which Sudell worked and a perfect summation of the philosophy that he articulated to his neighbours on Roehampton, his colleagues at the ILA, and the millions of readers of his books, magazine and newspaper articles. The Square itself, 1,250 flats surrounding his 1.4-hectare (3.5 ac) garden and completed in 1937, is located on the busy Grosvenor Road near the Thames.

In 1990 Westminster City Council designated it a conservation area, recognizing the special position it has in the early twentieth-century social history of central London. In its appraisal the council states that Dolphin is 'a highly visible landmark on this part of the Thames' and that 'the attractive and generous landscaping in the courtyard contributes to a more informal and peaceful space, which feels sheltered from the busy routes around.'[2] This was recognition that, despite its proximity to the Houses of Parliament, Sudell designed a garden that gives residents of this densely populated development the refuge from the 'turmoil of the day' and 'exclusion from the world' he had so often stated was the chief purpose of a garden. Buffered by the high-rise, Art Deco-style blocks of flats, the noise of the city is almost non-existent. Sudell's design also skilfully allows its hundreds of residents to find solitude. The garden is striking yet also modest, as if a collection of suburban gardens. Writing in the residents' magazine *The Dolphin* in July 1937, Sudell told readers exactly what his aim was: 'In every respect the gardens are designed to make you forget they are in the centre of a great city.'³

Originally the project of New York businessman Fred French, who wanted to import the concept of serviced apartments from the United States, Dolphin Square was taken over by British builder Richard Costain when the American failed to find financial backing. There were two aspects of the scheme that would certainly have appealed to Sudell. The first was that French wanted the Square to offer high-quality homes but with rents that could be afforded by those in middle- and lower-income brackets, many of whom worked in central London's public service and clerical sectors. Second, the courtyard garden was to serve as both a symbol and practical application of Dolphin's community spirit. 'One of the largest private gardens in London', said the developers, 'is for the health and

Dolphin Square in Pimlico, London, 2018.

enjoyment of the Dolphinians.'[4] It was almost as if the philosophy Sudell supported for Roehampton had been synthesized and transferred to the banks of the Thames, and even if there were no privet hedges behind which to shelter there were plenty of spaces in the courtyard for contemplation. In 1937 the list of community facilities, of which the garden was to be the jewel, was astonishing. A gymnasium and underground swimming pool, restaurants, bars, parade of shops, beauty parlour, nursery, library, palm court, underground car park and thirty guest bedrooms were just some of the attractions. However, proving modernity only went so far in the 1930s; *The Dolphin*, while lauding the combination of separate house and communal areas, half-jokingly warned that the amenities available raised concerns that 'fortunate wives will not have enough to do. A little drudgery is good for wives, perhaps. The Dolphin lady may be spoiled.'[5]

It is not known how Sudell won the contract to create the garden, although it is thought Costain approached him directly.[6] Sudell created communal gardens that highlighted his expertise as a plantsman together with his understanding of geometric delineations, which would create different experiences and vistas depending on where the resident was situated, either in the garden or looking down from their windows. He realized that much of the gardens, surrounded by blocks of flats mostly ten storeys high, would be in deep shade for large parts of the day and yet, as he explained to residents, he created something for them to enjoy all year round: 'The planting scheme is planned to display colourful flowers in season and to give a changing panorama of colour.'[7]

In essence, the gardens are aligned north–south with three large gardens of different character and function dominating the central section. The most southerly is the main lawn, divided by an avenue of horse chestnut trees that leads to a fountain and rose garden, and finally up through a loggia to a higher-level Spanish or Mexican garden, planted because it received the most sunlight. Around the outside of the central gardens Sudell cleverly then created five pairs of smaller, more ornamental planted gardens that sit in recesses allowed by the spurs of the building. These showcase styles as diverse as Italian, Japanese, Dutch and an Old English sunken garden, which combined with the three central gardens create an astonishing complexity of sightlines and intimate spaces. Box plants clipped as birds and animals feature in the Dutch garden, clipped cypress bay in the Italian, bridges and stone lanterns in the Japanese, while crocus and snowdrop in the English section add to this variety and difference.

Sudell clearly used his skill as a suburban garden pioneer to introduce pathways, recesses, raised walls for impromptu seating and pergolas to create a sense of intimacy. In fact, Dolphin itself is largely a roof garden, the central fountain lawn built over an underground car park for three hundred cars. Air vents to the car park are disguised by trellis-work and climbing plants under the pergolas, and the higher Spanish gardens sitting over a sports club and restaurant. Along the south front of this raised garden is a copper-roofed loggia three steps above the ground-floor garden, designed by architect Gordon Reeves, with painted timber columns supporting an extended canopy. Crazy paving is, not surprisingly, evident as is brick, stone and concrete in other paved areas in different patterns and Arts and Crafts styles, which help make each garden area distinctive, yet they transition easily to the next to create a unifying feel to the whole. Additionally, low stone walls facilitate informal places to sit, with large ornamental pots placed on plinths in recesses and steps marking the journey around the garden. In its submission to Historic England, the preservation society concluded: 'These are all the essential elements of the garden, idiosyncratic of the period, and all together convey an exotic feeling relating to the different garden styles, a sense of elegance and also of fun.'[8]

Sudell himself appears to have been more than aware of the scale of the task he was taking on, and probably understood that it would be the grandest project of his career, arriving as it did relatively late in life. He was now 45, three decades on from the beginning of his horticultural career. By now he had a confidence in his garden philosophy that was easily conveyed to the new Dolphinians. All who met Sudell considered him a modest, gentle man who rarely boasted – albeit with a rod of steel running through him when it came to politics and landscape. As we know he left no record of his work. Indeed, his grandchildren had no idea he had designed the Dolphin courtyard until taken there by this author to meet campaigners and have a picnic in the courtyard. However, in 1937 he was all too certain of the importance of the work he was undertaking. He told residents that Dolphin would reinstate the importance of London's square gardens, which were recognized throughout the world but were, in many cases, being turned into 'nothing but car parks'.[9] He explained that his gardens would have consideration for children, the elderly, 'invalids' and even tradesmen, and possess planting schemes that would give colour for as long as possible throughout the year with the minimum of supervision. And, of course, it should be a restful place. Here lawns were important, Sudell referencing the opinions of unnamed psychologists that green was a colour soothing to the nerves. He explained that:

> One of the most pleasing features in any garden, private or communal, is an expanse of smooth lawn unbroken by flower beds. At Dolphin Square, the two main lawns flanking the avenue of shady, pink chestnuts, create a feeling of restfulness and quiet the minute we leave the busy Embankment.[10]

Indeed, the garden seen roadside through the three magnificent arches that announce the southern entrance looks seductively and enticingly restful, a place for a secret rendezvous perhaps. 'All bright colour is kept to the sides and background of the picture as seen from the main archways.'[11] Everywhere, insisted Sudell, was restfulness, even the planting of alpines to the sides of the paved walks: 'another example of our effort to make the garden as restful as possible without impeding its usefulness'. This was, in essence, his definition of a suburban garden transferred to a 1.4-hectare (3.5 ac) plot, or in his words, 'a modern adaptation of an old idea'. The creation of the garden, of course, was anything but restful. Over a year and a half Sudell and his team brought in 3,000 tons of soil, 6,000 turfs, 10 hundredweight of grass seed, 16 tons of fertilizer, 2,000 tons of paving and walling stone, 10,000 bulbs and 5,000 plants.

That the project was considered a success can perhaps be evidenced from the decision to replace elements of the garden like for like when seventeen bombs fell around the site, including one direct hit on the fountain garden and another on the chestnut lawn, during the Second World War.[12] Some thirty people were killed and eighty injured in these attacks. The whole effect of the garden, as we have seen, can be described as idiosyncratic with its riot of different features quelled by the serenity of the planting and the quiet spaces created. It is a style entirely in keeping with the philosophy Sudell outlined in his writings, and entirely consistent with the characteristics of a twentieth-century garden philosophy he helped to pioneer, even if his role is only now beginning to be properly recognized.

That recognition has been helped hugely by the efforts of campaigners to save Dolphin Square from the redevelopment plan. Its American owners, Westbrook Partners, planned to demolish the six-storey northern block and replace it with a ten-storey building and add one floor to the remaining ten-storey buildings. Most of the redevelopment proposals in the north were for a new hotel and short-term letting. In June 2019, against the recommendation of its officers, Westminster City Council's Planning Committee rejected the redevelopment, although at the time an appeal by Westbrook was thought likely. If the plans had been approved, the northern half of Sudell's gardens, down to the fountain garden, would have been replaced with a modern design by renowned landscape architect Todd Longstaffe-Gowan to accommodate the new building, and the rest of the garden altered. Historic England's registering of the building was not in itself enough to have stopped the development, but such a listing requires planning authorities to take material consideration of the recognition. This was enough for Westminster councillors who rejected advice to give the go-ahead, citing the importance of the garden alongside the square's location in the council's own conservation area. The committee also considered the plan contained too many short-term let apartments in a residential area.

Rather than proceed with a costly appeal and a continued fight against doughty campaigners and with the Mayor of London's office, which could have called the proposal 'in', signalling sympathy for existing residents, in 2020 Westbrook threw in the towel. The company sold the building to AXA Investment Managers for a price believed to be around £850 million. The global asset management company has embarked on an extensive, carbon-reducing upgrade focusing on interiors while leaving the essential structure of the building intact. As for the garden, it is clear AXA has got the message about the importance of the work of the 'important and influential figure' who designed it. Senior Asset Manager Roshan Ramlugun described the garden as 'amazing'. 'You only have to go out into the gardens to see the community engagement that happens on a day-to-day basis.'[13] Landscape architect Sally Prothero, who specializes in revitalizing historic landscapes, public parks and gardens, has the contract to breathe fresh life into the courtyard. Unlike the previous plan, hers will be 'to conserve the best of what remains and undertake new design that complements the garden to meet the needs of today'.[14] Providing planning permission has been given, work starts in 2024 and is finally due to finish in 2028, such is the complexity of reviving both buildings and garden. For Prothero the garden has a clear and powerful intent. She understands what Sudell was trying to do even though his garden is now in desperate need of a change of fortune, its lustre and sparkle returned, after years of neglect:

The variety of scales is obvious but clever, flexible but intimate. It is formal but with areas of fluidity. It has both drama and simplicity. You can choose your own space for whatever mood or social activity or even antisocial frame of mind you may be in. It can accommodate groups of people and single people at the same time and everyone can be 'at home' and comfortable in their space.[15]

Her work will start to the north of the courtyard with a new Moroccan/Spanish rooftop garden connected by ramps to a new terraced balcony on the northside buildings and starting to revive the inset small gardens. The years of neglect have had one positive, in that she and her team have been able to dig into the garden ruins to find what the original plans were in the absence of any Sudell drawings. For instance, it was discovered in the Japanese garden in the northeast that there had originally been a small tea hut and waterways long since filled with soil. Prothero aims to restore these features. There will be much to replant, and rogue bay trees to be removed along with others, so the garden can breathe, and many of the shrubs taken out as well as areas of repaving to be undertaken. The aim will remain that it will be a garden to be used by visitors and residents themselves. In AXA's Design and Access statement submission to Westminster City Council as part of its bid for planning approval, Prothero and fellow landscape architect Annabel Downs, who did much research to enable the garden to be listed by Historic England, speculate that the reason for the appearance of different styles of gardens from around the world might be a 'living library'.

Here they hark back to 1933's *Landscape Gardening* in which Sudell allowed guest writers to pen chapters on world gardens such as Japanese, Dutch, Italian and Spanish. Or, they submit, did Sudell bring the gardens of the world into the courtyard at a time when discord and hostility was growing throughout the world including with Spain, Japan and Italy? Did Dolphin reflect a desire for peace both throughout the world and for the residents using the gardens? They conclude:

> The garden is of national and international importance as an example of a large-scale residential garden including roof gardens, for its association with the designer Sudell and his role in the founding of the ILA, his beliefs as a conscientious objector, and his design philosophy embracing different styles and themes to create an attractive, characterful and distinctive garden of its time and place. The garden deserves to be more widely known.[16]

As for Sudell, Prothero believes he is an important figure in the story of early twentieth-century landscape history:

> His understanding that landscape design needed to respond to the process of change in what he calls the 'new social order' was important. The creation of new landscapes for people to use, as well as to appreciate their beauty. He recognizes that there is a requirement for these landscapes to provide a variety of roles in everyday life – for new institutions, for the rise of sports grounds and how they all fit together in a beautiful way. These ideals seem to have got lost along the way though.[17]

Historic England agrees with Prothero's assessment and confirms that Dolphin Square's courtyard garden is of importance to the landscape history of the time. More than eighty years earlier, Sudell himself was very clear about what he had created. In uncharacteristically ebullient tones he told readers of *The Dolphin* in October 1937: 'There will be nothing in London to equal the Square when it is completed. London's eighteenth-century squares are beautiful indeed, but Dolphin Square will surpass them all in brightness, variety and originality.'[18]

It is perhaps typical of Sudell's forgotten status in the history of twentieth-century landscape architecture that evidence of his work on the gardens fronting the new de Havilland Aircraft Company headquarters in 1933 has to be stumbled upon. Certainly, Sudell himself never referred to the commission and in the voluminous literature around Hatfield Aerodrome's pivotal role in post-First World War aviation history there is no mention of the planning or landscaping of the development. The only clue that he did indeed design the grounds is the appearance of a caption in an article in the winter 1936 edition of the Sudell-edited ILA journal *Landscape and Garden*. The article, on factory gardens, does not mention de Havilland, but a picture of the striking Art Deco frontage of the building with fountain pond is captioned: 'Gardens Designed By Richard Sudell F.I.L.A.'

Hatfield has a key place in the history of British aviation. When Captain Geoffrey de Havilland moved to its aerodrome in 1930 to establish a new headquarters and factory, his eponymous company was already a multinational business. He had designed his first plane in 1909 and in 1912 established a British altitude record of 3,200 metres (10,500 ft) flying one of his own designs. By the First World War many of his aircraft were used in combat by British and U.S. forces. He set up the de Havilland Aircraft Company Ltd in 1920. His Gipsy Moth aircraft proved particularly successful, so much so that he outgrew his Stag Lane Aerodrome base in Edgware and moved to Hatfield in 1930.[19] His two-storey headquarters building was designed and built by James M. Monro & Son of Glasgow and originally included a clubhouse, swimming pool and sports complex at the rear, none of which remains. The remaining building is Grade II listed by Historic England. Sudell's task was to complement the striking building, but rather than create sightlines that could be viewed from the offices, as he had advised his suburban readers with their homes, this small, narrow garden was to serve the boldness of the structure, to enhance its design clarity as the gaze went towards it. Sudell was to help Monro give de Havilland a 'statement of intent' headquarters reflecting its pre-eminence in a rapidly growing industry.

We have already seen that *Landscape Gardening*, published in the year Sudell began designing for de Havilland, had referenced 'the modern tendency... towards simplification... rationalization', and here he was putting it into practice, with a garden perfectly sympathetic to the architectural disciplines of Art Deco or, more accurately, its 'Streamline Moderne' derivation. Within both the ILA and the pages of *Landscape Gardening* Sudell was insistent that the aerodrome or airport be properly planned and landscaped: 'In the future visitors will receive their first impressions as much from its airports as its harbours. The present arrangements... will be inadequate.'[20] Indeed in his ILA conference speech during the Second World War, Sudell predicted an explosion of airport development catering for long-distance travel post-conflict, the increase in passengers demanding that standards of planning and design would have to be raised: 'The public will be able to see all your mistakes! They will see the landscape from a new angle, the air.'[21] While there is no written record of Sudell's work for de Havilland, it is from the air that we have testimony to the development of both building and garden.

Determined to record the establishment of the new headquarters for posterity, a series of aerial photographs, now commonplace but rare in 1933, were commissioned by the company, which showed it taking shape. What can clearly be seen is that Sudell's design was minimalist and formal in the extreme, subsuming itself to the demands of Streamline Moderne with its long, simple straight lines, rounded corners and reinforced concrete structures that were invariably kept to a disciplined white. A manicured lawn runs parallel to the frontage of the building with sporadic tree planting, mainly willow, and a row of small rectangular, evenly spaced, planting beds interrupting the turf nearest the offices. At centre stage is a fountain

Aerial view of the beginning of work on the grounds at the front of the new de Havilland headquarters at Hatfield, 1933. Sudell warned landscape architects that in future their mistakes would be seen from the air.

and lily pond, bordered by paving stone and turf, and crowned by a stone font and fish-shaped waterspout that perfectly complements the central, defining fascia and entrance to the building, the eye drawn through the water to the main doors. Indeed, how successfully it harmonizes can be seen by a ground-level, night-time picture of the building in which the neon-lit frontage reflects beautifully in the tranquillity of the lily pond. Perhaps most strikingly Sudell borders the lawns, the immediate outside of the building and pond with clipped and triangular-shaped yew, a nod to the French Baroque style of gardens such as at the Château de Vaux-le-Vicomte, which in 1953 he would describe, somewhat frugally given its majesty, as 'one of the loveliest little things in the whole of Europe'.[22]

While the de Havilland garden might be thought atypical of Sudell's 'suburban-style' – and certainly it has differences with his later and only other surviving works at Dolphin Square and the City of London Cemetery – it would be a mistake to imagine him unable or unwilling to adopt a little classicism or modernism into his gardens. As we have seen, de Havilland contained elements of both, and twenty years later at the cemetery he had planned the sort of sunken garden he so admired at Hampton Court: 'To peep through the gates on a summer day and see the tiny jet fountain in the centre gives some idea of the dignity and distinction that the Sunk Garden can add to the garden scheme.'[23]

While Sudell never strayed far from his own formal, minimalist, plantsman, suburban style, which served his philosophy and politics well, it does not follow that he was unable or unwilling to adopt or appreciate the shifting garden trends of past and present. Within the ILA Sudell had been the key advocate that landscape architecture had a role in the development of aerodromes. We have also seen his displeasure at the fact that, in 1942, the ILA ducked the issue of setting up an aerodromes committee to look at post-war development. ILA files appear to show this committee was to include members of the

Sudell's minimalist design for de Havilland drew the eye towards the new prestigious landmark building of a cutting-edge company.

London County Council, but the idea had been vetoed by the LCC's chief architect John Forshaw, who at the time was busy preparing the County of London Plan, which was to address the replanning of the capital post-war and was published in 1943. Sudell clearly felt the aerodromes that surrounded the capital should be included in the remit, sending a copy of a memo to Forshaw that spoke of the employment possibilities they would bring, the importance of research in the United States and elsewhere, and the 'need to make Aerodromes attractive and efficient'.[24] Not for the first time Sudell's ambition was thwarted. There is no record that he worked on any other such project. Today the aerodrome at Hatfield is no more and the headquarters is a police station. The garden is in a poor state, the land to the right of the building, looking towards it, lost to a car park, the yew long gone, the lawns uncut, the pond now without water, its font crumbling and its fountain defunct.

A corner of the 80-hectare (200 ac) City of London Cemetery, Manor Park – one of the largest such municipal sites in Europe – unmistakably belongs to Richard Sudell. Opened in 1853, the cemetery was designed by William Haywood, the chief engineer of the City of London Commission of Sewers, amid concern about the health risks of continued burial within individual parish churchyards. Haywood created his cemetery landscape on a grand scale, designed to awe visitors with its park-like spaces, wide avenues and woodland trees.[25] The Victorian individualistic tradition of lavish memorials and grandiose, ornate tombstones set within wide open spaces quickly gave character to the new site. Today those graves remain but the cemetery's reflection of changing social attitudes to death, and the landscape design that gave them expression, is evidenced in Sudell's memorial garden. This is a striking example of mid-twentieth-century landscape history, a series of vignettes that articulate the combination of a philosophy witnessed in his writings and evangelical zeal for suburban gardens while also referencing his previous design work, particularly Dolphin Square.

Sudell's plan for the Memorial Gardens reflects much of postwar and post-Festival of Britain design theory – egalitarian and determinedly modern. His design was characterized by its use of modern materials, extensive paving, bright colours in hard and soft landscaping, geometrical forms, economical choice of plants ... the design had close and reassuring affiliations with the domestic gardens of the mourners.[26]

Sudell was commissioned to design and build the 4-hectare (10 ac) Memorial Garden in 1953 to cater for the rising demand for cremations that followed the Second World War. Cremation had only been formally recognized and legally controlled by the passing of the Cremation Act of 1902 and even in 1953 there was residual resistance to the practice, arising from Christianity's Judaic-rooted belief in the resurrection of the body. The establishment of the Cremation Society in 1874 to push for this form of interment, together with the pressure on burial space at cemeteries, led to a gradual change of policy. The City of London built its first crematorium in 1902 but take-up was slow with only 69 cremations in the first four years out of a total of more than 4,000 body disposals a year.[27] Increasingly it was landscape that was seen as the answer to boost numbers of cremations, creating spaces of tranquillity and reflection for relatives. However, it was not until the early 1920s at the City of London Cemetery that a very small garden of remembrance was constructed near the crematorium and in 1930 a slightly larger memorial garden was created.[28]

The appointment of Sudell in 1953 was the first serious attempt to promote a coherent landscape plan to promote the service, which was by then handling 2,500 cremations a year. We have already seen that Sudell and others at the ILA saw cemeteries as one of the essential public spaces to be influenced by landscape architecture. For Sudell the importance of the development of these gardens was twofold. In a speech to a conference of the Cremation Society of Great Britain in the same year he began his work at the City of London Cemetery, he told his audience that without a full-scale switch to cremations burial sites would devour rural land in the same way New Towns were threatening to. Then he returned to a familiar concern, namely that land for food production be protected: 'We see that with cemeteries we are outstripping food, our vital heritage.'[29] As importantly, these spaces, either in churchyards or cemeteries, should be used to bring back beautiful open areas in blighted urban areas, for the use of all. Referencing his start at Manor Park, he told the audience: 'My belief is these gardens should become almost public parks where people can go, and believe me, in that part of London they do need open spaces.'[30]

Indeed, seven years later, at a symposium organized by the Society, Sudell went further, calling for the beauty of the holistic garden to take precedence over the practice of interring ashes alongside individual plant memorials, usually rose bushes. For Sudell a garden should be restful and spiritual for both mourners and the public. The integrity of the design could be protected by ceremonial scatterings of ashes and a Book of Remembrance. He told his audience: 'We haven't the space to do this dedicated plant material.'[31] It is likely many of his audience, thinking of the revenue implications, would have remained sceptical. Original Sudell design drawings for the memorial garden housed in back offices at the cemetery's management building reveal familiar tropes. On land that was a former burial ground but now lying neglected with many (what he called) 'scrubby trees', he designed a compartmentalized memorial garden with sections offering different experiences divided by straight lines. Everywhere there were geometric patterns created by paved surfacing, using York stone, gravel, brick or coloured chippings rolled in asphalt and interspersed with planting.

Most striking of these, perhaps to the point of incongruity, is a chequerboard that appears at the northern end of a straight gravel walk. As at Dolphin Square, his plantsman skills come to the fore

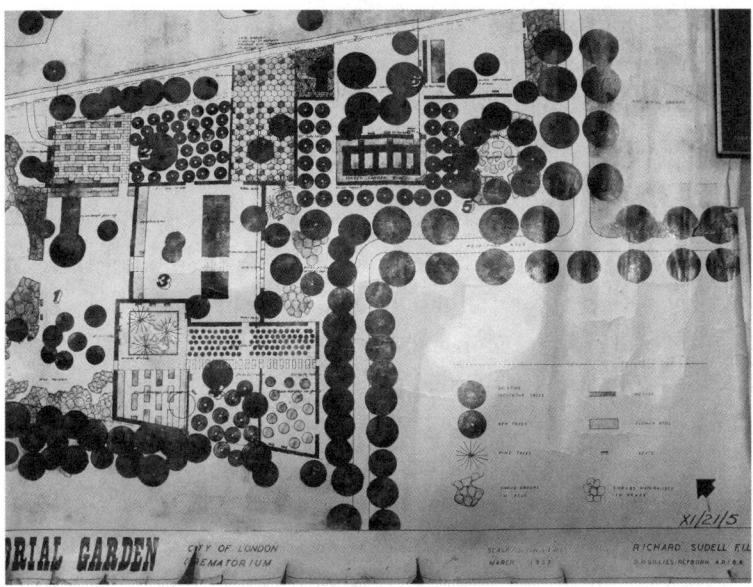

Sudell's original design drawing for the City of London Cemetery and Crematorium Memorial Garden.

with a horticultural plan to give all-year-round colour, including an informal Erica garden and enclosures of grass with scattered bulbs or shrubs such as roses and azaleas. Of course, formal beds of roses are to the fore, but he was careful to gently lead mourners to other options, planting dedicated beds of carnations, delphiniums, irises, azaleas and lilies, having warned society members in his 1953 speech that if they were not careful they would find their gardens full only of red roses, the firm favourite of the bereaved. Elsewhere he plans the removal of some trees but fits his design around others worth keeping, such as a horse chestnut he proposes to surround with bench seating. A sunken garden, beautifully cross-sectioned in the drawings, and a lily pond are also proposed. Changes of mood, tone and pace in the garden are rapid, just like many of the suburban garden plans he had drawn in his books. Mourners certainly had choice in Sudell's garden:

I have introduced a design which is a little out of the ordinary because I have broken it up into six little gardens. There I have planted, or I have indicated planting, about 5,000 dedicatable objects – plant material in the form of roses, shrubs, trees and so forth – as well as seats.[32]

The drawings show that most of Sudell's plans were implemented over the period 1953–7, although some were not executed. Possibly because of their not inconsiderable cost (for the time) of £10,000, the lily pond and the sunken garden were never started, a shelter replacing the former.

Manor Park was the biggest cemetery project Sudell undertook but it was not the only one. Cemeteries and, as we shall see, playing fields and sports grounds were to become something of a speciality for him. While other ILA contemporaries received large landmark commissions Sudell was not as successful here, but that should not be taken as evidence that his vision for landscape was entirely thwarted. Indeed, these significant pieces of land were the embodiment of his oft-repeated assertion that every corner of Britain could be beautified for the benefit of everyone. Improving publicly accessible land that all could enjoy rather than the private gardens of the rich suited his philosophy. His first commission in this field was the church of St Michael and All Angels in the picturesque Berkshire village of Highclere, near Newbury. Here he designed a rose garden as an extension to the churchyard. He told the audience at the 1953 conference that the vicar wisely decided against dedicating the garden straightaway for he knew what Sudell did not at that time: such was the success of the garden that requests for burials there came flooding in, the lure of the red rose again too hard to resist for many.

Sudell went on to advise on a garden for the innovative and naturalistic lawn cemetery Drake Memorial Park in Plymouth, something of a departure for the management. He designed a formal garden that could host both lawn interment and cremation burial. In the year of the conference, he told the audience he had worked to extend the garden of remembrance at Oxford Cemetery and mentioned similar work in Peterborough, Woking and Sunderland. At Oxford his rose garden had been a victim of its own success, growing to 1.6 hectares (4 ac) and continuing to expand, an illustration of the problem with dedication. The upside for Sudell was that in the early years, 'it has made such a beauty in town that people go to look at this garden.'[33] At both Society events, the 1953 speech and the 1960 symposium, what would have been notable to his audience – mainly crematoria managers and local authority officers – was his insistence that they needed to consider the balance between interment and burials and the beauty and spirituality of the landscapes he was creating.

For Sudell it should have been no contest; the beauty of the garden could not be sacrificed to a sea of red roses, no matter how much he personally loved them. But he was able to back up his point by suggesting alternatives grounded in an astounding knowledge of plants and flowers that he had garnered from the age of fourteen. He requested the owners of crematoria and cemeteries to think about all-year-round planting, urging them to gently suggest to mourners that they eschew roses in favour of shrubs or lilacs to mark the resting place of loved ones. Echoing his labour-saving garden philosophy, he was brilliant at identifying stunning blooms that needed little maintenance: 'The little purple daphne that blooms in the Spring [is] a dedicatable shrub that does not make a lot of waste growth. It comes into beauty and will give you 20 or 30 years of life without any trouble.'[34] As they furiously made notes, he told his audience of 'another lovely shrub, the viburnum, which is extraordinarily fragrant when in bloom. Go for the things which are easy to maintain and are permanently beautiful.'[35] His definition of beauty was, as always, a simplified one, unflashy. By way of example, during one conversation about the overuse of marble within crematoria and cemeteries,

Sudell managed to summarily dismiss what is thought of as one of the architectural marvels of the world, St Peter's Basilica in Rome, and thus reveal a puritanical Quaker sensibility: 'There is so much marble used, it was like Lyons' Corner House personified. It didn't strike me as a really beautiful place of worship. Too ornate beyond description. We must be simple and dignified.'[36] The last sentence could have equally applied to a Sudell suburban garden.

It was not just that these vital open spaces had to be at the service of mourners, giving them somewhere serene and spiritual to remember loved ones. It was also that they could be places of exploration and learning, healthy exercise for everyone – and that included children. A member of the audience at the conference recognized Sudell as a key player in the National Playing Fields Association, whose work we shall encounter shortly, and its London branch: 'I know his heart is in providing places for children to play.'[37] He had been asked about using religious spaces, particularly old churches with centuries-old tombstones, seven years earlier at the Society's conference. He harked back to the work of the Salters when answering: 'In London a great many of our little gardens – especially in the East End of London – are converted churchyards.'[38] And there was one place in London that in the early 1950s still suffered the grinding levels of poverty seen in Bermondsey, where Sudell himself helped to make a difference. This time it was just north of the river at Silvertown, a sliver of land sandwiched between the Thames and Royal Docks and dwarfed by grimy industrial factories such as the Tate & Lyle sugar refinery, the Brunner Mond munitions plant and the S. W. Silver & Co. clothing and rubber factory, from whose founder it got its name. Home to thousands of workers living cheek by jowl in terrible conditions, it was the location of one of the biggest explosions ever seen in Britain in 1917 at the munitions factory, which claimed the lives of 73 people and injured hundreds more. Its proximity to crucial British industries and ports led to persistent bomb attacks by the Germans during the Blitz of 1940. St Mark's church, sitting in the middle of Silvertown, remarkably survived, albeit with some damage, but all around was devastation.[39]

The vicar of St Mark's was a visionary parish priest, Rev. Joseph Stevens, a young man who was adored by the community. During the war he did all he could to keep spirits up including arranging for an orchestra to play a concert in the Tate & Lyle factory for workers and regularly visiting them as they made jam in the factory's air raid shelter. They in turn raffled a doll every year to raise money for the vicar's treats handed out to children at his Sunday school. When his vicarage was destroyed by the Luftwaffe in 1940, he turned the land into allotments to help feed the community. He refused to stop holding services, keeping morale up by running small evensong gatherings behind a curtained-off area in the side chapel.[40] In the early 1950s Stevens approached Sudell to help him utilize the grounds surrounding St Mark's, still effectively reduced to waste by the Luftwaffe, in a way that might help lift the spirits of his flock. Together they planned a memorial garden for the receipt of ashes from cremations, a children's playground and a garden to relax in for workforce members such as the refinery. Sudell and Stevens clearly got on very well, with the former helping the vicar to raise funds for the work. Here was a partnership with distinct echoes of both the LGG's work in the interwar years and the beautification of Bermondsey project. In his speech in 1953 Sudell told his audience with barely concealed disgust:

> You know how this industrial country of ours has been treated in the past. Industries have been dumped in districts and they have built houses between them without any thought of how people will live. That is the way in Silvertown. You have towering factories and wharves and there are still people living there.[41]

There was little difference, in other words, between communities immediately north and south of the Thames, conditions hardly changing in more than one hundred years. Sudell described Stevens as a 'very enlightened vicar who is doing jolly good work in the heart of Silvertown', who wanted to put church land to good purpose for the community. By 1953 the scheme was halfway to completion and fundraising was under way to finish the job. The few outsiders who made it to Silvertown could not help but be impressed by the pair's work. They heard the shouts of joy of children who had never had such facilities before, as they played on the brightly coloured swings and made home in the large colourful Wendy house described as 'lovely' by a woman in his 1953 audience.[42] Another member, a Dr C. White of the City of London Corporation, also commended the Silvertown project but described the district as 'dreadful'. While some of the big industrialists in the area had contributed, finance was still a problem and large areas surrounding the church, particularly where the rectory stood, were feet high in thistles. Dr White questioned how churches everywhere would be able to find the funds to build their own memorial gardens, let alone gardens for rest or play. Perhaps frustrated that the Silvertown companies had hardly shown largesse despite the mainly grim conditions they asked workers to put up with in their factories, Sudell's answer was terse. More efforts to raise funds from businesses in the area concerned would have to be made and charges for the dedications of the roses could make up the rest, he said. Willingness to make it happen would ensure it was so. Sudell appeared to have little time for negativity, particularly from someone representing one of the richest square miles in the world.

The next fifty years would see a different kind of future for Silvertown emerge as the docks declined and slum clearances made way for the siting of new factories and hundreds of new apartments. Unaffordable to local residents, a migration of the existing population began into other parts of Newham and further afield to Essex. Today almost £4 billion is being spent to revive the now much-desired riverside location for those who can afford it. A toll tunnel is being constructed under the Thames to link the area to Greenwich on the south bank. Silvertown is also the site of the City of London Airport, with high-class private jets taking executives on trips around the world. As the island strip was depopulated, industrial units and storage depots serving the airport took over. St Mark's itself was decommissioned in 1974 and is now home to the Brick Lane Music Hall. There is no trace of the gardens Sudell and Stevens created, with car parks for heavy goods lorries and industrial vehicles almost surrounding the building. What was important for Sudell was that cemetery gardens were designed as fitting tributes to the dead but, perhaps even more importantly, they were also one small step towards the realization of his lifetime landscape philosophy: 'We have here a fulcrum to bring into being a new beauty in our towns, cities and villages.'[43]

12
The Importance of Play

A journey from the East End to Southend in Essex would perhaps not be everybody's idea of a landscape magical mystery tour, although on the train from Fenchurch Street Station you would certainly pass close to the Becontree estate. You might choose to start out at the long defunct Beckton Gas Works at Barking Creek, near the Thames, once the largest gas works in Europe employing 4,500 people. Its one remaining spoil heap (collectively they were nicknamed the Beckton Alps) is still reckoned to be one of the highest artificial hills in London. The site is now a crisscross of roads and ruins. Heading north you could pass the Leigh Road Sports Ground on the North Circular Road in East Ham. Its redundant gas holder, surrounded by weed and thistle, reaches rustily to the sky and netless goalposts have long since ceased to be the backdrop for Sunday morning shouts for the referee to 'get a grip'. It speaks to a different era, one in which paternalistic companies built sports grounds for their staff to improve health, well-being and, of course, productivity. On the way to Southend more gas holders – some still used as safety valves to avoid too much pressure in pipes, but most now redundant – dot the landscape. All these sites were once owned by the North Thames Gas Board, formed through the nationalization of the industry in 1949 and dissolved when the company became part of the British Gas Corporation in 1972.

There is no archive of Sudell's work to which we can refer. His family believe all his papers were thrown out after his death since, while they remember a kindly, attentive grandfather, they could not possibly have thought that his work might be worth preserving for landscape history posterity. It was not a fate that awaited the files of Jellicoe, Colvin, Crowe and others, recognized as brilliant by their peers at the time. Much of their documented work and correspondence sits in the Landscape Institute archive held at the Museum of English Rural Life at the University of Reading. Sudell's file is confined to letters he wrote to the ILA and that were clearly filed by secretarial staff. We are left to piece together evidence from the clues he and others left behind. In truth, much of Sudell's landscape work could be considered mundane, evidence perhaps of a reputation that did not match those peers but also reflecting the need to win contracts to keep the business afloat. A remark sometimes heard in Sudell's office in the 1960s was 'Jellicoe's won another one', as the team was told they had lost out in another contract-bidding beauty contest.[1]

This brings us to the gas works. Sometime in the early 1950s Sudell's company won a contract with the North Thames Gas Board to design land around its works and gasholders. According to David Lee, who was a young partner in Sudell's company in the late 1960s, municipal and industrial contracts were food and drink for the company, the contract with the gas board one of them.[2] Lee could not be sure of the exact details but it is likely, given Sudell's subsequent success in sports pavilion and ground design – in 1957 he was co-author of the book *Sports Buildings and Playing Fields* – that this branch of his business started with modest efforts like the Leigh Road Sports Ground. We know he was giving speeches towards the end of his life about how the landscaping of spoil heaps could bring industrial areas back to life. Did he have experience of this with the Beckton Alps, which in the late 1980s became a dry ski slope for a while? We cannot be sure but it is certain those gas holders on the way to Southend bear the stamp of Sudell's grassroots philosophy that 'anything open to the air' should be properly landscaped to build a new Britain. Why should this not include the contoured grass slopes and planting schemes surrounding the iron monoliths of Essex?

As at Leigh Road, other ghosts of a vanished time, scenes of dereliction elsewhere in London, tell a forlorn story of a failed attempt at the reimagining of Britain but, in their ruin, speak powerfully of a lost history. It is doubtful motorists thundering past the waste land adjacent to the A1 at Stirling Corner, Barnet, directly northwest across the capital from Leigh Road, would be aware that within its 12 hectares (30 ac) lie the remnants of an award-winning sports pavilion and grounds designed by Sudell and his partner at the time, D. Tennyson Waters. The Modern Movement building was good enough to be photographed by the Royal Institute of British Architects as an example of excellence of the era.[3] The company name had changed to Sudell and Waters to reflect the latter's contribution as a cutting-edge architect in winning contracts. Now a shell of a building with no trace of the surrounding running track (except for a hollow dip to the south), sports fields, tennis courts, bowling green and caretaker's house, the Finsbury War Memorial Sports Centre is buried beneath brambles, a now not so blank canvas for offtrack graffiti artists. Like many opened in the era, it was funded by public subscription and donations as a fitting remembrance to those who had died in the First and Second World Wars.

A committee led by the chairman of the National Playing Fields Association (NPFA), Lord Luke, was established to raise the £70,000 needed for design and construction, with £10,000 of the sum donated by the Albany Club of Piccadilly, London, a private members establishment connected to one of the most prestigious blocks of flats in the capital and a bachelor refuge for prime ministers, actors and poets, including Gladstone and Byron. Finsbury was built in 1954–5 to replace a more modest playing ground. In many ways it represented a new and surprising direction for Sudell. As his practice

Sports pavilion for the Finsbury War Memorial Sports Centre, Barnet, London. D. Tennyson Waters designed the building while Sudell landscaped the sports fields.

expanded, he moved beyond pure landscape design and brought in architects, many of them like Tennyson Waters influenced by the Modern Movement, Le Corbusier and Frank Lloyd Wright, to complete holistic projects that involved both buildings and land. The 1950s and '60s were a time of rapid expansion, of towns, cities, businesses and industry, driven by the birth of consumer culture. One way to respond architecturally to this growth – to meet the demand – was to create utilitarian structures whose form and function reflected both the aesthetic and practicalities, including cheaper and more efficient construction, of the time. For industrial and municipal buildings, as well as housing, the Modern Movement's time had briefly come and was welcomed, except perhaps by those living in the latter. For Sudell the explosion of both municipal and commercial sports facilities was a rich new vein of landscape anthracite to mine. As mentioned, this was a time of large-scale industrial employers who took their social responsibilities seriously, at least for a while.

Almost all accepted the need to cater for the social and physical recreation of their employees. Social clubs and sports fields proliferated, and works teams playing football and cricket featured in local leagues in every town and city. As his business expanded, Sudell's skill at nurturing young talent came to the fore. First with Tennyson Waters and later with Michael Dixey, another award-winning Le Corbusier-influenced architect, the business began to win the odd showpiece contract alongside the municipal and corporation small-scale landscaping and private garden work.

Finsbury was a magnificent spectacle. Tennyson Waters's simple and functional glass and white concrete pavilion, gleaming like a giant harmonica, sat perfectly on a stage set by Sudell's 15-hectare (38 ac) grass landscape, all contours of the existing land and dotted oak trees, sweeping up to its front terrace, looking over an immaculate cricket pitch, from which the batting side could wait their turn at the crease.[4] A headline, 'Real Sizzler', accompanied a picture of the Duke of Edinburgh, who in 1948 had become president of the NPFA, in a sharp suit bowling a cricket ball on the strip as he officially opened the grounds in early May 1955. The facilities were open for all to use and were tremendously popular. Thirty years later, with spending cuts to the fore, its owners, the Metropolitan Police, could no longer afford to run the facilities – others had come to rival what is, thanks to the A1, a difficult site to access – and the land was sold. Various plans, including the possibility of Barnet FC building a new football ground on the site, have since come to nothing and the place, once a symbol of new endeavour and optimism, has been reclaimed by the wilderness, the constant hum of nearby traffic all that disturbs the peace.

Despite often losing out to Jellicoe and others the company, based both at Durford and in Georgian terrace offices at Guildford Place, Holborn, did begin to win some sizeable contracts, with Dixey and Tennyson Waters designing the buildings and Sudell planning the overall sites, using his talent for practical application to work out drainage, levelling, excavation, fertilizing, seed sowing, top- and subsoil work and planting. The sports business was fertile ground. Probably sometime in between the Leigh Road and Finsbury projects, Sudell and Waters had teamed up to design the pavilion and sports grounds at the giant EMI Factories Ltd plant in Hayes, Middlesex, which produced all the vinyl for its record labels as well as defence electronics, and employed 22,000 people at its peak. Again, reflecting the times, EMI had a vibrant social and sports club for its staff. Sudell and Waters built a small pavilion with five football and hockey pitches and an artificial cricket square (unusual for the time), bowling green and long jump pit. Bordering the Grand Union Canal and situated at the edge of the busy factory, they used hedges and trees, especially holly and yew, to create a definable and separate space for workers to enjoy their leisure time without the bosses watching over them from the fifth floor next door. Even at factory sports grounds, privacy and relief from the turmoil of the working day were important: 'On a very hot summer's day it is extremely enjoyable to watch a cricket match from the ease of a deckchair beneath a shady tree.'[5] Vinyl production moved from the site in the 1970s. Although other production limped on, in 2000 the site, renamed the Old Vinyl Factory, was acquired for flats, retail and leisure and is still under development. There is now no trace of the sports pavilion and grounds.

The company did not always start from scratch. A notable development, another sports ground, involved an extension to existing facilities and the conversion of a large house into a pavilion at Bignores estate, Dartford, Kent, in the late 1950s. The commissioning company was J. & E. Hall Ltd, which started as a one-man workshop in the town in 1785 and grew to become one of the world's most successful specialist refrigeration engineering companies. The ivy-clad house had been the home of a successful Kentish family of French Huguenot stock, the Pigous, who made their money in the gunpowder industry. It was bought by Hall when the Pigou bloodline ran out and the house began to run into disrepair. Sudell and his team were tasked with extending the small sports centre into the large garden of Bignores and converting the house into a sports and social pavilion:

> By removing an avenue of nondescript pine trees it is possible to provide an additional football pitch with a new cricket square near to the house. Tennis courts and a miniature golf course... are sited to harmonize with the existing landscape pattern and are related to the development of the clubhouse.[6]

By the early 2000s the company had ceased to use the site for sports. The land was sold and the house demolished to make way for the Princes Park stadium of Dartford Football Club. When Michael Dixey joined Sudell and Walters in 1958, as a young trainee architect not long out of National Service in the Far East, the first job he had was to supervise the construction of the Private Banks Sports Pavilion and Grounds in Catford. Waters had designed a pavilion straight out of the Lloyd Wright playbook, while Sudell as usual busied himself landscaping the sports field. Private Banks was a leisure centre for workers of London banks, including Coutts.

The pavilion was a striking modernist building with a wide concrete staircase reaching up to a spacious overhanging terrace, which again looked over the cricket pitch. It was modest yet bold, a striking statement that such facilities could be both utilitarian and eye-catching.[7] The sports ground is now owned by independent school St Dunstan's College. The pavilion has been much altered, with the wide confident balcony largely gone and the staircase replaced. The importance in this period of Sudell's links with the NPFA cannot be overstated. His practice was almost entirely reliant upon it for work, as at Private Banks where the charity would have effectively acted as a consultant on the project. The NPFA had a huge influence over the fundraising for and design of playing fields and playgrounds throughout the country, and later in the Commonwealth. Sudell's success in adding his name to the preferred suppliers list, through his role at the ILA, ensured a steady stream of work. The NPFA was established as a charity in 1925 at a meeting at the Royal Albert Hall, London, hosted by the then Duke of York, who would go on to become King George VI. Like other interwar movements it was formed to meet the challenge of creating a healthier population through open space and exercise. Supported by then Minister of Health and future prime minister Neville Chamberlain, its aim was to secure sufficient playing fields and playgrounds for the population and to save some open spaces within congested towns and cities for the purpose. For Chamberlain and others the poor state of health revealed among the soldiers of the First World War was a wake-up call.

> It seems to me that the National Playing Fields Association has come into existence at an extraordinarily opportune moment, when the country is beginning to realize the crying need for playgrounds, and when it is not too late to repair at any rate some of the errors of the past.[8]

The association estimated that up to 4 million young boys and girls had no access to playing fields, playgrounds or organized games in the interwar years. In 1932 King George V granted the association a Royal Charter, which imbued it with huge influence and power. His son George VI became patron of the association after his coronation in 1937, strengthening its hand considerably, and this role passed to Queen Elizabeth II on her father's death. HRH the Duke of Edinburgh became president in 1948 and continued for 64 years. On the death of George V, a foundation was established to buy open spaces to be called King George V Playfields: 471 of these were in existence by 1965, managed by the association. After the Second World War the association's focus was placed on play. During the 1950s the association's Children's Playground Committee ensured it maintained a record of helping to bring a playground into existence almost every other day for six years in a row (1952–8), by making grants in aid of their layout.[9] Sudell undoubtedly benefited from this as did Marjory Allen. Importantly the NPFA produced guidelines on how sports pavilions and grounds should be laid out, with minimum standards for facilities and equipment. Michael Dixey himself eventually wrote one of these, *Local Recreation Centres: A Research Study*, in 1974.

After Private Banks the company, now called Sudell and Partners after the departure of Waters, designed and landscaped Old Dean Common Pavilion and Sports Ground for Frimley and Camberley Urban District Council and a smaller pavilion for the same authority at Frimley Green. The Enfield Rolling Mills sports pavilion and ground in north London was another contract that Sudell and Dixey worked on in the early 1960s. None of these works remains. So it is that Sudell's work largely disappears from view, hanging on in scraps here and there and only really intact at Dolphin Square and the City of London Cemetery. The factory sports grounds that gave him a brief taste of recognition from contemporaries fell out of fashion as economic downturns arrived and industrial behemoths involved in full-scale production needing hundreds and even thousands of workers began to crumble under the pressure of global competition. They took with them an ethos that companies had a duty to provide for the social welfare and leisure opportunities of staff and could benefit from loyalty in return.

In addition, the squeeze on local government finance in the late 1960s and into the '70s also saw large-scale innovative sports and recreation centre work for municipalities dry up. However, in 1966, just two years before his death, Sudell did work on another project that survives to this day and, thanks to Michael Dixey, rivals that of more prestigious companies and architects. Sudell and Partners designed the Merton College sports pavilion and grounds in Oxford. Given the earlier backdrop of debate that coincided with Sudell's pioneering suburban garden work in the 1920s and '30s, it might again be thought ironic that Dixey, like Tennyson Waters, was another disciple of Le Corbusier with particular interest in concrete finishes to his buildings. The pavilion's modernist clear-lined look was widely praised. In 1969 the *Architects' Journal* compared its 'prestigious nature' favourably with other sports centres in the country and suggested that other sponsors of such facilities in Britain should use it as an example of how standards should rise to meet increasing leisure time demands of users, as was happening in the USA. Once again the building, with its uncompromising lines and sharp angles, stands confident, all blazing white concrete and reflective glass among Sudell's perfectly contoured landscape framed with a striking selection of oaks, yews and cypress extending the existing grounds.

According to Historic England the pavilion 'stands out from most contemporary sports facilities for the quality materials and particular attention to detail expended on it'.[10] The public body charged with preserving the country's historic environment points out that Merton stands close to Danish architectural functionalist and furniture designer Arne Jacobsen's Grade I listed St Catherine's College, which was being built at the time. It thus needed to reflect the general character and rhythm of the new college's buildings. According to Dixey, Merton had looked at a possible design for the pavilion by Jacobsen and had dismissed it. The college managers saw Dixey's much more modest design for Old Dean Common Pavilion and preferred it, awarding Sudell the contract. Dixey explains: 'I went away on holiday to Yugoslavia and stayed in a very modern hotel with a huge balcony running along the front which was really quite striking and bold ... that gave me the idea for Merton College.'[11] Historic England notes the concrete boardmarking at Merton is 'precisely executed, and all the materials – concrete, grey brick and timber fittings – are carefully chosen'. It describes Sudell as a specialist in sports fields. 'Rather than standing alone, the pavilion has its own informal landscape of birch trees and boulders, again a reflection of Scandinavian influence and similarly pioneered in Oxford at St Catherine's.'[12] Still working at the age of 74, with sixty years of horticultural expertise behind him, Sudell's incredible attention to detail and practical application remained in evidence as he employed landscaping, drainage, fencing, soil quality and grass seeding to help incorporate the pavilion within existing sports grounds. The pavilion building is Grade II listed by Historic England. Architect Peter Collymore, most famous for redeveloping Benjamin Britten's Red House at Aldeburgh, revisited Merton for the *Architects' Journal* in 1974, considering it one of the best in the country: 'This was no conventional pavilion. It was rather a grand affair.'[13]

Despite the exclusive air of Merton in the 1960s and '70s, the University of Oxford was not home to a classless meritocracy. At the heart of Sudell's work was a philosophical thread that still stretched back to the interwar period. In his seventies his contention that landscape architecture should seize any chance it could to reimagine Britain was still felt keenly despite the obvious dashing of the postwar dream that there could be an overarching nationwide contribution to be made. However, the work on sports pavilions and playing fields also reflected his belief that open space and health-giving activity should be accessible for everyone, especially the poor. Here the call of the Salters echoed down the years. Sudell's experience of the joyous churchyard playgrounds of Bermondsey undoubtedly helped forge a lifelong interest in providing children space to enjoy themselves. Sudell was a long-time member of the NPFA and, when president of the ILA in 1955, had asked to be added to its list of preferred suppliers. He told the ILA secretary to put his name forward: 'I have been responsible for quite a number of playing fields before and after the war.'[14]

Perhaps as influential as the Salters in promoting the health of children in the early twentieth century was Sudell's friend Marjory Allen, Baroness Allen of Hurtwood, whose lifetime in the field was unsurpassed. After the death in 1939 of her husband Clifford, who as we know never recovered from his incarceration during the First World War, Lady Allen, one of the founder members with Sudell of the ILA, threw herself into work for underprivileged children. She was one of the movers behind the 1948 Children's Act, which created the first comprehensive child welfare service, placing an onus on local authorities to take into care anyone without parents or whose parents could not provide for their offspring. Her socialist roots led her to believe that early intervention and education for all children could improve their life chances and in 1942 she became president of the Nursery School Association of Great Britain. Extremely doughty, with a mischievous side, she told *The Times* in 1968, 'I'm not sure that I'm particularly fond of children but I hate injustice.'[15]

In the area of play she was a pioneer, constantly urging governments and local authorities to provide facilities, especially in high-rise inner-city areas where children often had no open-air space at all, and writing books about how they should be constructed. Primarily she recognized that children loved play activities that were, in her words, 'delightfully messy', but which made planners, 'mostly tidy-minded', unhappy. Setting about changing this mindset she coined the term 'adventure playground' to describe areas of waste or junk where children's imaginations could run wild. Even though she argued that paid supervisors should be employed at some of these places, some of her ideas for what children might get up to within them might result in a bout of the vapours for today's health and safety inspectorate. In a letter to *The Times* in 1952, she wrote:

> Municipal playgrounds are often as bleak as barrack squares and just as boring. You are not allowed to build a fire, you would head straight for juvenile court if you started to dig the expensive asphalt to make a cave, there are no bricks or planks to build a house, no workshops for carpentry, mechanical work, painting or modelling and of course, no trees to climb.[16]

Sudell was obviously inspired by his friend, taking up cudgels for such play in old derelict land, even unreclaimed Second World War bomb sites. 'The sort of area needed is one where there are old bricks, pipes, wood and iron sheets, old dugouts, caves and preferably also a water supply. The idea is that children will . . . gradually learn the best way . . . to make something out of nothing.'[17] Fresh air, activity, creativity and practical application, and even a sense of risk, were important.

Of course there was space for more orthodox play too. Sudell designed a playground and garden in the corner of Hainault sports ground in Essex that included swings, see-saw and carousels, miniature golf, paddling pools and a maze of shrubs in which youngsters could lose themselves, all situated around a large boating pool. However, it did have a stationary old disused school bus for them to clamber around in, just in case anyone thought it was too risk-free.[18] At Finsbury War Memorial Sports Ground he created a small space for a playground using the natural slope to create a very steep

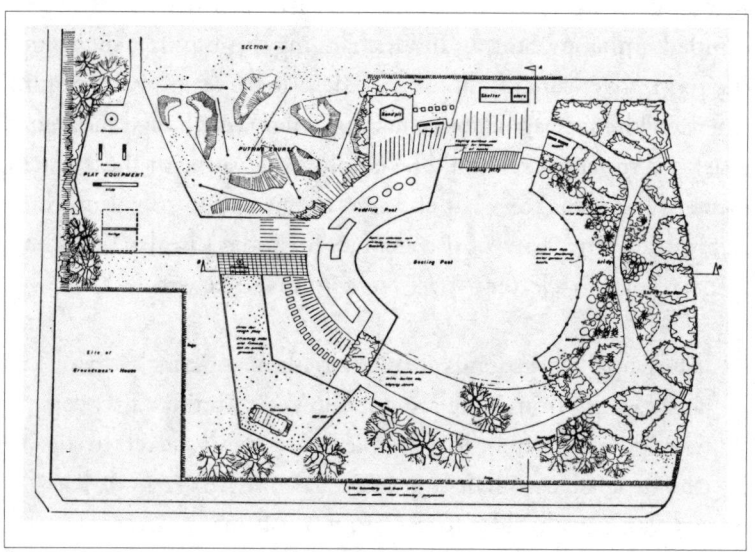

Sudell's drawing for a playground at Hainault sports ground in Essex; the disused bus for children to play in is at the bottom.

slide, which no doubt gave parents a moment's trepidation as their offspring sped down it. It too had a disused school bus on which to play. Children always had a place in the landscape for Sudell, both in the garden and playing field. That thinking seems also to have influenced another successful landscape architect renowned for her housing estate work, Mary Mitchell.

Mitchell, who died in 1988, is slowly gaining recognition as one of the foremost designers of children's play areas influenced undoubtedly by Marjory Allen and Richard Sudell. Born in Wiltshire, Mitchell became articled to Sudell's practice just before the outbreak of the Second World War after brief training at the RHS Wisley and the Royal Botanic Garden in Edinburgh. Sudell loved encouraging young people and Mitchell was no exception. After the war she left Sudell fired by his vision of what could be achieved by the landscape architect and, after returning for more studies in landscape design and architecture, had spells working in South Africa and Europe. She returned to Britain to become landscape architect for Stevenage New Town Corporation and then became the first such professional employed by Birmingham City Council. There, and in later private practice, she earned a reputation for the innovation of her children's playground design. In their book *Landscape by Design*, Tony Aldous and Brian Clouston observe that 'few consultants have made more of an impact on the profession and its clients' thinking in a particular area of landscape design than Mary Mitchell in the field of children's playgrounds.'[19] The value of this kind of landscape – and the way architects like Mitchell, Allen and Sudell studied and observed how children interacted with it – is only recently being appreciated as the installations themselves are often undiscovered and even thoughtlessly dismantled.

During the pandemic lockdown in 2020 the removal of seven slides from a pioneering Mitchell play area in Workington, Cumbria, prompted the Twentieth Century Society (C20) to step in to attempt to safeguard it, submitting the landscape for entry onto Historic

England's Historic Parks and Gardens register. Dr Luca Csepely-Knorr, Reader in Architecture at the Manchester School of Architecture, told the campaign group: 'Landscapes of housing estates were key in creating a more equal distribution of green space in the post-war period, and children's play areas were a crucial part of them. Mitchell's design in Workington is a masterpiece from this period.'[20] Mitchell's work on another playground project, Camp Hill in Nuneaton in 1966, featured prominently in Marjory Allen's book *Planning for Play*, a bible for creating rumbustious environments for inquisitive children that is largely forgotten today. What was equally important was that as the modernists held sway in the 1950s, working with municipalities to build dense high-rise blocks in inner-city areas, landscape artists, as we have seen largely locked out of any partnership with project architects, could at least leaven the unremitting uniformity of the environment.

The crowded, cacophonous living conditions the planners and architects imposed on the largely working-class population could be somewhat mitigated by beautifully designed and enticing play areas for the young in any pocket of spare land the landscape architect could grab. Mitchell's work in Birmingham is a classic of this kind. Taking her cue from work she had seen in Zurich, Mitchell helped the City Council develop proposals that insisted toddler play areas had to be provided for all blocks of flats over four storeys high, and that these had to be in place before tenants moved in so that the young could quickly settle into their new and alien environment. As the council's first in-house landscape architect she was able to be in at the start of projects to insist on some open space for leisure, unlike many other schemes at the time, particularly in London, even if they were often tiny. Her play areas were able to use existing natural features, identified before construction began, to maintain grass, slopes, and trees for light and shade, creating intimacy and some eye-line escape from the towering blocks all around, while screening from the traffic noise and dust that was frequently pervasive:

Imagination in this context means more than the quality required by an architect on the drawing board, but a positive act of design aimed specially to stimulate the child's imagination. The need is to cater for developing the child's body and mind and give facilities for climbing, swinging, sliding, balancing, roller skating and street games.[21]

The commitment of Allen, Mitchell and Sudell to the development of inner-city children's play areas in the 1950 and '60s has a direct lineage to the interwar campaigns to relieve grinding poverty by providing open space, gardens, allotments, slides and swings for the majority. This is the bloodline so often forgotten by critics of suburbia, for there was never a distinction to be drawn between the churchyard slide at St James's, Bermondsey, and the neatly trimmed privet hedge of the aspiring middle classes of Metro-land. Ridiculing the latter would be to misunderstand the powerful, perhaps even primeval, pull that the canopy of open space, colour, scent, weather and seasonal rhythm had on people in Britain, across all economic classes, in the first half of the twentieth century despite the often dire economic circumstances of the times. Any understanding of the period cannot be complete without knowledge of its landscape history. A small steel slide on a hillock dwarfed by a 15-storey inner-city Birmingham tower block plays a part in the story too.

Evidence of Sudell's encouragement of young talent like Mitchell into landscape architecture and a tireless devotion to the need for the garden or landscape to serve the needs of all can perhaps best be summed up by the description of him in an obituary carried in the *Journal of the Kew Guild*, a magazine for alumni. An unnamed colleague who worked with him was quoted thus:

> He had many trainees learning and practising in his office from various parts of the world, and he was continuously encouraging the future landscape architects. He often

arranged tree planting schemes for children in new public parks. Richard was a great lover of flowers and generally sported a rose buttonhole and always had flowers in his offices. He was a born optimist and was always eager to experiment and to spend money on new projects. During his last year he was trying out prototypes of new ideas of playing equipment designed by his assistant. On his staff he had architects who specialized in sports centres and pavilions. He was a great believer in roof gardens and the creation of gardens in difficult situations.

The *Journal* ended its article by adding, 'Like so many Kewites, Sudell was a great and successful pioneer.'[22]

Another young talent who came to work with Sudell at the start of his career was Russell Page, who went on to have a glittering career partnering with Jellicoe and individually designed gardens all over Europe and America. He conceived the Grand Vista at the 1951 Festival of Britain Pleasure Grounds at Battersea Park and gathered an impressive array of clients including the Duke of Windsor, King Leopold III of Belgium, and food and beverage giant PepsiCo, for whom he designed sweeping gardens at its New York headquarters. In his autobiography *Education of a Gardener*, Page described how the start of his career was a struggle but that his next job was 'nearer the mark'. 'I found a very subordinate job in a landscape architect's office, designing plantings for the endless new blocks of cheap flats then being built in the London suburbs.'[23] This was Sudell's small but growing practice in the early 1930s. By now one might not be surprised by the dismissal of the type of work nor the fact that Sudell is not mentioned by name.

Another such young talent was David Lee, who confirms: 'Sudell was an unassuming, modest man who never pushed himself. He never forgot he was a gardener. As for work he went after anything and everything he could get.'[24] Geoffrey and Susan Jellicoe have stated that Sudell had an 'extensive overseas practice' and in his ILA membership files he did list a private garden in Bhutan, fertile territory for the hunters of exotic plants at the time, as a principal work, but Dixey and Lee insist the number of contracts undertaken abroad was overstated.

Sudell was, though, on his way to Pakistan, still trying to pitch for employment at the age of 76, when he died suddenly of a stroke in Kuwait on 19 November 1968.[25] After Pakistan, Sudell and Ida were planning to make their first visit to Australia to see middle daughter Dorothy in her new home for Christmas. Dorothy had even made up their beds when the news of the death of her father came through. Ida had to fly the body of her husband of the last 38 years back to England for cremation. 'My mother came out on her own at the end of January, but she only stayed for about three weeks. It was too soon after Dad's death and she was keen to get back home.'[26] In his ILA membership files Sudell lists Dolphin Square and the Bhutan garden, alongside a memorial park in Bath and an allotment park in Sunderland, as his principal projects, although, typically, there is no detailed record of his involvement in the latter two, nor evidence now of their existence.

Clues about any of his private practice work, either in the early days on Roehampton, in London or latterly in Surrey, are hard to find. But one garden can be traced, that of one of the early twentieth-century newspaper barons who, unlike others such as Beaverbrook and Harmsworth, is little remembered. Julius Elias was born into a family of Polish Jews whose father, after initial business success, established himself as a newsagent and confectioner in Hammersmith, London. Young Julius delivered the newspapers. Leaving school at the age of thirteen he eventually took a lowly office job with Odhams, a small printing firm. Even after his father's fortunes rose again, affording a relatively comfortable lifestyle, Elias remained with Odhams working his way up to become managing director and chairman of the company which significantly expanded under his leadership. He renamed it as Odhams Press Ltd when it took over the *John Bull* newspaper. Surfing the rising tide of newspaper circulation, the company founded the *Sunday People*, with a circulation of 2 million, and in 1929 took over the *Daily Herald*, the only pro-Labour national daily newspaper.[27]

Sudell joined the *Daily Herald* as gardening editor as soon as Odhams took over ownership from the TUC. He was already holding a similar position at the company's *Ideal Home* magazine, an innovative project launched in 1919 to serve an explosion of new interest in home and garden improvement sparked by the building of the new suburbs. Clearly Elias would have known Sudell and equally regarded him highly as a horticultural and garden design expert. In 1925 he and his wife, Alice, moved to a salubrious address, Southwood Court, Southwood Lane in Highgate, London. In 1937 he was ennobled as Baron Southwood of Fernhurst and was created 1st Viscount Southwood in 1946. Although they had no children themselves, the 1939 census has the couple, a cook, lady's maid, a chauffeur, his wife, their three sons and a daughter living at Southwood.[28]

At some time before the outbreak of the Second World War Elias, perhaps inspired by his gardening editor, bought the adjacent property and demolished it so he could expand his own land. The obvious person to ask to redesign the garden was Sudell, and his journalist set about the work with gusto, convincing his boss that a grandiose rock garden would be a fitting showpiece for the extra land. Sudell was an avid hill and rock climber, often accompanying Ida to her native Alps and regularly advising his readers to create small rockeries in their own gardens festooned with low-maintenance alpines. The finished plan was reported in the American journal *Landscape Architecture Magazine* in a feature that focused on a British exhibition of landscape architecture that took place in the Cotswold village of Broadway in June 1938. The exhibition was organized by the ILA, the first it had ever put on. According to the programme notes written by the then president, Dr Thomas Adams, the exhibition was focused on the aspect of its work that 'has the broadest and most intimate applications in relation to domestic life and architecture'. One of the ILA's key principles, he wrote, was 'affording a guiding and refining influence on the layout and planting of domestic gardens in towns and villages'.[29] Gardener Sudell would likely have welcomed the emphasis. Like Jellicoe he was concerned that the ILA should not move away from promoting good gardens, no matter how small, despite increasing numbers of his fellows now focusing on bigger ideals. For Sudell the beautification of Britain still had to come inch by hard-dug inch and everyone, amateur gardener included, had a part to play. The picturesque village of Broadway had been chosen for its 'unique charm'.

Among those whose work was exhibited were Christopher Tunnard with his formal gardens around a modernist house in Surrey, George Dillistone's update at historic Cannizaro House in Wimbledon, especially its woodland walks, and Sudell's undertaking for Elias at Southwood Court. According to the magazine article: 'A plan was prepared which took advantage of the old cellars to form a rock and water garden. Every fine tree was preserved and worked into the design.' The result was certainly epic and far removed from the tiny examples, sometimes adorned by fishing gnomes, that were inspired by Sudell in suburbia. Stretching back to a skyline of fir trees, the depth of the rock crevicing was remarkable, reaching into the foundations of the demolished house, with clear water trickling down to a pool, and mature alpines situated in every crack. The Alps had indeed come to Highgate. Compared to Tunnard's elegant modern enclosures and Dillistone's mellow rural walks it is not difficult to see why Sudell's work might sometimes have attracted sniffy condescension. Southwood Court's rockery is a jumble of angles compared to the smooth linear or curving lines of the other examples, an unlikely eruption of stone in the heart of leafy Highgate, even if you accept the district's own hills are created by the uplift of sandstone sitting above London Clay. One thing is for sure, though: Julius and

Alice and the extended family of servants would certainly have been transported to other lands, away from the turmoil of the capital, when sitting amid the scent of saxifrages and listening to the gently flowing water in Sudell's garden. Despite its apparent immutability there is no evidence of the rock garden in Southwood Lane today.

Residents of one block of flats in Richmond that Sudell and Partners designed, however, are trying to restore something of his legacy. Richmond Towers and Court on Lower Mortlake Road was another private development in which Dixey took the lead in the early 1960s. The development consisted of one ten-storey tower block, which even had a three-bedroomed studio apartment, and three smaller three-storey blocks surrounding. This was a very rare project for Sudell by this time – Dixey winning the architectural contract and his boss playing a supporting role; nevertheless his influence on the amount of outdoor space was clear. In total there were 72 flats or maisonettes for sale, but what was also noticeable was the spacious landscaping with trees, large lawns and gardens and play areas initially designed in. As the website for residents explains today: 'We are very lucky to have spacious gardens for everyone to use and enjoy. There is plenty of space for children to play, and for residents to sit outside in the summer.'[30] The land now consists of lawns, hedges and trees, with the play area and sandpit now shrubbery. Some parts have become overgrown, leading residents to begin a project attempting a restoration of the landscape to something close to its original. A gardens committee is replacing hedges and dead conifers and wants to create a herb garden. Committee member and London tour guide Angela Akehurst has been researching Sudell's history and leading the efforts to bring the gardens back to life, replacing shrubs, planting winter box, installing pots and hanging baskets, and starting off camellias in two new planters by the entrance to the development. She has bought a copy of Sudell's *The Secret of Successful Gardening* to help her and other residents understand his garden philosophy. The residents' website describes this as 'a friendly, safe and pleasant place to live, with its relatively spacious common parts and beautiful garden areas'. It is certainly a different response from that expressed by the current residents of the Alton Estate just a 5-kilometre (3 mi.) walk away.

Among those also included in the ILA's 1938 Broadway exhibition was Marjory Allen, whose two examples could be said to be a perfect summation of her lifetime's work. One is the design for a small nursery school in St Pancras with a sandpit and paddling pool that was emptied in winter and used for slides and see-saws, the other a tiny garden with sea-washed turf and wattle divides. What united them was that they were both roof gardens, sitting high above the London smog, so it is somewhat surprising that Sudell did not record in his ILA CV his partnership with his friend on one of the most successful roof gardens London had ever seen. At its peak, Selfridges Roof Garden in Oxford Street, London, created in 1930, attracted 35,000 people a week. It was Allen who had the idea of creating a roof garden at Selfridges even though she had never worked on one at this scale. Typical of her forthright manner, one day in the store she noticed maintenance men taking the lift to the roof and jumped in with them to take a look. What she saw, 'a vast, grey empty expanse', upset her, especially when she thought of the Selfridges staff having to take their lunch somewhere in the dark backrooms of the store. A roof garden was the answer. Sometime later she spotted founder Harry Selfridge, sporting a black silk topper at a rakish angle, walking the shop floor. Spying that he wore a carnation in his buttonhole, she concluded he must be a garden lover. Boldly arranging an appointment, Allen convinced the American magnate straight away that a roof garden would be good for business. None of the visitors, he told her, 'would be able to resist spending a few shillings'.[31] But that was only the start. Having convinced Selfridge, she now realized she would need specialist help for such a complex and risky task at such a prestigious landmark and turned to her friend and fellow of the gardening wing of the ILA, Sudell. The two horticulturalists set to work on the asphalt roof, and were allowed only 46 centimetres (18 in.) of topsoil to prevent collapse of the iconic building. The pair created an English garden, scent garden, rose garden, pergola water garden, lawns, cherry tree walk and herbaceous borders. Much of this compartmentalization would find echo in Sudell's Dolphin Square courtyard seven years later.

The whole enterprise required 60,000 plants a year, many of which were grown in the rooftop greenhouses, others at the store's sports ground. In total the pair shifted a thousand tons of material, including farmyard manure, onto the roof using the store's lifts before opening time. Such was the expertise with which Sudell devised ways of both watering and drainage, ensuring that enough moisture was retained in the ground, that, while London's parks turned brown during the 1930 heatwave, the roof garden lawns were 'velvety and brilliant'. The garden was such an instant success, crowds flocking to take tea or watch the summer fashion shows, that they were awarded a three-year contract to maintain it. However, towards the end of that time store management wanted to use a proportion of the space to display garden equipment including gnomes, toadstools and, what Allen described as, 'other colourful God-wottery': 'When we told them they would have to decide between the gnomes and us, they chose the gnomes.'[32] The roof garden was destroyed in the Blitz in 1940 and the space was not opened to the public again until 2009.

Silvertown, Leigh Road, Finsbury, EMI, Bignores, Hainault, even Selfridges, all have faded from memory, sit rusting or are poorly sketched in archives. Yet they too have a place in the story of twentieth-century British garden and landscape history. The thread running through them is Sudell, but their real importance is how they, in some small way, reflect a different way of thinking about how people could live in harmony with their landscape and nature. It was a philosophy, it could be argued, that failed to grow enough roots to thrive today and is now as symbolically ancient as the attempts of garden designers in the eras of antiquity, the Renaissance, the knot and parterre, the picturesque and parkland to similarly harmonize the relationship between landscape and people. Future psychogeographers might find rich pickings in the rusty goalposts, derelict pavilions and dusty drawings of flower bed patterns in order to understand what we could have been, and what we are now not.

13
Sudell Urges Us to Invite Betty Uprichard into our Garden

In a small plot of land, no more than 15 metres by 9 metres (50 × 30 ft) amid the continued building of a new housing estate, a tall man is slowly walking the perimeter, pencil and paper in hand. He is over 6 foot, with a gleaming, domed bald head on which tufts of brown hair cling around the ears, a look he has favoured since losing his hair prematurely at around thirty years old. He wears what we would nowadays think excessively formal clothes for outdoor work, especially as we are standing in mud and brambles. He wears a tweed jacket – pockets packed with lollies in case there are children to amuse – which he'll sometimes jettison in summer in favour of a white shirt, complete with tie of course, worsted trousers and sturdy shoes. He has a kind, scrubbed, rounded, almost feminine face. He also has a sense of purpose.

Let's momentarily imagine this land is ours. We are lucky, for this man can see what we cannot. He knows how this small patch of land can be transformed into a garden we can be proud of, work hard on, spend virtually all of our leisure time in, enjoying the fresh breeze and imbibing the almost year-round scent of flowers he will tell us to plant. Let's say it's just after the Second World War, as the country drags itself to its feet again for the second time in less than thirty years. It's our new house on a council estate in London but, after making our interiors the cosiest we can, we excitedly move outdoors to find what many have found before us: our front and back gardens are a wasteland abandoned by builders. It's good fortune to have one of the country's foremost suburban garden experts with us, a man whose instruction books fly from shop to shed shelf in their thousands. We've brought him to life from some of these editions, let's say *Practical Gardening and Food Production in Pictures*, published by Odhams in 1948, or their *Practical Home Gardening Illustrated* from a year later, or *The Town and Suburban Garden* by Ward Lock a year after that. That's three books in three years proving how insatiable is our demand for his advice.

Our imagined Sudell is pointing over our new neighbour's fence. 'Remember a tree or hedge in your neighbour's plot is part of your picture,' he says. 'Note the views, if any. See what is grown in gardens around. All these neighbouring details will help you in your own garden making.'[1] Now he wants us to think about clearing the plot, hacking away the brambles, so we can really see what we've got. He advises us to leave the old tree in the far corner. We may learn to love it. That evening, after back-breaking work on the debris, we gather around the kitchen table to watch Sudell, notes from the survey to hand, sketch out a plan. We will need lawn, vegetable and fruit spaces, essential paths only (he doesn't want us to pave over our garden), flower borders and perhaps shrubberies. It all looks daunting, but

Sudell showing us how to lay out a typical suburban garden oval bed.

gentle Sudell is there to assure us: 'In this ever-perplexing age we need to escape from our troubles. Gardening affords such an escape. It does more – it restores our faith in Nature.'[2] This Nature, he says, will meet us halfway and rectify any amateurish mistakes we may make. As he pencils out our plan, he also tells us we need to dig a few trial holes, about a foot square and 45 centimetres (18 in.) deep, so we can inspect the soil to ascertain whether it is waterlogged. We will need to think about drainage systems if so. He sees our anxious faces. He tells us that there are only a few rules that need to be followed. The rest is up to us. To our surprise, he says he likes a garden with idiosyncrasies. 'I look around at other forms of art and I notice that the little informal, even erratic touches are frequently the focus points of charm and delight.'[3]

There are, though, a few musts:

> Paths should be made straight and wide so that washing can be dried in the garden;
> Walls and fences are best kept low because plants need fresh air. If a high wall is already in place climbers should be used;
> Whitewash those high walls to avoid darkening the garden;
> The lawn, the 'carpet' for your outdoor room, should be as quiet and secluded as possible;
> A garden seat shaded by a tree or arbour is a must. Ornaments are fine but should be used sparingly;
> The views from our windows and, in the front garden, from the street must have something to catch the eye, a dahlia or Standard Rose, a sundial, archway or a fine shrub;
> Paths should, where possible, be situated in shady parts of the gardens and borders in the sun.[4]

He favours crazy paving because of the charm, a frequent Sudell word, of the plants that can grow between the stone, particularly scented thyme, which does not mind being trodden on and releasing its perfume. We can use brick if we wish, too. But he wants our garden to be used, he doesn't want a 'gardeners garden' where children, animals and even grass would be banished: 'An unfriendly garden and unworthy of the name.'[5]

While he loves a miniature rock garden he spares us this complication, but he wants us to invest in an arbour so we can sit and enjoy what we have created. That is the point. His drawing for our back garden has an archway near the house, which announces the entrance to a diagonal path that bisects the lawn. The option of a circular flower bed or ornament appears halfway along our journey to the arbour. Bordering the lawn on both sides he makes it easy for us by suggesting we plant standard rose trees at uniform intervals, but says we could swap one of those rows for a flower border if we are feeling adventurous. A combination of rose hedge and fruit trees about 10–11 metres (35 ft) into the garden from the house forms a border, beyond which lies a kitchen garden. We will be able to grow most of our own fruit and vegetables.

He's given us a separate drawing if we feel emboldened to try the border. It has space for lupins, delphiniums and papaver at the rear with phlox, eckia speciosa, summer heleniums, gypsophila and

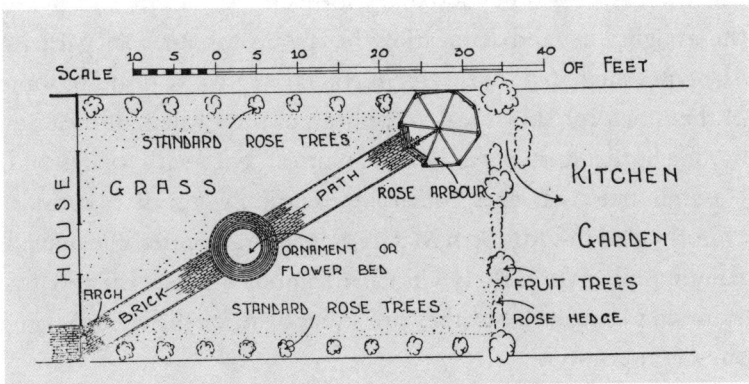

Here's a simple garden that Sudell might draw us.
Note the labour-saving rose trees.

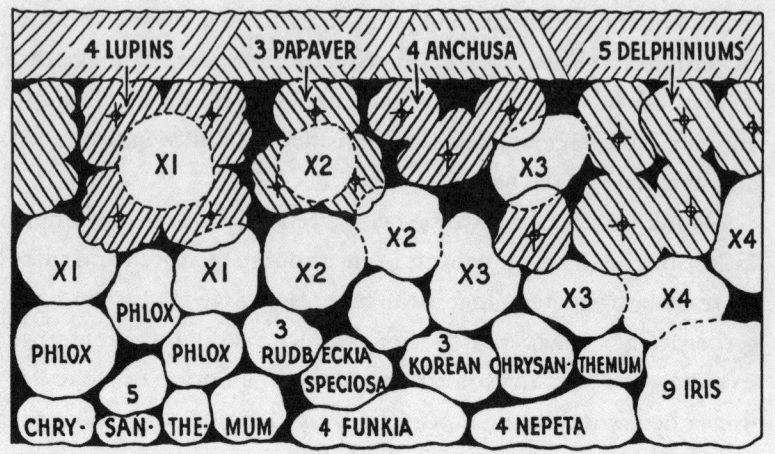

Sudell tells us that if we are feeling bold we could replace one of the lines of rose trees with a plant border: diagram showing interplanting scheme.

chrysanthemum in the middle, funkia, nepeta and iris towards the front with some thrift auricula and pinks at the edge. He assures us all these can be grown from seeds and will give colour from spring to autumn, some coming on strongly as others begin to fade. We can just plant and mostly sit back and watch. However, should we still baulk at this, the fragrant standard rose tree options for both sides are classic Sudell labour-saving options. Planted individually half a metre (2 ft) apart, they add to the formality of our plot and give us the straight lines and delineations he favours for our small gardens. The types suggested for this regimented line? We've heard of some of them before. They speak of politics in the garden, of meaning beyond horticulture, of symbols of suburbia loaded with condescending connotations. For yes, Sudell enthusiastically urges us to consider Dorothy Perkins, Mrs Sam McGredy, and the wonderfully named, salmon pink, hybrid Betty Uprichard among others.[6] They are fragrant and beautiful, but they are so redolent of the suburbs on a Sunday afternoon.

Those bold, blowsy blooms have been created for the early twentieth-century explosion of small British gardens, marketed as a gateway to peace and tranquillity, an Eden and a history we barely understand. And oh so vulgar, yet popular. They appear everywhere across this land, splashes of vibrant colour cheering us as we walk down the street, sit under our arbour, pass by on the commuter train. We remain blissfully unaware of any other meaning they might contain beyond the joy they give. And there's more to come. Sudell wants us to plant three or four morello cherry trees to mark the divide between our restful leisure plot and our productive kitchen garden. We could substitute a couple of pear or plum trees for variety if we wish. He never ceases to push the morello cherry or any kind of cherry trees for that matter, whether in garden or forming an urban avenue. The morello is easy to grow and looks spectacular in spring when it blossoms and in July when its vibrant red fruit appears. And, while more sour than conventional sweet cherries, the fruit can be used in pies, jams and tarts. In between these trees we will grow more roses, this time bushes. Our garden scents will drift far and wide. And in the kitchen garden we will start with potatoes, as favoured by the new allotment holders of the interwar years, even though our space for vegetables is a mere 4.5 metres by 3 metres (15 × 10 ft). They will require less maintenance and thus we are unlikely to be discouraged by too much failure in the early years. However Sudell urges us to move as quickly as we can towards French and runner beans, tomatoes, celery, cauliflower and other fresh greens, maybe even run a line of radishes and lettuces between green crops such as peas, so that we can have the salads in summer and the peas and beans later. He tells us:

> A lettuce from your own small plot not only tastes better but has more vitamins in it than one transported from a distance. I like to think in these days of 'mechanical everything' our gardens still come direct from Mother Earth, and we are still free to do what we wish with them.[7]

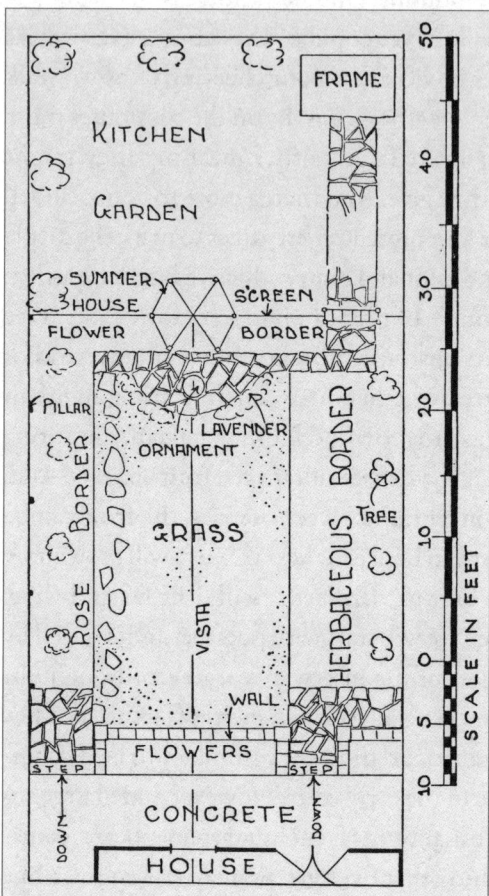

Perhaps in time we might try something a bit more advanced.

As he leaves us to begin our gardening odyssey, we know it's inevitable we will need him again, for things will certainly go wrong and we will need to consult him to lift us from our despondency with his motivating practical solutions.

It is not too far-fetched to posit that Sudell was indeed 'invited' into the kitchens, sheds and gardens of the new suburbanites on a weekly basis. Whether residents took the *Daily Herald*, splashed out on the aspirational *Ideal Home* magazine or brought down one of his 47 well-thumbed garden books from the shelf, his voice, gentle and encouraging, was undoubtedly one of the pre-eminent of its day as gardens and gardening became a national obsession. Of course, there is no such thing as a typical Sudell garden, but there are tropes and themes. He himself was happy for people to experiment and get things wrong, but because it was important that millions of new, time-poor, gardeners did not become discouraged and because the beautification of Britain was too important to him, the basics were important. Lawns, wide paving, small rock gardens, roses, fruit trees, statuary and kitchen gardens, formally laid out in straight sightlines so as not to become unwieldy, were important. Discipline was needed if the new spaces were to give relief from the turmoil of the day for gardeners, but also to contribute to the patchwork of colour that was spreading throughout the country. Of course, as Sudell became a potting shed name his audience expanded, and some of the gardens he showcased became larger, and could even incorporate tennis courts and sunken gardens. However the symbols largely remained the same: lawns were immaculate, roses neatly pruned, pride on show, whether in Roehampton or Dunroamin.

While estates like Roehampton did eventually evolve in a different socio-economic direction from those of Metro-land and Downham from Dunroamin, the suburbanite – council tenant or new mortgage holder – had one interest in common: the garden. A gnome was a gnome whether fishing in a fountain pool in Ruislip or pushing a wheelbarrow in a small front garden on Becontree. Dunroamin might have had more space for a herbaceous border but the small circular flower bed in a front garden of the Watling cottage estate still held the same perennials, still had the same colourful impact. It was not the house but the garden that remained the key space for individual creativity, albeit within instructional guidelines laid down by Sudell and others. Residents could make their mark on nature and then, of course, enjoy the fruits of their labour with a semblance of solitude and privacy. This need for space and low-density housing was enshrined in the 1919 Tudor Walters Report, driven by the desire for the post-war working classes to have the opportunity of a decent new environment in which to live. Both council estate planners and speculative builders took their lead from this seminal report, not least because private developers knew it was best to pay homage to its principles if they were to sail smoothly through planning processes, such was its influence and the regard in which it was held by the government.

One such widely accepted principle in both cottage estate and Dunroamin was that living rooms should open straight out to gardens, whereas many pre-war terraced houses had a dingy backyard, coal store and maybe even an outside toilet. The cul-de-sac in both council estate and private development was largely a Tudor Walters invention, giving both space and privacy. However the report was open to interpretation and builders of both types could take away from the committee report elements they wanted. For example, it stressed the need for uniformity of design for groups of housing in one breath while discountenancing monotony on the other.[8] Thus began the slow evolution of two types of new housing estate. For local authorities, particularly the LCC, there was an overriding need to build community, which was thought to have been lost over the past one hundred years of industrialization.[9] With varying degrees of success, although sometimes stymied by economics, local authorities insisted on communal open spaces, public realm, where people could meet, and tried to ensure a mix of people from different backgrounds and family size was catered for in the various sizes of houses built.

An area of common land called The Pleasance on Roehampton (now Dover House) still serves as a meeting place, with its play area and seating shaded under mature oak trees. It remains a gorgeous oasis of serenity with not a sound of nearby snarling London traffic penetrating its green canopy. Small clumps of cottage estate terracing were also recommended to enhance community spirit. Over in Dunroamin, however, speculative builders, obviously looking to entice new buyers, began to promote individualism with the key message that the house and land was theirs. They could have their own version of those manor houses of the seventeenth century owned by the minor gentry. The one-family semi-detached house became the building block of a new estate that developed in an accumulative way with little overall design and with scant public realm. This ended up placing a heavy burden on the front garden to brighten the neighbourhood as well as advertise some form of gardening prowess. A sense of community might further be dampened by lack of facilities such as shops and cinemas, which were beyond the economic remit of the speculative builders.

However, private space was a demand that united Metro-lander and council estate dweller. On the latter, the public realm was fine as long as it was not a substitute for a garden. Tudor Walters committed to uniting clumps of terraced houses by joining the gaps with walls and outbuildings, but this foundered on the desire for front gardens. Trying to work around this problem, the committee looked towards American estates with their system of communal landscaping at the front of houses, which eliminated the need for front gardens. The committee, however, had to conclude there was one thing that divided the British and their American cousins: 'In this country . . . there appears to exist a general desire for some enclosure.'[10] The halfway house for the committee was to suggest that individual front gardens could still promote a sense of unity and enclosure if a, by now familiar, horticultural feature was adopted: 'If the suitable type of hedges is planted, they will very soon grow so as to afford an effective screen.'[11] In Roehampton and many other places like it, the privet hedge's time had come. Neatly trimmed to a uniform height, often by council gardeners, it became the leitmotif of suburbia. And not just on council estates, for the gardens of Dunroamin also needed to be maintained to a high standard that showed off both beauty and privacy, not least because the quality of the individual house and garden was now a selling point for the new mortgage holders looking to climb the property ladder. Sudell's horticultural attempts to have residents experiment with options other than the privet hedge were going to be met with resistance.

And what of today? How fares the privet? A walk around some of the neighbourhoods where an estimated 84 per cent of Britons live reveals it is alive and well and growing lustily.[12] Listen to the sound of electric pruning shears at the weekend and the curses of the gardeners as they battle a shrub that will grow 30 centimetres (12 in.) a year if you let it, but who could not do without that verdant screen keeping away prying eyes and the noise and pollution of traffic. The RHS tells us when to prune it, while selling online specimens priced from £10.49. Presenter Monty Don on the BBC's *Gardeners' World* shows us how he cuts a window for a glimpse of the outside world through his hedge at his Longmeadow house, while his colleague Catherine Mansley for the programme's tie-in magazine tells us we should have no worries about hard-pruning our privet. It'll take it and come back even stronger. What is not always recognized is that in June and July it comes out in clusters of fragrant white flowers that are excellent pollinators. It has new life as a weapon in the fight against climate change. And yet, just like the standard tea rose, the privet is still political. Meaning is projected on its glossy green foliage whether the residents behind are aware of it or not. In March 2022 the then co-chairman of the Conservative Party, Oliver Dowden, placed the privet hedge at the centre of British politics.

> As I walk with my children through the calm suburbia of Hertfordshire, its values so derided by the Left, I actually reflect on the great fortune we have to live in a nation defined by stability, security... and, yes, Conservatism. For me, the privet hedges of suburbia are the privet hedges of a free people. And I will make it my mission as Chairman to defend those values and those freedoms.[13]

There is much to unpack here, but in two sentences during a speech to the Conservative Party Spring Conference the MP for Hertsmere (and from autumn 2022 the Chancellor of the Duchy of Lancaster and Deputy Prime Minister) placed the privet hedge just where the critics of suburbia have always suspiciously viewed it. In suburbia the shrub creates calm, stability, security and – alongside suburbia itself – is a symbol of Conservativism and freedom. These characteristics can so easily morph into other adjectives for critics: try dull, conformist or narrow-minded for size. It is worth repeating Dowden's words: the privet hedges of suburbia are the privet hedges of a free people. No definition of free is given and one would probably not include freedom from ever-spiralling mortgage payments, nor whether there are actually other kinds of privet that might imprison. We are a long way here from the Quaker Socialism of Richard Sudell and other reformers from the early part of the last century. Sudell may have had horticultural qualms about privet itself: 'It is dull and characterless and in a small garden it impoverished the soil.'[14] However, this was not the same as telling his readers and neighbours they should have no hedge at all. The hornbeam, *Berberis stenophylla* or *Escallonia macrantha*, would give perfect alternative cover to serve what Sudell always described as a 'crying demand' from the housing estate, for 'exclusion from the world'. So the Conservative Party chairman confirmed the stereotypes that have been associated with the privet hedge and suburbia since the end of the Second World War, even though it cannot be statistically possible that the majority of British people who live there conform to the type of person who might give Mr Dowden their votes.

 Perhaps predictably the Left rose against Dowden's garden provocations. Journalist John Lubbock of the website *Left Foot Forward* described the privet hedge of the Tory Party chairman's vision as 'putting up a shield of privacy and control around their sacred and inviolable property rights'. It was a bourgeois sense of security, of the family values of middle-aged homeowners who have moved out of the chaotic city to commuter towns. If I want to be more uncharitable, it's a very white image of Britain, a psychogeographic boundary between urban and rural life, and maybe between a nostalgic set of values and a progressive one.[15]

Strube's Little Man is back and with him the garden-obsessed people who eschew community and progressive politics, pull up the drawbridge, sit in their arbours and admire their voluminous Betty Uprichards. In truth he never went away. Anyone who might attempt to understand what the suburbs have often meant to many of the residents themselves is here caught in the crossfire. Once again they appear not to have a voice in the debate. Trampled underfoot also are the historical roots of the early twentieth-century mass migration to the suburbs, why this was often a lifesaver, and why those homes and gardens were often a source of pride and fulfilment, not dullness and conformity. In politics the Left and the Right continue to misunderstand suburbia today.

Writer and suburbia defender Paul Barker ploughs a different, idiosyncratic furrow, one that might find little favour with Sudell, Dowden or those who damn its residents and their conservatism. 'I have sometimes thought I should start a Privet Hedge Preservation Society,' he writes.[16] Barker rejoices in the suburbs and dismisses the modernists who would force residents out of them and into the high rise. Although he doesn't name them, his book *The Freedoms of Suburbia* starts in celebratory fashion as Hackney Borough Council lays on a party for locals as it demolishes two 22-storey blocks of flats, Sutherland and Embley Points, on the Nightingale Estate in 2000. They will be replaced by a housing association estate of two- and three-storey houses. Suburbia has won, says Barker, who sees the interwar estate-building programme as a high point of British urban design, a phenomenon no one will understand until they also appreciate residents' love of gardens. He takes a picaresque journey to the suburbs around the country in the 2000s, which frankly could have been taken eighty years earlier with very little noticeable difference. Along the way he takes down modernists like Clough Williams-Ellis and moves his sights on to 1960s brutalist architects Peter and Alison Smithson, described as an unsmiling couple still in thrall to Le Corbusier. They favoured 'streets in the sky', tower blocks, and despised suburbia, dismissing the arguments such estates were what people wanted as 'invalid': 'They sneer at the love of gardens and at "the simple well-wishers, of the back-to-gentle-nature era".'[17] Urban togetherness in the sky, all elevated walkways and concrete stretching upwards, was the real solution for modern living, they argued.

Barker visits their 'nightmare creation', the Greater London Council's Robin Hood Gardens in Poplar, east London. He finds two 'seven storey workhouses facing each other'. The balconies are narrow, and netting is in place to stop children falling. Rain-soaked concrete and a derisory playground add to the bleakness for Barker, who goes on to detail how the flats started leaking almost immediately after they were built in 1966. Soon the elevated walkways were rat runs for thieves and drug dealers and the crime rate was thirty times higher than London council estate averages. 'To go there was to see a tombstone to progressive public housing. The Smithsons themselves lived in a Victorian house in Chelsea.'[18] For Barker this monolithic design crushed the spirit in the name of mythical community living. What was so good about the interwar suburb was its basic blandness. It offered new residents a chance to express their own personalities and idiosyncratic tastes. As Richards, Roberts and – in his own way – Sudell had argued before, the suburb allowed the community to grow their built environment organically, watching each other (and yes, sometimes trying to better each other) to create a living whole. The suburb could never be represented by one individual building or garden or cul-de-sac. It was an entity in itself. It eschewed distinctions between urban and rural. It was both. It was not eating up rural idyll nor destroying architecturally interesting cities. Citizens mostly had no access to the former and had fled the latter for space and privacy. No, the suburb was something different altogether, a new way of living that engendered pride and, yes, community spirit. It's worth pausing momentarily to also consider the suburban garden's replacement of the countryside's vast tracts of publicly inaccessible, chemically boosted agricultural wastelands as the home of British wildlife. Every suburban gardener will have experienced the holes in their hedges as a host of sparrows, finches, tits and wrens colonize those cool inner spaces. Some species of butterfly are now found solely in the suburbs and the fox finds food and shelter in our gardens.

Yet at this point Barker travels a different garden path from early twentieth-century planners, gardeners and politicians such as Abercrombie, Unwin, Barnett, Salter and even Sudell with his Garden City ethos. The libertarian former editor of *New Society* magazine adopts a Left/Right hybrid free-market and anarchic philosophy to eschew any planning at all. It stifles creativity, he says, and the suburbs should be free to grow where the suburbanite takes it. Except for some obvious examples of open spaces such as national parks, moors and already protected lands, the creative working classes should be able to establish homes where they like, instead of being crammed by planners into far too few and undersized homes on unsuitable urban sites. He celebrates the Arcadian self-help communities of Jaywick Sands, near Clacton-on-Sea, Essex, and Peacehaven, Sussex, built on bought land by entrepreneurs in the 1920s and '30s whose 'temporary' shacks and bungalows have become plotland settlements of idiosyncratic character, featuring garden ornamentation that is often semi-surreal with giant squirrels dwarfing flowerpot men. Snobbish dismissal has inevitably followed. It is doubtful that Jaywick and Peacehaven found favour with the governments, planners, landscapers and politicians of the Left in the early twentieth century, wedded as they were to a paternalistic vision of how the working class should live and keen to regulate that both indoors and out. Nevertheless, Jaywick and Peacehaven in their own way – like Roehampton, Becontree and Dunroamin – speak to the aspirations of people to create their own homes, their own space and make a mark that says: this is mine. The rest is a matter of taste.

This story has been about the interwar birth of the suburban garden as we know it today, and the forgotten man Richard Sudell's role as a pioneering evangelist for the cause. It is entirely wrapped up in debates over definitions of landscape and who it belonged to, at a time when the garden was one part of a vision that had Britain at the beginning of a new egalitarian era in which beauty of land and design was for the benefit of all. It is important to reflect on those times today, for what we did not become and what lessons we did not learn. Despite the views of the odd libertarian, it would appear evident that the deregulated free-for-all house building of the last thirty years – free from any national planning policy dreamed of by some in the interwar period and riding roughshod over defanged local authority control – has not created Arcadia. It has certainly not provided anywhere near enough the quantity and quality of new homes for those who desperately need them.

In the present age of Generation Rent, with young people unable to afford to buy their own homes or live in accommodation with open space to enjoy, the garden history of the early twentieth century and the benefits it brought to sizeable numbers of the population stands as a salutary lesson. Yet it still seems strange that this progress a century ago is hardly recognized today even though we virtually all still live there. Wherever suburbia and its gardens occur in popular culture it is mostly to be sniffed at or laughed at. Witness the petty snobberies of Margo Leadbeatter in the hit BBC TV comedy *The Good Life*. Poor Margo was too busy with her Surbiton social life or pruning the odd rose to get that the joke was on her, although Sudell would surely have given a nod of approval to neighbours Tom and Barbara Good's attempts at food self-sufficiency, animal husbandry and shallot growing. *The Good Life* and a host of other comedies continue to generate easy laughs from aspiration amid the asters. *Keeping Up Appearances*, *The Fall and Rise of Reginald Perrin*, *Terry and June* and *Abigail's Party* are just some of the sitcoms and plays mining easy seams for humour, perhaps because we are still a little nervously embarrassed not to be living in cutting-edge city or manor house rural bliss. Ricky Gervais's hit comedy about the tedium of working in a stationery supply company, *The Office*, was based in Slough, surely now a byword for dull conformity. While the action – such as it was – was set firmly within the office, it would not be too far-fetched to imagine that some of Wernham Hogg's middle managers had the odd Dorothy Perkins in their small gardens.

In 2019 the singer-songwriter Tracey Thorn published her well-received memoir *Another Planet: A Teenager in Suburbia*. For Thorn and other artists (perhaps David Bowie in Bromley?), dreams of escape from humdrum suburban surroundings were the rocket fuel to make a success of a creative career and get a one-way ticket out. Brought up in the commuter settlement of Brookmans Park in Hertfordshire, Thorn's teenage years were largely spent not doing anything, not quite getting anywhere: 'A life described by what's missing, and what fails to happen.'[19] She describes her part of suburbia as 'a stage set dropped on to an empty landscape' and is amazed that her parents moved out of London to this place, while admitting it was safer than the capital.[20] Beneath the order she detects minor differences morphing into bigger issues, one neighbour dismissed as 'the kind of person who has too many annuals in the front garden'.[21]

Just like almost everyone else's, her own front garden had a small lawn surrounded by 'flower beds full of peach and yellow roses', with her father gardening in neat rows. Like the accountant he was, said her mother. Thorn is fully aware that her garden was symbolic of class. Not for her neighbourhood the country-house style of shrubby perennials and 'untidy opulence'. Here were half barrels of bedding plants and hanging baskets, rows of conifers and crazy paving patios.[22] She knows a peony is Yew while a marigold, found in her garden, is non-Yew. Thorn's gentle and amusing dissection of her home town is full of the tropes that surround suburbia. It is difficult to find any piece of art that really celebrates its diversity, the quirkiness, the sheer difference of what you might find if you look hard enough, what Barker calls its 'vigour and unexpectedness'. It is, he insists, 'a land of pleasantness, friendship and hope'.[23] For Thorn it is a place from which to depart, much like the radio waves radiating from her town's landmark, its transmission tower. And yet what we are really talking about here is a rite of passage. Thorn is a sometimes bored, sometimes confused adolescent in this story. It is doubtful she, or most other teenagers for that matter, would have been deliriously happy in Xanadu – especially if their mothers had the habit of poking around in their bedrooms. At some point everyone wants to leave the family home for adventure and a new life. It just so happens that the place most of us will eventually escape from is suburbia, even if a return at some point is a distinct possibility.

Perhaps it is not surprising that after all these decades of dismissal the suburb of today is facing something of an identity crisis. It might continue to be viewed in some quarters as the land of the small-minded, materially aspirational; those citizens with narrowed cultural horizons, privately mowing lawns behind a privet hedge (or alternative), getting on with life without making a fuss. Yet dark clouds are gathering over the dahlias and fuchsias. Almost without the rest of society (a much smaller but culturally much more powerful subset) noticing, suburbia has problems. A report by independent thinktank the Smith Institute in 2016 entitled *Towards a Suburban Renaissance* assumed we even knew such a revival was needed, so under the radar had the decline been.[24] The report's author Paul Hunter found that in the suburbs 'this technicolor ideal has rapidly started to fade'. His report, focusing on Greater London, Greater Manchester and the West Midlands, revealed a decades-long reversal of fortunes for the suburb as investment in inner cities brought new life and jobs there.

Continued government policies to support these inner cities were continuing to drain the lifeblood from the suburbs. The proportion of the most-deprived areas within cities was rising rapidly in suburbia, and in London there were now more poor people living in outer boroughs than inner ones. In turn this change had forced up property prices in the inner city, driving the poorest out into the suburbs whose relative affordability also attracted a new immigrant population, both groups moving out to find little employment in the suburbs.

The gradual death of local shopping areas, replaced by shopping malls built on old industrial parks, was also adding to the air of depression, with surveyed levels of satisfaction soaring in inner-city Hackney at the same time they were dipping in Havering and Harrow. The report suggested a range of measures that could be adopted to revive the suburbs, including a government-sponsored taskforce to study how they could adapt and grow. More remarkable still was the suggestion that the government consider creating ministerial responsibility for the suburbs and establishing an agency to provide information and best-practice guides for a suburban renaissance. A Minister for the Suburbs might bring predictable laughter from predictable quarters, but it is not so funny when the issue at hand is increased levels of deprivation and poverty among vast swathes of the population.

> With so many people living in the suburbs, the state of the nation rests on their fortunes. The failure to act is only storing up problems for the suburbs of tomorrow. And if left unchecked the trends, which should be much higher up on the political agenda, could end up being as significant and far reaching as the inner-city deterioration of the post-war era.[25]

This was powerful testimony, recognizing as it did that the suburbs are the bellwether for the state of the nation, and that seventy years after the Second World War the problem they were established to solve – inner-city deprivation – was now being visited upon them. The report also called for more investment and an exploration of the idea of 'Supurbia', whereby existing suburbs are intensified, especially around railway stations and other transport connections, for example by increasing building sizes from two storeys to four and creating high-tech business hubs there. How this would square with the characteristics of the suburb that enticed people there in the first place – open space, privacy – remains open to question.

In response to the report, the chief executive of global market research company Ipsos, Ben Page, added more bad news. One of the most marked social trends he had seen in the last thirty years was that outer areas of towns and cities had become more miserable than inner: 'All these ideas we have about leafy suburbs have changed. They are losing their distinctiveness and reasons to be. Family homes have been denatured. They have been made into mini apartment blocks and their gardens are torn up and turned into car parks for all their residents.'[26] So we have come to this. The suburbs are becoming denatured, and their gardens turned into off-street parking bays. Since the Smith Institute report in 2016, it does not appear as if much action has been taken to reverse these trends. The suburbs remain undemonstrative and unremarked upon. Their residents continue not to make a fuss and as a result a toxic mix of neglect and ridicule might threaten a bleak future. If the Sudells, Salters, Barnetts, Allens and Unwins were around today there would be much work for them to do: not in the inner cities but in the places they thought might be a salvation.

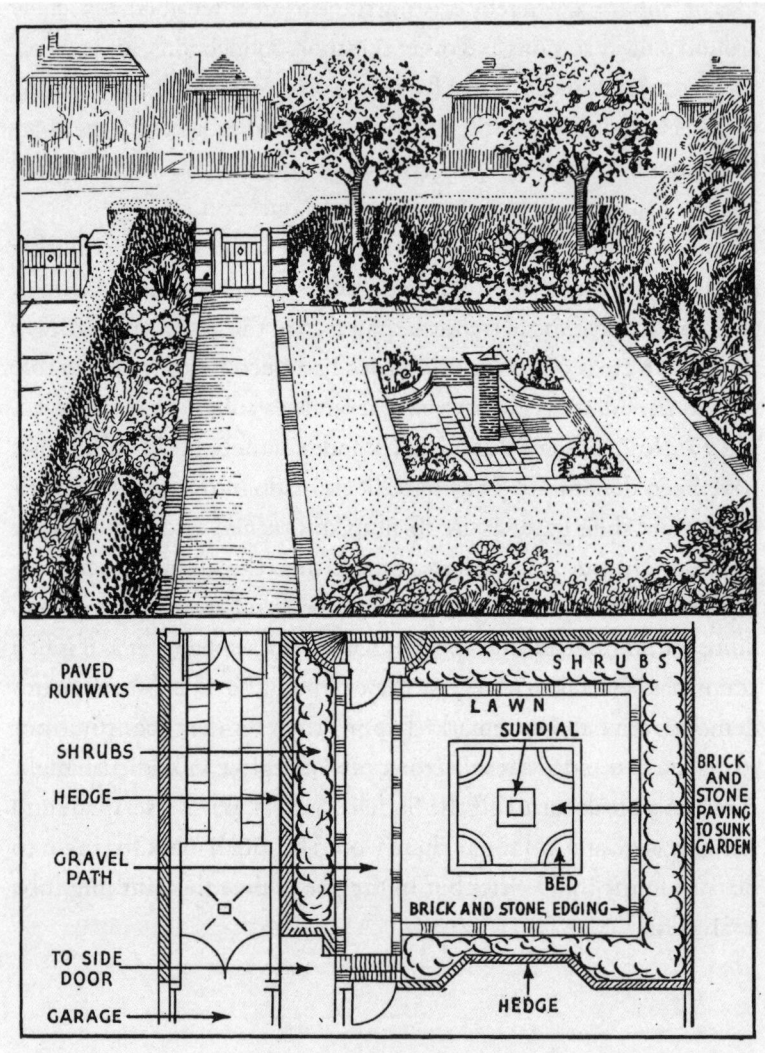

An easily tended garden.

14
'Sudell has been proved right'

Helen McKinnon has lived on the Dover House Estate for 35 years. No one is entirely clear when and why the estate changed its name from Roehampton, but as the surrounding district continued to grow, some distinction was clearly needed. If Sudell were still holding his 'clinics' and chairing his garden society meetings it is likely Helen would be one of his star pupils. She's actually followed the Sudell playbook, both taking initial advice about her small garden from an expert and then stamping her own creativity on it as she gained the knowledge and confidence to experiment. When she moved in, the original hedges were overgrown. A small patch of untended grass formed the front garden, and flower beds under the windows, unfortunately sheltered from the rain, struggled to thrive. Now her side and front garden is a picture in spring and summer. She has a smaller plot at the back of her house. Two large flower beds, one of white plants and the other blue, have been planted, with paving cambering down to channel rainwater into the soil. Hedges have all been replaced with lower and slimmer versions so that the air can reach her beds. You can almost hear Sudell applauding.

> I really enjoy people stopping to chat about the plants and take on ideas about what I could try – especially for the blue border as proper blue plants are harder to find. I find the

admiration really rewarding. My garden shows my expression of what I think is beautiful and people do understand what I am trying to achieve.[1]

Over at the main allotment site, reached via a gate to The Pleasance, Maria Sforza is happily tending her summer vegetables. It looks like a bumper crop this year. She has lived on the estate for 32 years and revels in the community spirit created by garden and allotment. Her children went to the now closed school and were encouraged to have fun on the allotment once the family successfully reached the top of the waiting list. The youngsters even entered their produce into the annual show. But she feels there are now some storm clouds gathering over Dover House, perhaps a spirit in danger of being lost. She wants the council to be more proactive in defending the conservation area, for example by refusing to allow front gardens to be pulled up and privet hedges removed to create off-street parking. Allotments have become a middle-class hobby, she fears, unlike in Sudell's day, and she wishes more newcomers would get involved in the garden society, which relies on a few stalwarts to keep it going. She doesn't want to go back to the days when 'you may have been told off by someone in a hat and wearing a tie but at the same time there was a respect'.[2] There is one hope: she is seeing more children coming to the allotment to explore and play. 'I'm looking forward to my granddaughter coming to the allotment,' Maria says. Neighbour Lindley Maitland, who has had her plot for ten years, agrees: 'I love being outside. I enjoy the peace and quiet of the allotment but also take pleasure in the children who enjoy it and [in] hearing their screams of laughter. I love it in the winter because it gives me somewhere to go to check if my plot is OK.'[3] For allotment holder Jackie Savage, past president of the RGS who saved for posterity the minutes of the garden society of 1922, the founder's legacy is clear: 'Sudell's ideas of gardens, those private spaces, were criticized over the years but he has been proved right.'[4]

A walking tour around Dover House today does reveal evidence to back up Maria's fears. There are quite a few off-street parking bays where front gardens once stood, just as the chief executive of Ipsos reported across suburbia in response to the Smith Institute report. Very few houses are now rented by the council. Ground-floor maisonettes within houses that were once rented by one family of inner-city dwellers after the First World War are now on the market at starting prices of £500,000. A legacy of regulations created a garden suburb of space, light and air within striking distance of the centre of London. The existence of a coordinated pattern of brightly coloured gardens across the whole estate, which Sudell spent years promoting, has been fragmented but many of the gardens, like Helen's, are still beautiful evidence of hard work, trial and error and, yes, they still provide privacy and give joy. Green spaces like The Pleasance remain protected. Recognizing the special nature of the estate and the risk it was under led Wandsworth Borough Council in 1978 to apply conservation area status to the estate, meaning that attempts to develop the site that are not in keeping with the original ethos of the garden suburb are limited. The council urges residents, virtually all homeowners, to consider replacing brick walls and fences with privet hedges and gives advice on how to do this. As we have seen, the Roehampton Garden Society is still going strong and in the 1970s successfully saved two of the estate's three allotment sites from the threat of housing development.

Meanwhile over at Alton efforts to improve the living conditions of residents are moving slowly. In May 2022 Labour took control of Wandsworth Borough Council for the first time since 1978 and scrapped a 'once in a generation' redevelopment plan put forward by the Conservatives. The £105 million plan would have seen the demolition of some blocks, although not the Le Corbusier-inspired slabs, to be replaced by 1,100 new homes including 261 council homes. The proposals would have also delivered new community facilities including a library, youth centre, community hall, GPs' surgeries, a children's nursery and children's centre, together with new shops and business space. Labour has halted the procurement process, claiming there were far too few social housing units, and the community facilities were inadequate. It has pledged to bring forward new plans. In June 2022 a local newspaper, the *Wandsworth Times*, reported local resident and father-of-two Terry Baker's claims that the estate is plagued by crime gangs coming from nearby Battersea and Clapham and that many of the lifts are frequently out of order. High-rise homes are freezing in the winter because residents are still waiting for double glazing.[5]

Slowly, via Dover House, Dolphin Square and, perhaps, new research such as contained here, the forgotten man of twentieth-century garden and landscape history is emerging from obscurity. It should not be forgotten that it is a remarkable personal story too. A largely uneducated fourteen-year-old apprentice gardener from a poverty-stricken background who would not abandon his beliefs, even if it meant imprisonment, and whose faith and politics ran as a powerful thread throughout his life, was destined to be an outsider. That he remained so even while playing a major role in the story of early twentieth-century garden and landscape history, lobbying governments and influencing millions of first-time gardeners to play their overlooked part in the chapter, makes his achievements all the more worthy of record.

Although it cannot be confirmed, there is one other strand of his life that may have added to his outsider status. After his death, Ida shared with Anne, his elder daughter, that her husband was homosexual. This had not prevented the couple sharing forty years in what all their grandchildren remember as a happy and loving marriage. 'He really was the kindest and gentlest man and was very much loved by us all.'[6] Homosexuality was only decriminalized for over-21s in the UK a year before his death. Against this backdrop, Sudell, along with thousands of others, kept his sexual preference secret during his lifetime. One grandchild, Sarah Adamson, one of six daughters of Richard and Ida's first daughter Anne, feels all of the aspects of his background worked against him when it came to recognition for his pioneering work. Sarah believes her grandfather's spirit of encouraging debate, political and otherwise, which passed down through the generations, probably influenced her. In 1983 she was imprisoned for a short time after refusing to pay a fine imposed on her and other women protestors for cutting a hole in the fence of the USAF airbase at Greenham Common in Berkshire and lying down on the runway in protest at the stationing of nuclear cruise missiles on the base. 'Just a week in Holloway was nothing compared to what Richard had to endure. I have always admired his bravery to stick to his principles, which I am sure were from his political and humanitarian views.'[7]

While his name is largely missing from historical accounts and records of the time, what he and others believed about the place of gardens and landscapes in a new Britain has, it can be argued, stood the test of time. Richard Sudell is long overdue a restoration to the story of what was a pivotal moment in British garden history, as huge societal changes ushered in a time when land, no matter how small, became available to the many, not the few. In the suburban gardens themselves, in the pages of newspapers and magazines and within letters and meetings connected to a newly professionalized landscape architectural movement, Sudell's words and, as importantly, actions show he was a key figure. In advocating the democratization of the land, the beautification of Britain for the majority, the right of all to enjoy open spaces and find refuge in them from the strains of everyday life, he offers a fleeting glimpse of what might have been possible. Politics cannot be separated from landscape in the Sudell story. He lived at a time, particularly interwar, when demands for an egalitarian society were heightened. While many took to the street, the meeting hall and the polling booth to argue for this, Sudell's contribution was to plant trees, show the working classes how to sow for all-year-round colour, lay their crazy paving to save labour, and argue that roadsides,

Richard Sudell in later life.

cemeteries and any open spaces could be uplifting environments for the whole population.

This modest man's vision was sweeping in intent, 'any area open to the sky', but destined never to be realized. Britain today is certainly not planned, designed and landscaped in the way Sudell and many of his contemporaries wished for. For all his efforts he has been overlooked and even, at times, quite brutally dismissed. Sudell's work was of the age, but he was not a Modernist and for that he would be associated with all the 'conservative' connotations that came with the suburban gardener. Yet that is to overlook the radicalism of what he was doing, the gentle cajoling of millions of people to create their own spaces, understand the rhythms of seasons, grow their own food, create their own environments. Having lived the experience, Sudell understood what those small suburban gardens meant to residents in a way any number of theorists simply could not. While his style of garden and landscape did become linked with an alleged suburban conformity, it can be argued that such gardens, together with those inspired by the Arts and Crafts Movement, still hold sway in Britain today. Perhaps this is because those compartmentalized, delineated, colourful, private spaces still give relief from the 'turmoil of the day' as they did when Sudell embarked on his life's quest. Sudell sits somewhat uneasily in the space between the suburban garden and the reimagining and planning of the country, the former often heaped with derision for its conservatism and the latter stretching the horizons of the possible. That Sudell was able to play significant roles in both fields makes him an important though hitherto overlooked figure, worthy of study for those interested in this period of British social history.

This book does not argue that Sudell was at the centre of the intellectual debate about landscape and architecture in the first half of the twentieth century, nor is it a restoration of the reputation of his key works, the existing evidence of which serves powerfully to illustrate a philosophy and historical significance rather than necessarily standing as examples of excellence. And yet through words and deeds he allows us a glimpse into the suburban garden. That garden, just like any house or building, tells us much about the times and can be read as an historic document as full of meaning as any manuscript. He allows us, almost step by step, to follow the hard work, trials and tribulations of the new wave of gardeners. He helps us to understand the social, political and economic context in which they became symbols, negative and positive, of a time of change. Finally, he guides us out of the garden gate and is our conduit into the thoughts and arguments of horticulturalists, architects, planners, politicians and campaigners grasping for new definitions of land. In this story there is a confluence of tumultuous social history, a revolution in our relationship with landscape and a fierce debate about the environment in which people lived. It is here that we find Richard Sudell.

References

Introduction

1. D. H. Lawrence, 'Nottingham and the Mining Country', *New Adelphi* (June–August 1930), pp. 298–309, available at www.spokesmanbooks.com, accessed 14 August 2023.
2. Alison Flood, '"Cat Torturers Names Withheld": Edith Sitwell's Gossipy Address Book Found', *The Guardian* (27 August 2021).
3. Paul Oliver, Ian David and Ian Bentley, eds, *Dunroamin: The Suburban Semi and Its Enemies* (London, 1981), pp. 19–21.
4. James Mayer, 'The Run-Down London Estate on the Edge of Posh Richmond Park Where some Days It's "Hell"', *MyLondon*, 28 August 2021, www.mylondon.news.

1 'A little garden city'

1. Editorial, *Roehampton Estate Gazette* (December 1922).
2. Ibid. (September 1924).
3. David Lloyd George, quoted in A. E. Holmans, *Housing Policy in Britain* (London, 1987), p. 298.
4. Quoted in John Burnett, *A Social History of Housing, 1815–1970* (Newton Abbot, 1978).
5. Richard Reiss, *The Home I Want* (London, 1918).
6. Sophie Seifalian, 'Gardens of Metro-Land', *Garden History*, XXXIX/2 (2011), pp. 218–38.
7. Peter Batchelor, 'The Origin of the Garden City Concept of Urban Form', *Journal of the Society of Architectural Historians*, XXVIII/3 (1969), p. 48.
8. Richard M. Andrews, 'The Development of the Residential Suburb in Britain, 1850–1970', *Urbani Izziv*, 28/29 (1995), p. 18.
9. Michael Harrison, *Bournville: Model Village to Garden Suburb* (Chichester, 1999), p. 39.

10 J. H. Barlow, 'Housing and Health, with Special Reference to the Lessons from Bournville Village', *Journal of the Royal Institute of Public Health*, XVII/2 (1909), pp. 105–10.
11 'Roehampton's New Club and Institute', *Wandsworth Borough News* (June 1924), p. 13.
12 R. Sudell, *Roehampton Estate Gazette* (December 1922).
13 Antonia Rubinstein, *Just Like the Country* (London, 1991), p. 36.
14 R. Sudell, 'Layout a Lovely Garden', *Ideal Home* (May 1930), p. 36.
15 R. Sudell, 'Small Gardens and Labour Saving', *Ideal Home* (February 1939), p. 125.
16 Mark Meredith, 'Dover House', *HouseHistree*, 1 April 2020, https://househistree.com.
17 *London Suburbs*, intro. Andrew Saint (London, 1999), p. 81.
18 Ibid.
19 Technical Services Department, Wandsworth Council, 'Dover House Estate Conservation Area Appraisal' (2007), available at www.wandsworth.gov.uk, accessed 14 August 2023.
20 Darrin Bayliss, 'Council Cottages and Community in Inter-War Britain: A Study of Class, Culture, Politics and Place', PhD thesis, Queen Mary University of London, 1998, p. 91.
21 Mark Swenarton, *Homes Fit for Heroes: The Politics and Architecture of Early State Housing in Britain* (London, 1981), p. 177.
22 Ibid., p. 25.
23 Bayliss, 'Council Cottages and Community', p. 100.
24 Rubinstein, *Just Like the Country*, p. 11.
25 Ibid., p. 24.
26 Letters, *Wandsworth Borough News* (May 1919), p. 4.
27 Bayliss, 'Council Cottages and Community', p. 167.
28 Ibid., p. 168.
29 REGS Committee Minutes, Wandsworth Heritage Service, January 1922.
30 Ibid., October 1923.

2 'An industrial slave? Never'

1 Diary Entry, *Woodbrooke Chronicle* (May 1916).
2 Editor's Note, *The Guild Gardener* (February 1927).
3 Annabel Downs, 'Sudell, Richard', *Oxford Dictionary of National Biography*, 8 January 2009, www.oxforddnb.com.
4 Sudell File, Library, Royal Botanic Gardens, Kew.
5 Ibid.
6 Ibid.

7 Thomas C. Kennedy, 'The Quaker Renaissance and the Origins of the Modern British Peace Movement, 1895–1920', *Albion: A Quarterly Journal Concerned with British Studies*, 16 (1984), p. 260.
8 Ibid., p. 250.
9 Ibid., p. 265.
10 Cyril Pearce, 'The Pearce Register of WWI British Conscientious Objectors', material available at *Lives of the First World War*, https://livesofthefirstworldwar.iwm.org.uk.
11 Margaret Willes, *The Gardens of the British Working Class* (London, 2014), p. 265.
12 Conscientious Objector Information Bureau report on Sudell, NCF/COIB Report LXXIII, Working Class Movement Library (WCML).
13 Ibid.
14 Ibid.
15 Pearce Register.
16 Ibid.
17 Kennedy, 'Quaker Renaissance', p. 267.
18 Blunt Mss. Box 54/Salter, West Sussex Record Office.
19 Ibid.
20 Wandsworth Detention Barracks (June 1916), at www.hansard.parliament.uk.
21 Thomas C. Kennedy, 'Public Opinion and the Conscientious Objector, 1915–1919', *Journal of British Studies*, XII/2 (1973), p. 110.
22 Ibid., p. 111.
23 Ibid.
24 Ibid., p. 115.
25 Editor's Note, *Guild Gardener* (December 1926).
26 Fenner Brockway, *Bermondsey Story: The Life of Alfred Salter* (London, 1949), p. 12.
27 Ibid.
28 Noel Buxton, *Guild Gardener* (May 1927).
29 Note, *Guild Gardener* (May 1928).
30 Willes, *Gardens of the British Working Class*, p. 213.

3 Trouble at the Whit Monday Garden Show

1 Note, *Estate Gazette* (August 1922).
2 REGS Committee Minutes, Wandsworth Heritage Service (May 1923).
3 Ibid. (June 1923).
4 Ibid. (August 1923).
5 Note, *Estate Gazette* (November 1925).
6 Ibid. (August 1924).

7 Ibid. (May 1923).
8 Ibid., p. 20.
9 Ibid., p. 47.
10 Ibid., p. 28.
11 Ibid., p. 67.
12 Ibid., p. 36.
13 REGS Committee Minutes (November 1923).
14 Notes, *Estate Gazette* (April 1924).
15 Ibid. (May 1924).
16 R. Sudell, *Estate Gazette* (December 1922), p. 11.
17 Ibid. (February 1923), p. 7; (May 1923), p. 12; (July 1923), p. 13; (January 1924), p. 8; (February 1924), p. 8.
18 R. Sudell, *The Town Gardener's Handbook* (London, 1924), p. iv.
19 Ibid., p. 2.
20 Ibid., p. 5.
21 REGS Committee Minutes (November 1923).
22 Interview with Mrs Murphy, in Darrin Bayliss, 'Council Cottages and Community in Inter-War Britain: A Study of Class, Culture, Politics and Place', PhD thesis, Queen Mary University of London, 1998, p. 102.
23 Ibid., p. 146.
24 Ibid., p. 103.
25 J. M. Richards, *The Castles on the Ground: The Anatomy of Suburbia* (London, 2011), p. 13.
26 Correspondence RETA/London County Council, London Metropolitan Archive (LCC/HSG/GEN), 8 October 2022.
27 Ibid.
28 Ibid.
29 Ibid., 27 December 2022.
30 Ibid., 5 January 2023.
31 R. Sudell, *Estate Gazette* (August 1924), p. 6.

4 The Birth of Beautification

1 Letterhead address, Sudell letter as Secretary of LGG, London Metropolitan Archive (LCC/CL/GP), 21 April 1922.
2 Jeffrey Scheuer, 'Origins of the Settlement House Movement, in *Legacy of Light: University Settlement's First Century* (New York, 1985), available at www.socialwelfare.library.vcu.edu, accessed 10 October 2020.
3 Ibid.
4 C.V.J. Griffiths, 'Buxton, Noel Edward Noel-', *Oxford Dictionary of National Biography*, 3 January 2008, www.oxforddnb.com.

5 Peter Kemp, 'Meyer, (Horace) Rollo', *Oxford Dictionary of National Biography*, 23 September 2004, www.oxforddnb.com.
6 Noel Buxton, *Guild Gardener* (May 1927).
7 Letterhead address, Sudell letter (LCC/CL/GP), 21 April 1922.
8 Fenner Brockway, *Bermondsey Story: The Life of Alfred Salter* (London, 1949), p. 93.
9 Ibid., p. 43.
10 Graham Taylor, *Ada Salter: Pioneer of Ethical Socialism* (London, 2016), p. 50.
11 Elizabeth Lebas, 'The Making of a Socialist Utopia and Horticulture in the London Borough of Bermondsey after the Great War', *Garden History*, XXVII/2 (1999), pp. 219–37.
12 Brockway, *Bermondsey Story*, p. 88.
13 Lebas, 'Making of a Socialist Utopia', p. 230.
14 Brockway, *Bermondsey Story*, p. 92.
15 Ibid., p. 93.
16 Peter Mayer, 'Small Owners Limited', at www.hartley-kent.org.uk, accessed 10 January 2021.
17 Ibid.
18 R. Sudell, Gardening Column, *Herne Bay Press*, 9 November 1929, p. 11.
19 Ibid.
20 John W. Graham, *Conscription and Conscience* (London, 1921), p. 328.
21 Taylor, *Ada Salter*, p. 161.
22 Ada Salter speech, MBB Bermondsey Borough Council Minutes (1924–5), Southwark Archives.
23 John Boughton, 'Healthcare in Bermondsey: Reaching for the "New Jerusalem"', *Municipal Dreams*, 10 September 2013, www.municipaldreams.wordpress.com.
24 Beautification Committee report, MBB Bermondsey.
25 Lebas, 'Making of a Socialist Utopia', p. 230.
26 Beautification Committee, MBB Bermondsey.
27 Lebas, 'Making of a Socialist Utopia', p. 233.
28 Beautification Committee, MBB Bermondsey.
29 Author interview, 20 October 2022.

5 Sudell the Flower Evangelist

1 Editorial, *Guild Gardener* (July 1937), p. 4.
2 Ibid. (October 1927), p. 4.
3 Ibid. (December 1926), p. 4.
4 Ibid. (February 1927), p. 4.
5 Ibid. (August 1926), p. 4.

6 Ibid. (October 1926), p. 4.
7 Ibid. (July 1937), p. 4.
8 Note, *Guild Gardener* (January 1927), p. 12.
9 Ibid. (March 1927), p. 5.
10 Report of the Commissioners of Prisons (March 1923), Cmd.2000, p. 46.
11 'Women Prisoners Turn Holloway Dump into Blooming Garden', *Manchester Guardian* (19 August 1930).
12 Editorial, *Guild Gardener* (May 1929), p. 4.
13 Note, *Guild Gardener* (February 1929), p. 5.
14 Ibid. (February 1928), p. 10.
15 Advertisement, *Guild Gardener* (July 1927), p. 2.
16 Note, *Guild Gardener* (May 1926), p. 6.
17 Decree Nisi, National Archives (J77/2812/7064).
18 Note, *Guild Gardener* (December 1930), p. 16.

6 'Taste is utterly debased'

1 R. Sudell, 'Layout a Lovely Garden', *Ideal Home* (May 1930), p. 36.
2 Jane Brown, *The Pursuit of Paradise: A Social History of Gardens and Gardening* (London, 1999), p. 149.
3 Susie Barson, 'Infinite Variety in Brick and Stucco, 1840–1914', in *London Suburbs*, ed. Julian Honer (London, 1991), p. 61.
4 Ibid., pp. 61–101.
5 Ibid., p. 81.
6 Raymond Unwin, *Town Planning in Practice: An Introduction to the Art of Designing Cities and Suburbs* (London, 1909), pp. 3–4.
7 Roger Bowdler, 'Between the Wars: 1914–1940, in *London Suburbs*, ed. Honer, p. 104.
8 Sophie Seifalian, 'Gardens of Metro-Land', *Garden History*, XXXIX/2 (2011), p. 219.
9 Stephen Games, ed., *Betjeman's England* (London, 2010), p. 167.
10 Quoted in David Matless, *Landscape and Englishness* (London, 1998), p. 53.
11 Ibid., p. 56.
12 Ibid., p. 59.
13 D. H. Lawrence, 'Nottingham and the Mining Country', *New Adelphi* (June–August 1930), pp. 298–309, available at www.spokesmanbooks.com, accessed 14 August 2023.
14 Ibid.
15 George Orwell, *Coming Up for Air* (London, 1939), p. 32.
16 J. B. Priestley, 'Houses', *Saturday Review* (11 June 1927), pp. 897–9.

17 Quoted in Paul Barker, *The Freedoms of Suburbia* (London, 2009), pp. 64–9.
18 Paul Oliver, Ian David and Ian Bentley, eds, *Dunroamin: The Suburban Semi and Its Enemies* (London, 1981), p. 42.
19 Matless, *Landscape and Englishness*, p. 55.
20 Ibid., p. 57.
21 Oliver, David and Bentley, eds, *Dunroamin*, p. 21.
22 Judith Roberts, 'The Gardens of Dunroamin: History and Cultural Values with Specific Reference to the Gardens of the Inter-War Semi', *International Journal of Heritage Studies*, I/4 (1996), p. 230.
23 J. M. Richards, *The Castles on the Ground: The Anatomy of Suburbia* (London, 2011), p. 17.
24 Ibid., p. 14.
25 Ibid., p. 15.
26 Ibid., p. 69.
27 Ibid., p. 22.
28 Ibid., p. 67.
29 Ibid., p. 77.
30 R. Sudell, 'Gathered Ideas for the Garden', *Ideal Home* (May 1930), p. 27.

7 'There were little bridges, gnomes and things'

1 R. Sudell, *The Town Gardening Handbook* (London, 1927), p. 2.
2 Jane Brown, *The Pursuit of Paradise: A Social History of Gardens and Gardening* (London 1999), p. 4.
3 Paul Barker, *The Freedoms of Suburbia* (London, 2009), p. 154.
4 Alison Ravetz, 'Gardens and External Space', in Alison Ravetz and R. Turkington, *The Place of Home: English Domestic Environments, 1914–2000* (London, 1995), p. 180.
5 J. Roberts, 'The Gardens of Dunroamin: History and Cultural Values with Specific Reference to the Gardens of the Inter-War Semi', *International Journal of Heritage Studies*, I/4 (1996), p. 229.
6 Brown, *Pursuit of Paradise*, p. 156.
7 Matthew Hollow, 'Suburban Ideals on England's Interwar Council Estates', *Garden History*, XXXIX/2 (2011), p. 206.
8 Brown, *Pursuit of Paradise*, p. 159.
9 Hollow, 'Suburban Ideals', p. 207.
10 Marguerite James, *The Family Garden* (London, 1937).
11 Antonia Rubinstein, *Just Like the Country* (London, 1991), p. 31.
12 Hollow, 'Suburban Ideals', p. 207.
13 Laurence Fleming and Alan Gore, *The English Garden* (London, 1979), p. 229.

14　George Orwell, *Coming Up for Air* (London, 1939).
15　Paul Oliver, Ian David and Ian Bentley, eds, *Dunroamin: The Suburban Semi and Its Enemies* (London, 1981), p. 170.
16　Hollow, 'Surburban Ideals', p. 207.
17　Roberts, 'Gardens of Dunroamin', p. 234.
18　Editorial, *Gardening Illustrated* (May 1930), p. 313.
19　Roberts, 'Gardens of Dunroamin', p. 226.
20　Esmond de Beer, ed., *The Diary of John Evelyn*, vol. III : *Kalendarium, 1650–1672* (Oxford, 1955), pp. 495–6.
21　Ibid.
22　Ibid.
23　R.O.A.M. Lyne, 'Introduction', *Virgil: 'The Eclogues' and 'The Georgics'*, trans. C. Day Lewis (Oxford, 2009), p. xxv.
24　Carola Small and Alastair Small, 'John Evelyn and the Garden of Epicurus', *Journal of the Warburg and Courtauld Institutes*, LX (1997), pp. 194–214, p. 196.
25　Mark Bhatti, Andrew Church and Amanda Claremont, 'Peaceful, Pleasant and Private: The British Domestic Garden as an Ordinary Landscape', *Landscape Research*, XXXIX/1 (2014), pp. 40–52, p. 45.
26　Ibid., p. 50.
27　B. Seebohm Rowntree, *Poverty and Progress: A Second Social Study of York* (London, 1941), p. 234.
28　Brown, *Pursuit of Paradise*, p. 160.
29　Ibid., p. 164.
30　Hollow, 'Suburban Ideals', p. 213.
31　Barker, *Freedoms of Suburbia*, p. 59.
32　Rubinstein, *Just Like the Country*, p. 36.

8 An Unrivalled Influence on a New Nation of Gardeners

1　R. Sudell, *The Town and Suburban Garden* (London, 1950), p. 17.
2　Interview with Susan Johanknecht, Course Leader MA Book Arts, Camberwell College of Arts, 21 January 2019.
3　E. Percy Scholfield, quoted in Sophie Seifalian, 'Gardens of Metro-Land', *Garden History*, XXXIX/2 (2011), p. 225.
4　R. Sudell, 'Making a New Garden', *Ideal Home* (May 1928), p. 22.
5　Seifalian, 'Gardens of Metro-Land', p. 227.
6　R. Sudell, 'New Ideas in Garden Design', *Ideal Home* (April 1929), p. 26.
7　R. Sudell, 'Leisure in the Garden', *Ideal Home* (July 1929), p. 53.
8　R. Sudell, *Landscape Gardening* (London, 1933), p. 9.
9　R. Sudell, 'Joy of the Rock Garden', *Ideal Home* (August 1929), p. 76.
10　R. Sudell, 'Your Seed Order', *Ideal Home* (January 1935), p. 96.

11 R. Sudell, 'The Flowers in Your Garden Now', *Ideal Home* (July 1936), p. 92.
12 R. Sudell, 'Layout a Lovely Garden', *Ideal Home* (May 1930), p. 36.
13 R. Sudell, 'The New Garden', *Ideal Home* (August 1936), p. 31.
14 R. Sudell, 'No More Back-Breaking Gardens', *Daily Herald* (17 October 1937), p. 15.
15 R. Sudell, 'Rest in the Garden', *Daily Herald* (5 May 1933), p. 17.
16 Editorial, 'Herald Debate', *Daily Herald* (19 December 1938), p. 10.
17 Editorial, www.historic-uk.com, accessed 2 March 2019.
18 In total the British Library has 47 titles and revisions authored or edited by Sudell, although not all published by Odhams. These include *The New Garden* (London, 1935), *Everybody's Gardening Guide* (London, 1935), *The New Illustrated Gardening Encyclopaedia* (London, 1937), *Herbaceous Borders and Waterside* (London, 1938), *Secrets of Successful Gardening* (London, 1939), *Practical Gardening and Food Production in Pictures* (London, 1948) and *Practical Home Gardening Illustrated* (London, 1949).
19 Ian Woodward, *With Heart and Voice: The Life and Times of Ray Sherry* (Seven Mile Beach, Tasmania, 2005), p. 60.
20 Ibid., p. 61.
21 Ibid.
22 Sudell, *Landscape Gardening*, p. 11.
23 Ibid.
24 Ibid., p. 30.
25 Ibid., p. 370.
26 Letter from Sudell to Geoffrey Jellicoe, 31 March 1941, Museum of English Rural Life (MERL), SRLI AD2/2/3/4/19.
27 Patrick Abercrombie, *Town and Country Planning* (London, 1933), p. 11.
28 Letter from Sudell to Jellicoe, 31 March 1941, MERL.
29 Editorial and Book Review, *Landscape and Garden*, 1/1 (1934), pp. 54–6.
30 Sheila Harvey, ed., *Reflections on Landscape: The Lives and Work of Six British Landscape Architects* (Aldershot, 1987), p. 108.

9 'A new Britain must arise on better lines than the old'

1 Sheila Harvey, ed., *Reflections on Landscape: The Lives and Work of Six British Landscape Architects* (Aldershot, 1987), p. 12.
2 Ibid., p. 88.
3 Ibid., p. 11.
4 Annabel Downs, 'Sudell, Richard', *Oxford Dictionary of National Biography*, 8 January 2009, www.oxforddnb.com.
5 R. Sudell, *Landscape Gardening* (London, 1933), p. 24.
6 Notice, *Gardeners' Chronicle* (February 1929), p. 16.

7 Downs, 'Sudell, Richard'.
8 Harvey, ed., *Reflections on Landscape*, p. 12.
9 Tony Aldous, *Landscape by Design* (London, 1979), pp. 120–29.
10 David Mawson, 'T. H. Mawson (1861–1933), Landscape Architect and Town Planner', *Journal of the Royal Society of Arts*, CXXXII/5331 (1984), pp. 184–99.
11 John Crosby Freeman, 'Thomas Mawson: Imperial Missionary of British Town-Planning', *Canadian Art Review*, II/2 (1975), pp. 37–47.
12 First Constitution, Museum of English Rural Life (MERL), SRLI AD2/1/1/23.
13 Letter from Sudell to Geoffrey Jellicoe, 31 March 1941, MERL, SRLI AD2/2/3/4/19.
14 Geoffrey and Susan Jellicoe, 'Introduction', *The Landscape of Man: Shaping the Environment from Prehistory to the Present Day* (London, 1975).
15 'Letter from Sudell to American Society', *Landscape Architecture Magazine*, XXXVII/4 (1947), pp. 132–4.
16 Letter to Jellicoe, MERL, 13 February 1942.
17 Letter from Jellicoe to Sudell, MERL, 22 April 1942.
18 Letter to Jellicoe, 30 April 1942.
19 Letter to Sudell, 4 May 1942.
20 Letter to Jellicoe, 31 March 1941.
21 Ibid., 21 March 1941.
22 Letter to Secretariat, MERL, 13 May 1941.
23 Ibid., 15 July 1944.
24 Memo to ILA, MERL, 6 January 1943.
25 Letter to Jellicoe, 18 May 1946.
26 Letter, *Landscape Architecture Magazine*, XXXI/3 (1941), pp. 153–4.
27 Jellicoe, *Landscape of Man*, p. 6.
28 Editorial, *Landscape and Garden*, I (1934).
29 R. Sudell, 'Review of Policy', *The War-Time Journal* (1943), p. 7.
30 R. Sudell, 'The Next 25 Years', *Journal of the Institute of Landscape Architects* (Spring 1956), p. 4.
31 Aldous, *Landscape by Design*, p. 128.
32 Editorial, *The War-Time Journal* (1941), p. 4.
33 Elain Harwood, 'Post-War Landscape and Public Housing', *Garden History*, XXVIII/1 (2000), p. 103.
34 Harvey, ed., *Reflections on Landscape*, p. 34.
35 Ibid., p. 33.
36 Sylvia Crowe note, MERL, SRLI AD2/2/1/59.
37 Harwood, 'Post-War Landscape and Public Housing', p. 109.
38 Ibid., p. 115.

39 David Jacques, 'Modern Needs, Art and Instincts: Modernist Landscape Theory', *Garden History*, XXVIII/1 (2000), p. 92.
40 Ibid., p. 89.
41 H. B. Dunington-Grubb, quoted ibid., p. 91.
42 Ibid., p. 94.
43 Ibid., p. 95.
44 David Mawson, 'T. H. Mawson', p. 199.
45 Sudell, 'The Next 25 Years', p. 4.

10 The Landscape Architect Struggles to Make a Mark

1 Brenda Colvin, speech, *Journal of the ILA*, XXII (1951), p. 4.
2 Peter Merrimen, '"A New Look at the English Landscape": Landscape Architecture, Movement and the Aesthetics of Motorways in Early Post-War Britain', *Cultural Geographies*, XIII/1 (2006), p. 82.
3 Brenda Colvin, 'Roadside Planting in Country Districts', *Landscape and Garden*, 6 (1939), p. 86.
4 Merrimen, '"New Look at the English Landscape"', p. 85.
5 Letter to Jellicoe, MERL, 22 June 1944.
6 Merrimen, '"New Look at the English Landscape"', p. 92.
7 Ibid., p. 89.
8 Ibid., p. 91.
9 Dacorum Borough Council, 'Jellicoe Water Gardens', www.dacorum.gov.uk, accessed 14 August 2023.
10 Ibid.
11 Robert McKown, 'Great Britain: Green Belts and New Towns', *Official Architecture and Planning*, XXVIII/11 (1965), pp. 1556–9.
12 Quoted in Sheila Harvey and Stephen Rettig, eds, *Fifty Years of Landscape Design* (London, 1985), p. 46.
13 Luca Csepely-Knorr and Karen Fitzsimon, 'Post-War Designed Landscapes: "A green place in which to live and work": Landscapes by Sylvia Crowe and Janet Jack', *Society of Architectural Historians of Great Britain*, 8 March 2021, www.sahgb.org.uk.
14 Jonathan Glancey, 'Sylvia Crowe (1901–1997)', *Architectural Review*, 23 February 2017, www.architectural-review.com.
15 Tom Turner, 'Obituary: Peter Youngman', *The Guardian* (17 June 2005).
16 'Understanding Historic Parks and Gardens in Buckinghamshire', *Buckinghamshire Gardens Trust*, August 2018, www.bucksgardenstrust.org.uk.
17 R. Sudell, 'The Next 25 Years', *Journal of the Institute of Landscape Architects* (Spring 1956), p. 4.

18 Ibid.
19 Ibid.
20 'Papers of Creech Jones', at www.archives.bodleian.ox.ac.uk, accessed 16 November 2023.
21 Horace B. Davis, 'The Decolonization of Sugar in Guyana', *Caribbean Studies*, VII/3 (1967), pp. 35–57.
22 Tota C. Mangar, 'The Leonora Strike and Riots (Part One)', *Guyana Chronicle*, 14 February 2022, www.guyanachronicle.com.
23 Guyana Government Department of Public Information, 'Remembering the Enmore Martyrs', 16 June 2020, www.dpi.gov.gy.
24 Hansard, HC, vol. CDLII, col. 23 (23 June 1948).
25 Archives of the Cheddi Jagan Research Centre, www.jagan.org.
26 Cheddi Jagan, 'Memorandum on the Sugar Industry of British Guiana (1948)', Archives of the Cheddi Jagan Research Centre, www.jagan.org, accessed 10 January 2024.
27 Archives of the Cheddi Jagan Research Centre, www.jagan.org.
28 'Biography of Dr Cheddi Jagan', www.jagan.org.

11 'An important and influential figure'

1 'Dolphin Square Gardens', *Historic England*, 13 July 2018, https://historicengland.org.uk.
2 Editorial, *C20 Magazine*, 2 (2017), p. 72.
3 R. Sudell, 'The Garden at Dolphin Square', *The Dolphin* (1937), p. 5.
4 Editorial, *The Dolphin* (1937), p. 3.
5 Ibid., p. 5.
6 Dolphin Square Preservation Society submission to Historic England, December 2017.
7 Sudell, 'The Garden at Dolphin Square', p. 5.
8 Preservation Society submission, December 2017.
9 Sudell, 'The Garden at Dolphin Square', p. 5.
10 Ibid.
11 Ibid.
12 Preservation Society, December 2017.
13 AXA Investment Managers, 'Dolphin Square, London', www.youtube.com, accessed 6 December 2022.
14 Sally Prothero, interview with the author, 16 November 2022.
15 Ibid.
16 For further information, see Dolphin Square Restoration Programme, www.dsqrestoration.co.uk, accessed 7 March 2024.
17 Prothero, interview with author.

18 R. Sudell, 'Riverside Rendezvous: How Your Garden Will Soon Appear', *The Dolphin* (October 1937), p. 9.
19 De Havilland Heritage Trail leaflet, published by the University of Hertfordshire. See www.hatfield-herts.co.uk/aviation/avhistrail.html and www.herts.ac.uk/heritage-hub, accessed 28 November 2023.
20 R. Sudell, *Landscape Gardening* (London, 1933), p. 417.
21 R. Sudell, 'Policy Review', *The War-Time Journal* (1943), p. 7.
22 R. Sudell, 'Planning the Garden of Remembrance', *Report of Proceedings: Annual Cremation Conference, Llandudno, 29 June–1 July 1953* (London, 1953), pp. 17–20.
23 Sudell, *Landscape Gardening*, p. 148.
24 Memo to John Forshaw, 27 February 1942, Museum of English Rural Life (MERL), SRLI AD2/2/3/4/19.
25 City of London Cemetery History leaflet, n.d.
26 Cemetery Research Group, *City of London Cemetery Conservation Management Plan* (London, 2004), p. 203.
27 Ibid., p. 253.
28 Ibid., p. 254.
29 Sudell, 'Planning the Garden of Remembrance'.
30 Ibid.
31 J. P. Chaplin and R. Sudell, 'Symposium on Planning a Crematorium', *Report of Proceedings: Annual Cremation Conference, Peterborough, 1960* (London, 1960).
32 Ibid.
33 Ibid.
34 Ibid.
35 Ibid.
36 Ibid.
37 Audience member of Sudell, ibid.
38 Ibid.
39 See 'Abandoned Communities: Central Silvertown', *Abandoned Communities*, www.abandonedcommunities.co.uk, and 'The Silvertown Explosion', *The History of London*, www.historyoflondon.co.uk.
40 Ministry of Information Photo Division, 'Parish Priest: The Work of the Vicar of St Mark's Church, Victoria Docks, Silvertown, London, England, UK, 1944', Imperial War Museum cat. no. D 21016, www.iwm.org.uk.
41 Sudell, 'Planning the Garden of Remembrance'.
42 Ibid.
43 Ibid.

12 The Importance of Play

1. Author interview with Michael Dixey, Sudell practice partner, 3 November 2022.
2. Author interview with David Lee, Sudell practice partner, 12 January 2019.
3. Sports pavilion for Finsbury Memorial Sports Centre, Barnet, London, RIBA, www.ribapix.com
4. R. Sudell and D. Tennyson Waters, *Sports Buildings and Playing Fields* (London, 1957), pp. 38–9.
5. Ibid., p. 27.
6. Ibid., p. 232.
7. Interview with Dixey.
8. 'Our History', *Fields in Trust*, www.fieldsintrust.org, accessed 20 January 2024.
9. Ibid.
10. 'Merton College Sports Pavilion', *Historic England*, https://historicengland.org.uk, accessed 5 January 2019.
11. Interview with Dixey.
12. Paul Stamper, ed., *Designation Yearbook 2014–15* (2015), available at https://historicengland.org.uk, accessed 15 August 2023.
13. Ibid.
14. Letter to Secretariat, 6 July 1955, Museum of English Rural Life (MERL), SRLI AD2/2/3/4/19.
15. Susan Raven, 'Lady Allen and the Pursuit of Happiness', *The Times* (25 September 1968), p. 9.
16. Marjory Allen, *Memoirs of an Uneducated Lady* (London, 1975), p. 232.
17. Sudell and Tennyson Waters, *Sports Buildings*, p. 80.
18. Ibid., p. 76.
19. Editorial, 'Pioneering Children's Play Area Under Threat', *Twentieth Century Society*, 4 July 2021, https://c20society.org.uk.
20. Ibid.
21. Mary Mitchell, 'Landscaping of Housing Areas', *Official Architecture and Planning*, XXV/4 (1962), pp. 193–6.
22. Obituary, 'R. Sudell', *Journal of the Kew Guild*, IX/76 (1972), pp. 64–5.
23. Russell Page, *Education of a Gardener* (London, 1962), p. 25.
24. Interview with Lee.
25. Geoffrey Jellicoe and Susan Jellicoe, *The Oxford Companion to Gardens* (Oxford, 1986), p. 323.
26. Ian Woodward, *With Heart and Voice: The Life and Times of Ray Sherry* (Seven Mile Beach, Tasmania, 2005), p. 114.

27 See 'Julius Salter Elias, Viscount Southwood, 1873–1946', at https://hornseyhistorical.org.uk, accessed 28 November 2023.
28 'Julius Salter Elias, Viscount Southwood', at www.londonremembers.com, accessed 28 November 2023.
29 'A British Exhibition of Landscape Architecture: Held at Broadway, Worcestershire, June 4th–25th, 1938', *Landscape Architecture Magazine*, XXIX/1 (1938), pp. 1–23.
30 'Richmond Towers and Courts, at https://richmondtowersandcourts.org, accessed 15 August 2023.
31 Allen, *Memoirs*, p. 99.
32 Ibid., p. 102.

13 Sudell Urges Us to Invite Betty Uprichard into our Garden

1 R. Sudell, *Practical Gardening and Food Production in Pictures* (London, 1948), p. 3.
2 R. Sudell, *Practical Home Gardening Illustrated* (London, 1949), p. vi.
3 Ibid.
4 R. Sudell, *The Town and Suburban Garden* (London, 1950), pp. 13–14.
5 Ibid., p. iv.
6 Sudell, *Practical Gardening and Food Production*, p. 143.
7 Sudell, *Practical Home Gardening Illustrated*, p. 4.
8 Paul Oliver, Ian David and Ian Bentley, eds, *Dunroamin: The Suburban Semi and Its Enemies* (London, 1981), p. 108.
9 Ibid., p. 109.
10 Ibid., quoting Tudor Walters, p. 112.
11 Ibid.
12 Paul Barker, *The Freedoms of Suburbia* (London, 2009), p. 15.
13 Oliver Dowden, speech to Conservative Party Spring Conference, Blackpool, 18 March 2022, available at www.ukpol.co.uk, accessed 15 August 2023.
14 R. Sudell, *The Town Garden* (1930), p. 78.
15 John Lubbock, 'Oliver Dowden's Nostalgia for 1940s Britain and the Privet Hedges of Suburbia', *Left Foot Forward*, 23 March 2022, www.leftfootforward.org.
16 Barker, *Freedoms of Suburbia*, p. 17.
17 Ibid., p. 120.
18 Ibid., p. 122.
19 Tracey Thorn, *Another Planet: A Teenager in Suburbia* (Edinburgh, 2019), p. 2
20 Ibid., p. 13.
21 Ibid., p. 29.

22 Ibid.
23 Barker, *Freedoms of Suburbia*, p. 32.
24 Paul Hunter, *Towards a Suburban Renaissance: An Agenda for Our City Suburbs* (London, 2016), available at www.smith-institute.org.uk, accessed 15 August 2023.
25 Ibid., p. 4.
26 Rowan Moore, 'With the Good Life Over, How Can Suburbia Regain Its Place in the Sun?', *The Observer* (10 July 2016).

14 'Sudell has been proved right'

1 Interview with author, 2 November 2022.
2 Interview with author, 12 September 2021.
3 Ibid.
4 Ibid.
5 Charlotte Lillywhite, 'Life on Alton Estate Roehampton "Plagued by Gangs"', *Wandsworth Times*, 20 June 2022, www.wandsworthguardian.co.uk.
6 Jane van den Broeke, interview with author, 18 November 2022.
7 Sarah Adamson, interview with author, 21 October 2021.

Acknowledgements

I would like to thank Annabel Downs, landscape architect and chair of FOLAR (Friends of the Landscape Archive at Reading), for her generous help and foundational research; Dr Barbara Simms, landscape historian, for her wise advice; Richard Sudell's granddaughters Jane van den Broeke, Sarah Adamson and Clare Grimes for their enthusiastic support; Jackie Savage for all her help; and Edwin and Joseph Gilson for their precise, tireless and patient editing.

Photo Acknowledgements

The author and publishers wish to express their thanks to the sources listed below for illustrative material and/or permission to reproduce it:

BAE Systems Heritage: pp. 242, 243; City of Westminster Archives Centre, London (2518/2): pp. 162, 163; from Trish Gibson, *Brenda Colvin: A Career in Landscape* (London, 2011): p. 193; photos Michael Gilson: pp. 6, 15, 26, 164, 165, 166, 167, 168, 232, 247 (courtesy City of London Cemetery and Crematorium); from the *Guild Gardener*, photos © British Library Board: pp. 78 (June 1927), 95 (May 1927); courtesy John Holder: p. 181; © London Metropolitan Archives: pp. 16 (SC_PHL_02_0853_A2835), 97 (SC_PHL_02_0906_A5866), 106 (SC_PHL_02_0906_A8155), 128 (SC_PHL_02_0906_A6899), 143 (SC_PHL_02_0905_A8111); London Transport Museum (2004/25040): p. 161; from Richard Sudell, *Practical Gardening and Food Production in Pictures* (London, 1947): pp. 160, 282, 298; from Richard Sudell, *Practical Home Gardening Illustrated* (London, 1949): pp. 137, 145, 279; from Richard Sudell, *The Town Garden* (London, 1950): p. 281; from Richard Sudell, *The Town and Suburban Garden* (London, 1950): p. 284; from Richard Sudell and D. Tennyson Waters, *Sports Buildings and Playing Fields* (London, 1957): pp. 257, 266; courtesy Sudell Family Archive: pp. 24, 178, 179, 180, 304.

Index

Page numbers in *italics* refer to illustrations

Addison Act 21
aerodromes 192, 195–7, 221,
    240–44
Allen, Clifford 39, 43, 91, 97, 173,
    264
Allen, Marjory, Lady Allen of
    Hurtwood
  children's playgrounds 152, 264–7
  London Gardens Guild 97, 102
  Selfridge roof garden 173, 275–6
allotments
  history of 57–62
  on Roehampton 14–15, 18, 29,
    127, *167*, 300–301
  St Mark's, Silvertown 251
  wartime 40
Alton Estate 11–12, 125–6, *168*, 206
  living conditions in present day
    301–2
  see also Howell, William
Asquith, H. H. 38, 44

Baillie Scott, M. H. 139
Barker, Paul 290–92
Barnett, Henrietta 50, 74–5
Barnett, Revd Samuel 50, 74, 77
Beautification Committee,
    Bermondsey 44, 82–3, 100
Becontree estate 23, 68, 116, 154, 293

Bermondsey
  Ada and Alfred Salter in 43, 75,
    79–84, 220
  beautification of 42, 91, 100
  poverty 48–9
Bernard Shaw, George 46
Betjeman, John 118–19, 123, 151, 214
Blunt, Wilfrid Scawen 44
Boumphrey, Geoffrey 123–6
Bournville 20, 22–3, 36, 123
British Guiana 223, 225–8
Brockway, Fenner 39, 85
Brown, Jane 140, 150
Butcher, Gerald 60–61
Buxton, Noel 49–50, 73–8, 91, *95*, 106

Cadbury, George 20–23, 36, 101
  see also Bournville
Cadbury, John 123–4
cemeteries 192, 203, 245–8, 253
cigarette cards 176–7
City of London Cemetery *166*,
    244–6, *247*
Colvin, Brenda
  definitions of landscape 207–8
  Institute of Landscape Architects
    169, 180–82, 188, 190, 198–9,
    201–3
  lasting effect 219

conscientious objection
   absolutists 43
   Conscientious Objector Information Bureau 41
   letter from Christine Gregory 42
   No-Conscription Fellowship 39, 41
   Quaker position on 38–39
   Richard Sudell 18, 25, 36–9, 42–4
   Wandsworth Detention Centre 44–5
Council for the Protection of Rural England 119, 124, 202–4
Crowe, Slyvia
   Harlow new town 218–20
   harmony of the cosmos 208
   Institute of Landscape Architects 204–6
   new M1 211–14

Daily Herald 172–7, 272, 284
De Havilland headquarters 195–6, 208, 240–43, *242*, *243*
Dixey, Michael 258, 260, 262–3, 271, 274
Dolphin Square *162*, *163*, *165*, 209, 244, 276
   campaign to save 236
   garden design 233–5
   Historic England 230–31
   history of 232, *232*
   Sally Prothero on 237
   The Dolphin magazine 232–3
Dover House Estate (Roehampton Estate) 6, 11, 12, *26*, 29–33, 52, 124, *164*, *167*, *168*, 286, 299–301
   known as 'Uniform Town' 30
Dowden, Oliver 288–90

Elias, Julias 271–3
Evelyn, John 148–9

Fairby Grange
   convalescence at 88
   farm at 86
   flowers, fruit and vegetable at 89–90
   Salters at 85–7
   Sudells at 91
   young mothers and children at 89
Festival of Britain 10, 28, 245, 270

garden gnomes 28, 108, 142–4, 276
gasworks landscape 222, 254–5
Gloag, John 122–3
Guild Gardener 48, 93–4, 100, 106–8, 110–11

Hampstead Garden Suburb 30, 50, 75, 100, 137
Hartley, Kent 85–7, 90–91, 109–10
Harvey, Edmund 41–2
high-rise living 12, 125–6, 206, 231, 268
   children's play space in 265
   see also Alton Estate
Hollow, Matthew 142, 151–2
Hortus conclusus 113
Howard, Ebenezer 21–3, 75, 216
Howell, William 11–12, 125–6, 206, 222

Ideal Home 160, *160*, 169–72
Independent Labour Party 82, 85, 91, 104, 120, 173, 223
Institute of Landscape Architects 29, 108, *193*
   conference 210
   constitution 191
   founding members 190
   legacy 204–6
   M1 campaign 210–12
   name change 189
   presidential address 201–2, 220–22
   professionalism 192
   Sudell as founder 169, 187–9
   Sudell's correspondence with Jellicoe 192–8

Index

Jekyll, Gertrude 28–9, 135, 138, 140, 178
Jellicoe, Geoffrey 169, 184–5, *193*
    correspondence with Sudell 192–8
    emphasis on good garden design 273
    Hemel Hempstead 215–16
    on Institute of Landscape Architects foundation 187–90
    links between landscape architecture and painting 207–8, 212
    M1 campaign 210–13
    national reconstruction 211
    origins of landscape architecture 190
    praise of Sudell 203
    on role of landscape architect 200

Kew Gardens 37–8, 47, 66, 98, 188, 212, 269–70

Lancaster, Osbert 116
Landscape and Garden 185, 197, 200, 202–3, 240
Landscape Gardening 171, 180, 182, 185, 241
Latchmere Baths, Battersea 60
Lawrence, D. H. 8–10, 121, 138, 144
Le Corbusier 12, 25, 123–6, 132, 206, 257–8, 263, 291
Left Foot Forward 289
Letchworth Garden City 21–2, 50, 129, 216
Lloyd George, David 19, 45–6, 51, 75
London Gardens Championship 94–9, *95*, 101
London Gardens Exhibition 96
London Gardens Guild (LGG) 34, 48, *78*
    becoming national movement 98
    city of gardens 98
    conference dinner 102
    founding of 49–50, 78–9
    headquarters branch 102
    judges 96
    London branch guilds 100
    membership 97
    Roehampton joins up 34, 56
    Sudell at LGG 92–4
    Sudell's resignation 108–9
    Town Gardening Handbook 63
London Garden Settlement 73, 79, 85, 106

MacDonald, Ramsay 75, 82, 85, 104, 173, 197
Mass Observation Survey 149
Matless, David 119–20
Metro-land *161*
    Betjeman on 118
    conformity 50
    critics of 25–6
    nostalgia 151
    origins of 116–20
    reference to golden age 137
    twee gardens 143
    vegetable plots 146
Meyer, Rev. Rollo 49–50, 73, 76–7, 81, 97
Middleton, Cecil Henry 141, 153
Mitchell, Mary 267–9
Morris, William 21, 76, 114, 137–8, 200

National Gardens Guild 50, 98, 180
National Playing Fields Association 250, 256, 258, 260–64
New Towns 205, 215–21

Orwell, George 122, 143

Page, Russell 270
Parker, Barry 21, 50, 141, 169, 189

Practical Gardening and Food Production in Pictures 158, *169*, 279
Priestley, J. B. 122–3
Prison Gardening Association 103
Putney Park House 23, 29, 34, 53, 68, 124

Quakers (Religious Society of Friends)
  Ada and Alfred Salter 43, 81
  Cadbury and Rowntree 36
  conscientious objection 38, 43
  Fairby Grange 87
  pacifist network 91
  peace testimony 39
  socialism 39, 152
  Sudell 24, 36–7, 41–5

Ravetz, Alison 138
Reith, Sir John 197–8, 200, 205, 218
Richards, Sir J. M. 129–32, 134, 145, 149
Roberts, Judith 139, 146–8, 291
Roehampton Estate Gazette 18–19, 25–7, 33, *33*, *55*, 56, 63–7
Roehampton Estate Tenants Association 17, 19, 32, 52, 56, 68–71
Roehampton Garden Society 7, 13–14, *15*, 17, 52, 68, 96, *167*, 301
Royal Horticultural Society 14, 29, 77, 83, 94–6, 171, 188, 267, 288

Salter, Ada 43, 72, 75, 79–85, 90, 97, 110
Salter, Alfred 43, 72, 79–85, 87–8, 110
Savage, Jackie 13, 54, 300
Silvertown 250–53, 276
Sitwell, Edith 9
Sharp, Thomas 120–21, 123, 126, 197, 202

Small Owners Ltd 86, 87, 91
Smith Institute 295–7
sports grounds 199, 204, 227, 239, 254–66, *257*, *266*
Strube 120–23, 153, 290
Stubbs, Margaret 97, 103
Sudell, Emily
  in Hartley 86
  at the LGG 73, 93, 97, 99–100, 110
  as Marguerite James 141
  resignation and divorce 108–9
  on Roehampton 34, 46, 55, 72
Sudell, Ida 109, 177–9, *178*, 179, *180*, 198–9, 225, 271–2, 302

Tennyson Waters, D. 256–8, *257*, 263
Thorn, Tracey 294–5
Town and Suburban Garden, The 157, 279
Town Gardening Handbook 63, 107, 134, 158, 182
Toynbee, Arnold 74–5
Tudor Walters Committee and Report 21–2, 69, 285–7

Unwin, Raymond 21, 23, 29–30, 50, 115, 297

Vacant Land Cultivation Society 40–42, 57–61, 73, 79, 103, 158

Wells, H. G. 114
Welwyn Garden City 22, 216
Williams, Sir Owen 212–13
Williams-Ellis, Clough 119–21, 153, 202, 213, 220
Wilson Grove, Bermondsey 85, 129
Woodbrooke College 36–7

Yew and non-Yew 135–6